THE MILLENNIUM

THE ROUGH GUIDE

There are more than one hundred Rough Guide travel, phrasebook, and music titles, covering destinations from Amsterdam to Zimbabwe, languages from Czech to Thai, and musics from World to Opera and Jazz

Forthcoming titles include

Chile • Dominican Republic
Jerusalem • Melbourne • Sydney

Rough Guides on the Internet

www.roughguides.com

Rough Guide Credits

Text editor: Orla Duane. Series editor: Mark Ellingham
Production: Henry Iles, Susanne Hillen, James Morris

Publishing Information

This second edition published May 1999 by
Rough Guides Ltd, 62–70 Shorts Gardens, London WC2H 9AB

Distributed by the Penguin Group:

Penguin Books Ltd, 27 Wrights Lane, London W8 5TZ
Penguin Books USA Inc., 375 Hudson Street, New York 10014, USA
Penguin Books Australia Ltd, 487 Maroondah Highway,
PO Box 257, Ringwood, Victoria 3134, Australia
Penguin Books Canada Ltd, 10 Alcorn Avenue,
Toronto, Ontario, Canada M4V 1E4
Penguin Books (NZ) Ltd, 182–190 Wairau Road,
Auckland 10, New Zealand

Typeset in Bembo and Helvetica to an original design by Henry Iles.
Printed in Spain by Graphy Cems.

Some mapping is based upon the Ordnance Survey maps with
the permission of the Controller of Her Majesty's Stationery Office,
© copyright

© Nick Hanna 1999. 320pp, includes index
A catalogue record for this book is available from the British Library.
ISBN 1-85828-405-8

THE MILLENNIUM

THE ROUGH GUIDE

by Nick Hanna

Acknowledgements

I first came across millenarian movements when studying social anthropology at Sussex University twenty years ago, and I remember thinking at the time that there would be a book in it as the year 2000 approached. Little did I realise then the extent to which millennium fever would take hold in the western world, nor indeed quite what this book would involve. I have known the Rough Guides team as friends and associates for many years and, despite a mutual wish to work together, never found the right project – until now. I'd particularly like to thank Mark Ellingham for his consistent support and numerous lunches, editor Orla Duane for dealing stoically with numerous last-minute revisions (again), Henry Iles for his creative input, and Russell Walton for his proofreading.

I am also grateful to my family for their support and encouragement (particularly my Dad for tirelessly sending newspaper cuttings). Thanks are also due to Simon and Jackie, as ever, for their hospitality in London. For their editorial help on various sections in this edition I am indebted to Sían Gower, Oliver Marshall and Melissa Shales. Sincere thanks also to Paula for being a single parent whilst I completed this edition.

Finally, many thanks to all those individuals in millennium organisations and tourist offices around the world who have responded patiently to my incessant emails and faxes.

Dedicated to my sons Luke and Oscar, who will
experience many wonders in the next millennium.

The Author

As a travel writer and photographer Nick Hanna has worked for numerous national and international newspapers and magazines and written nine guidebooks, including one that covered more than two hundred tropical beaches around the world. He has also written extensively on scuba diving, the marine environment, and the impact of tourism on host countries.

CONTENTS

PREFACE

The world is about to experience the biggest mass celebration in the history of humanity. Never mind that the millennium doesn't really start until 2001, it is the big, round figure of 2000 which has gripped the global imagination.

Thousands of parties are being planned in villages, towns and cities across Europe, the Americas, Australasia and the Pacific. Monuments to the millennium – pyramids, domes, spires, towers, and arches – are being built all over the world. Beacons, fireworks, lasers and light shows will light up the night sky as midnight arrives in each of the planet's 24 time zones. Dawn ceremonies will mark the sunrise, whether performed by druids in Britain, drummers in New Mexico or islanders chanting on a Pacific beach. Festivals, parades, carnivals, exhibitions, and wacky celebrations of all kinds will embrace the millennial *Zeitgeist*. Huge television screens will be erected at locations all over the world and, for the first time ever, the yielding of one thousand-year epoch to another will be observed simultaneously across the globe.

Most of us will want to celebrate the millennium in some way, even the party-poopers who protest that they're sick and tired of the hype. Thousands will party the night away at spectacular gala events, despite the huge hike in prices. Up-market hotels have been quick to cash in on the opportunity, in some cases raising their prices for millennium packages by 300 percent. One deluxe chain is even offering a three-night 'millennium experience' for the astronomical sum of US$100,000 (£60,000). Many top resorts and hotels are already booked out.

Another boom area has been cruises. Despite reports that most are sold out there is still some space available, partly because many potential passengers who had put down deposits backed off when they found out what the final price was going to be (in some cases, double the normal fare). New ships are also being launched just in time for the millennium, notably Royal Caribbean's mammoth 142,000 ton *Voyager of the Seas*, Radisson's *Seven Seas Navigator*, and Cunard's *Caronia*. Many of the sister ships in each fleet will rendez-vous in the Caribbean for parties and firework displays on New Year's Eve, 1999, whilst others will be performing aquatic ballets as they jostle for position to be first in or out of the Panama Canal. The most expensive cruises are to the South Pacific, where dozens of vessels will be steaming backwards and forwards across the International Date Line to give passengers the chance of celebrating twice.

Millions more of us will party in the streets, or join in with the scores of other celebrations listed in this guide. The rising cost of overseas holidays and fears about the effects of the millennium bug have also meant that a high proportion of people are now planning to stick closer to home, celebrating at local events.

As the pattern of what's likely to happen worldwide on New Year's Eve, 1999 has taken shape, one question remains an enigma: where are all the big-name rock bands and pop stars performing? Barbra Streisand is playing Las Vegas for a reported fee of US$6m (£3.5m), Celine Dion will sing in Toronto and Gloria Estefan in Miami. The organisers of the Gisborne celebrations in New Zealand claim David Bowie will be the guest of honour, while Jean Michel Jarre is apparently booked for both Tonga and Egypt. Although other international stars have not announced their plans as we go to press, one thing's for sure – as the date approaches, they'll be charging a king's ransom to appear.

As well as providing a compelling country-by-country guide to millennium celebrations worldwide, we've also explored what Internet users call FAQs (Frequently Asked Questions) about whether the world will really end, whether the computers will crash, and whether we should all be holding out for January 1, 2001.

Nick Hanna
March 1999

THE MILLENNIUM

FAQs

What is the 'millennium'?

Derived from the Latin *mille* (one thousand) and *annus* (years), a millennium is a period of one thousand years. The Millennium (with a capital M), however, has a far more specific meaning for theologians and social scientists, and refers to the belief in the dawning of a new age, a 'heaven on earth', during which all strife and suffering will be abolished and peace, justice and perfect harmony will reign supreme.

For Christians the Millennium is a period when Jesus Christ will return to rule the earth for a period of one thousand years, as set out in the last book of the New Testament, the Book of Revelation. The idea of the Millennium is, in fact, much older and more far-reaching than the Christian version in Revelation, and indeed some concept of a return to paradise seems almost universal throughout human belief systems.

When does the next millennium begin?

The next millennium begins on January 1, 2001. This date relates to the Gregorian calendar, which was drawn up when Roman numerals (which do not feature a zero) were still in use. It may seem strange today, but it was a perfectly workable system, using the numerals X (10), XX (20), C (100), M (1000) and so on.

Problems with this calendar first arose when a Scythian monk, Dionysus Exiguus, introduced the AD ('Anno Domini') dating system in the late fifth century. Not having use of a zero, he dated Christ's birth as 1 AD. His error was compounded two hundred years later by a Northumbrian monk, the Venerable Bede, who created the BC system by extending Dionysus's system backwards into the years before Christ's birth. Like his predecessor, he didn't have use of a zero and so the calendar went backwards, straight from 1 AD to 1 BC. This now seems absurd, rather like counting backwards from eleven to nine while missing out ten, but it is a calendrical anomaly that has persisted for twelve centuries.

According to this system, the first year of the first millennium ran from January 1, 1 AD, to December 31, 1 AD, and the one thousandth year ran from January 1, 1000 AD, to December 31, 1000 AD, making the first day of the second millennium January 1, 1001. The start of the next millennium, therefore, will be January 1, 2001.

Most people will celebrate the eve of the new millennium on the night of December 31, 1999/January 1, 2000, even though this is technically a year too early. A similar argument has also arisen in previous centuries. On December 26, 1799, *The Times* thundered that "the present century will not terminate til 1 January, 1801...We shall not pursue this matter further...It is a silly, childish discussion and only exposes the want of brains of those who maintain a contrary opinion to that we have stated."

But today even the Old Royal Observatory at Greenwich, whilst maintaining that 2001 is the start of the next millennium, is planning to celebrate in 2000. The weight of popular opinion, not to mention sponsorship opportunities, has held sway.

"There is no need for us to argue with those who tell us it is really 2001. It is the round thousands which have the magical power; that goes back to the ancient Etruscans and the ancient Jews."

Conor Cruise O'Brien, *On the Eve of the Millennium.*

"Some have made the argument that the next millennium does not even begin until 2001, so there is no real millennial significance to the year 2000...2000 is a big round number, teeming with prophetic and apocalyptic significance for the beginning of a new age."

Philip Lamy, *Millennium Rage.*

Why are people saying the millennium has already happened?

This is because of the confusion surrounding Jesus's actual birthdate. Most academics accept that if Christ was indeed born during the rule of Herod, then his birth must have been in 4 BC or earlier.

The seventeenth-century astronomer Johannes Kepler believed that Jesus was born seven years earlier because of cumulative errors made by Dionysus (see previous FAQ): not only did he fail to take into account the year zero, but Dionysus also omitted the four-year period when the Emperor Augustus was on the throne under the name Octavian (31–27 BC) and left out the first two years of his stepson Tiberius's rule after Augustus died. Kepler reckoned that this seven-year error tied in with the conjunction of Jupiter and Saturn in 7 BC, which St Matthew identified as the Star of Bethlehem.

But recently a leading Italian astronomer, Professor Giovanni Baratta, has claimed that Kepler also got it wrong, and that Jesus was born in 12 BC when an unusually bright 'travelling star' was observed between the constellations of Leo and Gemini. This comet was noted by Chinese as well as European astronomers at the time.

Depending on which theory is correct, the two-thousand-year anniversary of Jesus's birth could therefore have been in 1988, 1993, or 1996.

Why do we need calendars?

Calendars are essentially devices that adjust and regulate the differences between the natural divisions of time so that we can impose order on the astronomical clock of the universe. There are three basic cosmic sequences that define time – the rotation of the earth on its own axis, which defines the length of a 24-hour day; the rotation of the moon around the earth, which defines the lunar month; and the rotation of the earth around the sun, which defines a year. The other main sequence defining time is the week, but this is a purely artificial construct, based on the biblical story of creation.

The first calendars are thought to have been invented by the Egyptians. They knew that the best time to plant their crops was immediately after the River Nile flooded each year, and the priests calculated that between each flooding the moon rose twelve times. They therefore counted twelve *moon*ths, or months, and arrived at the first approximation of the length of a year.

The Egyptians also noticed that at floodtime each year a certain bright star would rise just before the sun did. They counted the days before this occurred again, and arrived at a figure of 365 days in the year. They then divided the year into twelve months of thirty days each, with five (sometimes six) extra days which became holy days.

How did leap years evolve?

Unfortunately, the natural cycles that define time are not easily divisible one into another. For instance, there are a variable number of days in the lunar month, and the number of days in the year don't add up to a round figure.

Despite this, the Egyptian calendar was eventually switched from a lunar one to one based on the rotation of the earth around the sun (365.25 days). But the extra quarter of a day in the solar calendar began to cause more and more confusion.

How was the problem of leap years resolved?

It was left to the Romans to sort out the confusion. Julius Caesar ordered that the year 46 BC should have 445 days to 'catch up', and that every fourth year from then on would have 366 days to use up the fractions left over from preceding years, thus introducing the concept of leap years.

The Julian calendar was in use up until the sixteenth century, but it then became apparent that too many 'extra' days were piling up and Easter and other holy days were not falling where they should. Easter, for example, was coming closer and closer to Christmas, the reason being that the true length of the cycle of the seasons (technically known as the tropical year) is 365.24219 days, not 365.25 days.

Pope Gregory's solution was to change the rules so that centurial years would only be leap years if they were divisible by 400. Effectively, this creates an adopted average of 365.2425 days in the year, an approximation that is within 30 seconds of the length of the tropical year and that the Royal Greenwich Observatory calculates will amount to a one-day error within 4000 years.

Italy adopted the Gregorian calendar in 1582, when ten days were 'dropped' from the year to make up the difference. Britain didn't adopt the calendar until 1752, by which time the margin of error was eleven days. During that particular year, September 2 was immediately followed by September 14.

Although various religions around the world maintain their own calendars for religious purposes, for everyday reckonings the Gregorian calendar is in use virtually worldwide.

Will 2000 be a leap year?

Yes. The rule is as follows:

"Every year that is exactly divisible by 4 is a leap year, except for years that are exactly divisible by 100. These centurial years are leap years only if they are divisible by 400. As a result, the year 2000 is a leap year, whereas 1900 and 2100 are not leap years."

The Explanatory Supplement to the Astronomical Almanac, 1992.

What will the first decade of the next century be called?

Various suggestions have been made, including the 'noughties', the 'naughties', the 'nothings', the 'noneties', the 'oughts', and the 'zeroes'.

Why is there so much interest in the year 2000?

Ever since humanity became conscious of the fact just over a few hundred years ago that it was living 'in' a particular decade or century, people have tended to define their era by reference to groups of ten or a hundred years. We review a decade in terms of society's achievements and failures, natural disasters and other events, while at the same time looking forward to what might be on the horizon in the decade ahead. A century-long span offers an additional nuance, since it is at the upper limits of human life expectancy.

It is hardly surprising, therefore, that the year 2000 should carry with it some conceptual force, not to mention the weight of religious and millennial expectations. The magnetic pull it exerts is partly explained by the fact that it is the first time in history that so many people have shared the consciousness that a thousand-year time cycle is about to come to a close.

Even though cynics maintain that it is no more than a roll-over of digits on the clock, and party-poopers claim that the millennium doesn't start until 2001, the year 2000 has already generated a huge volume of features in the media, dozens of books on everything from millennial prophecies to the millennium time bomb, and hundreds of Web sites.

"The millennium is the comet that crosses the calendar every thousand years. It throws off metaphysical sparks. It promises a new age, or an apocalypse. It is a magic trick that time performs,

*extracting a millisecond from its eternal flatness and then, poised
on that transitional instant, projecting a sort of hologram that
teems with the summarised life of a thousand years just passed
and with visions of the thousand now to come."*

Time, Fall 1992.

What is a bimillennium?

A bimillennium is the anniversary of any event that took place
2000 years previously – a double millennium celebration.
Strictly speaking, the anniversary of Christ's birth is a bimillennium celebration.

What is *fin de siècle malaise*, and is it catching?

The phrase *fin de siècle* ('end of century') was first used in
France in 1885, and was soon taken up as the title for a novel
by Emile Zola and also a play which was performed in Paris in
1888. By the 1890s the term was in widespread use in
English-speaking countries, indeed to such an extent that one
august journal complained in 1891 that "everywhere we are
treated to dissertations on *fin-de-siècle* literature, *fin-de-siècle*
statesmanship, *fin-de-siècle* morality".

'*Fin de siècle malaise*' (literally 'end of century disquiet') may
have had its origins in the writer Chateaubriand's earlier use of
the phrase *mal de siècle* but passed into the vernacular as a term
describing a general sense of fatigue, self-doubt, disenchant-
ment and weariness as the nineteenth century neared its end.

A similar sense of overwhelming morbidity is echoed today
in the predictions of environmentalists, millenarian groups and
Doomsday cults, but *fin de siècle malaise* is unlikely to become a
fashionable complaint at the end of the twentieth century.
Instead, you are much more likely to succumb to less dramatic
anxieties – whether or not, for instance, you have been invited
to the best and biggest New Year's Eve party.

What is premillennial angst?

A more modern and intense manifestation of *fin de siècle malaise* is the experience of premillennial angst – an acute sense of foreboding and heightened expectation relating to the arrival of the Millennium and/or the Second Coming. Most likely to apply to Doomsday groups, evangelical churches, UFO enthusiasts and other millennial cults, premillennial angst also manifests itself in a general feeling of unease about 'endings'. Dwelling on personal or global cataclysms, experiencing a sense of hopelessness in the face of overwhelming events – in a millennial context, this is premillennial angst. Fears about potential Y2K catastrophes (see pp.22–36) have also given currency to the term 'Millenniumitis".

What is premillennial tension?

Premillennial tension is the name given to outbreaks of hysterical behaviour amongst members of evangelical groups in anticipation of the Rapture to follow in the year 2000. The Toronto Blessing, for instance, has been described as a classic incidence of premillennial tension. In 1994 thousands of worshippers at a small church near Toronto were overcome with 'Holy Spirit Fever' during services, which caused them to fall over, laughing uncontrollably, or to lie perfectly still with beatific smiles on their faces. The phenomenon also spread to England, where it was given the name Premillennial Tension, or PMT (pun intended), by Dr Andrew Walker of King's College, London. Premillennial tension also has a secular meaning, since it has become a fashionable label for any manifestation of contemporary culture with a vaguely apocalyptic theme.

What is millenarianism?

Millenarianism is a term that can be applied to any set of beliefs which envisage imminent salvation. In his classic work *The*

Pursuit of the Millennium, Norman Cohn defines millenarian sects as those which picture salvation to be collective (the faithful will be saved), terrestrial (it takes place on earth rather than in heaven), imminent (it will come both soon and suddenly), total (life will be completely transformed), and miraculous (supernatural agencies will be involved). Within these parameters there is still enormous scope for imagining how the millennium is going to happen and the route to reaching it.

Over the centuries the millennial myth has surfaced in countries and cultures all over the world, from medieval Europe to eighteenth-century China and from Melanesia to twentieth-century America. Its broad sweep has led to the accommodation of beliefs as diverse as those of survivalists, Raëlians, UFO freaks, conspiracy theorists, utopians, and a whole bevy of latter-day prophets. The New Age movement has powerful millennial resonances, as does the environmental movement.

What is chiliasm?

Chilias, derived from the Greek *khilioi* meaning 'thousand', is an alternative word for millenarianism. Its main use to date has been by millenarian scholars.

What on earth (or in heaven) is meant by pre-millennial, amillennial and postmillennial beliefs?

The cryptic language in which the Book of Revelation is written does not allow for a single, unambiguous interpretation of the text. Christian scholars, amongst others, have been debating its precise meaning for centuries and are continuing to do so today. Essentially, the premillennialists believe that the millennial party can't get going until humankind has been redeemed through the Second Coming of Christ; the postmillennialists believe that the party has already started; and the amillennialists think that there isn't going to be a party after all.

According to the premillennialists, the Second Coming will be preceded by signs such as wars, famine, earthquakes and other tribulations, along with the appearance of the Antichrist. Christ will then descend, vanquish the Antichrist at the battle of Armageddon, and reign over a millennium of peace and righteousness. During this golden age dead believers will be raised and will mingle with the rest of the world's inhabitants (in their 'glorified bodies'), and at the end of the millennium the rest of the (non-Christian) dead will be raised, and the world divided into the eternal states of heaven and hell.

By contrast, the postmillennialists believe that Christ already reigns through his church on earth, and that when Christianity is eventually accepted throughout the world, Christ will return to rule for a thousand years of spiritual harmony.

Amillennialists do not believe in the literal truth of Revelation, or in the thousand-year reign of Christ. For them, the millennium of Revelation is a description of the kingdom of heaven where Christ already rules over deceased believers.

Jesus on Film

Numerous films and animated features are being planned on the life of Jesus Christ. The Bible Society is sponsoring *The Trial*, an account of Christ's arrest, interrogation, and condemnation, which has been shot with a cast of thousands in Turkey. Producer-director John Brierley has made a crib-to-crucifixion biopic, *Son of Man*, which was filmed in the Moroccan desert. Neither has been filmed in the Holy Land because film industry insurers are wary of arousing sectarian passions.

Channel Four Wales is producing *The Miracle Maker*, a full-length animation made in Russia, using unusual animation techniques which include two-dimensional cartoons and three-dimensional models. The BBC in Britain is also producing a full-length animation, *In My Father's House*, which tells the story through the eyes of a young girl who meets Jesus at the start of his ministry and is a witness to the Passion and the Resurrection.

What is Jerusalem Syndrome?

Jerusalem Syndrome is a psychological state that often grips newly-arrived pilgrims in the city, who are overwhelmed by the urge to take on the identity of biblical characters (principally Jesus, John the Baptist or Mary Magdalene). The outbreak is expected to be particularly severe as apocalyptic fever grips the evangelical community, and the city authorities are even building an extension to the psychiatric hospital to cope with casualties.

Why is Jerusalem 'Ground Zero' for millennialists?

Jerusalem is 'ground zero' for many apocalyptic cults, and many see January 1, 2000 as the key date for the return of

Jesus and The Great Rapture. Thousands of fundamentalists are planning to travel to the Holy Land and by early 1999 over a hundred millennialists (mostly from the US and Canada) were already living in Arab villages near the Temple Mount, preparing for the event.

The Denver evangelist Monte Kim Miller arrived with his Concerned Christians cult and vowed to die on the streets and be resurrected three days later. But his movements were being shadowed by Israeli intelligence, who expelled the cult in January 1999 when it transpired that its members were planning to bring on the Apocalypse with 'violent acts'.

Police believe that at least three more mass suicide cults are on their way, and they've expressed concern that if The Rapture doesn't arrive some fundamentalists may take matters into their own hands to bring on the Apocalypse. To counter these potential threats £8 million (US$13.4m) is being spent on extra protection for the Temple Mount and other religious sites, and border security is being improved to exclude unwanted cult leaders – and those with one-way tickets.

Where will the sun rise first on January 1, 2000?

The issue of where the sun will rise first has prompted a heated debate in the South Pacific between different contenders for the title. The difference between competing claims is only a matter of minutes (or, between some locations, mere seconds), but it is enough to separate winners from losers and to challenge the authenticity of rival millennium parties and television companies planning to sell their sunrise footage to the global networks.

Some 500 miles east of Christchurch in New Zealand, the Chatham Islands lie 155 miles from the dateline and are confident of their claim to be the first inhabited landmass to witness the millennium dawn. According to their calculations, the sun will rise over the 231m summit of Mount Hapeka on

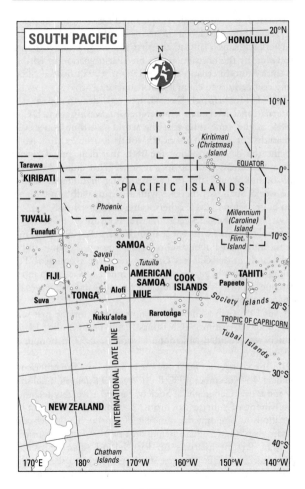

Pitt Island, the most easterly inhabited island in the group, at 3:59am (15:59 GMT) on the morning of January 1, 2000.

The Chathams' claim to the first sunrise was cast in doubt, however, by the decision of the tiny Pacific nation of Kiribati to 'move' the International Date Line in 1995, thus leap-frogging competitors to claim the first sunrise.

The International Date Line was drawn up at the International Meridian Conference in Washington, DC in 1884, at the same time that the world's 24 time zones were created. For most of its north-south journey through the Pacific the dateline follows the 180° meridian, but it zigzags around landmasses for obvious reasons – if it didn't do so, the inhabitants would find themselves living in different days of the week. Such was the case with Kiribati, with some islands ten hours behind GMT, others fourteen hours ahead.

On December 23, 1994, the Republic of Kiribati announced that: "with effect from January 1, 1995, all islands in the Line and Phoenix Groups shall be on the same day as the islands in the Gilberts Group within the Republic." This ruling created a huge, one-thousand-mile eastward loop in the dateline's course, shifting the easternmost islands from 'yesterday' to 'today'.

Several of Kiribati's islands are now in line for the first sunrise, notably Kiritimati (Christmas Island) and Caroline Island, which was renamed Millennium Island in 1997 in honour of this position.

But the change has not gone unchallenged by the other contenders. In November 1997 the *Geographical Journal*, published by the Royal Geographical Society, carried a weighty technical assessment of sunrise isochrons, declinations and complex equations to pinpoint the moment of sunrise. The paper concludes that "the Chatham Islands area of New Zealand, in particular certain hilltops on Pitt Island (also known as Rangiauria), will be the first inhabited places to see the first light on January 1, 2000 AD." It pours cold water on Kiribati's claims, by stating that the dateline change "lacks sensibility" and that the "arbitrary and unilateral moving of time zones or the International Date Line does not give rise to any level of credibility in the international navigation community."

The criticism displays a rather high-handed attitude towards the Kiribatians, for whom the change is eminently sensible. The Pitt Islanders, it might be noted, set their own time 45 minutes ahead of New Zealand for what they no doubt also consider valid reasons. More pertinently, the journal's findings (which have been widely reported in New Zealand) are open to accusations of commercial bias. One of the three co-authors is Norris McWhirter (founder of the *Guinness Book of Records*), whose Millennium Adventure Company has snapped up the rights (surprise, surprise) to film on certain hilltops on Pitt Island.

So who is right? The Old Royal Observatory at Greenwich comes down in favour of Pitt Island. "The international date-line has not been changed", says Maria Blyzinsky, astronomer at the Old Royal Observatory. "Although the time they're keeping in the Line and Phoenix Islands now puts them on the west side of the dateline, for scientific purposes they're not on the other side of the dateline and it won't be recognised by scientists or navigators."

"It all depends on which system you want to measure time by", says Blyzinsky. "The time zones system is a convenience which allows us to know roughly what time it is somewhere else in the world in comparison to ourselves, but it is just a social convention", she says. "The official system is Universal Time Coordinated (UTC), which is based on Greenwich Mean Time and the meridian, as determined by the Meridian Conference in Washington in 1884."

Confusingly, Dr Robin Catchpole of the Royal Greenwich Observatory in Cambridge believes that Kiribati's decision is legitimate. "There are good administrative reasons why Kiribati put all of its islands on the same day, and a not unrealised

consequence is that the Line Islands will be the first to see the local sunrise at the millennium. Our calculations show that it rises there at 15:43 GMT, and that Pitt Island will see it around 16:00 GMT."

Undoubtedly the debate about where the sun really rises first will continue until dawn itself on January 1, 2000 – after which everybody will wonder what on earth all the fuss was about.

Millennium Babies

The first baby born in the next millennium could become very rich. Sponsorship by baby clothes and equipment makers as well as lucrative television and media contracts are likely to be offered to the 'Millie', 'Milo' or 'Miles' who pops out first. Several countries in the South Pacific, including New Zealand and Tonga, are hoping that the first millennium baby will arrive in their maternity wards – although the ongoing row about where the millennium actually starts will evidently affect any 'first baby' claims. In Britain, television companies have clashed in an undignified struggle to sign contracts with maternity wards in the big cities, with the BBC's *Babies of the Millennium* competing against ITV's *Birthrace 2000*. ITV has signed up ten couples whose progress will be followed as they try and deliver a millennium baby – although the early hours of January 1, 2000 are not an auspicious time to give birth, given that hospitals may be suffering millennium bug chaos, compounded by the increase in casualties from all-night parties.

Sunrise times at the start of the year 2000

		GMT	LOCAL
Millennium Island, Kiribati	Dec 31, 1999	15:43	5:43
Flint Island, Kiribati	Dec 31, 1999	15:47	5:47
Antipodes Island	Dec 31, 1999	15:55	3:55
Pitt Island, NZ	Dec 31, 1999	16:00	4:45
Kiritimati, Kiribati	Dec 31, 1999	16:31	5:31
Mt Hikurangi, NZ	Dec 31, 1999	16:39	4:39
Katchall Island, Nicobar	Jan 1, 2000	00:00	6:00

Source: Royal Greenwich Observatory

Doesn't the New Year begin at midnight in Greenwich?

There is a twist in this tale of sunrise squabblings – they might all be wrong about where the new millennium actually begins. According to the International Meridian Conference, the universal day begins when it is 'mean midnight at the cross-hairs of the Airy transit circle in the Old Royal Observatory' at Greenwich. So the start of the new millennium is at 00:00 on January 1, 2000, measured in Universal Time. 'This would have to be regarded as the astronomical definition of the instant of the New Year', says the Royal Greenwich Observatory's Astronomy Research Council.

As the sunrise comes up over the Pacific, technically the New Year hasn't yet started since it is still around noon on December 31 in Greenwich. And it will remain 'yesterday' until noon the following day.

This fact introduces a surprise contender into the global sunrise sweepstakes. When it is midnight on December 31 in Greenwich, where is the sun actually rising at that moment? The answer is in the Nicobar Islands, which lie within Indian territorial waters. "The sun is rising along half a great circle, across Russia, China and out over the Bay of Bengal, and at midnight GMT it will just be rising over an island called Katchall in the Nicobar group", says Dr Catchpole.

Located around 300km south of the Andaman Islands on the eastern side of the Bay of Bengal, the Nicobars are a restricted area with almost impossible access. A media race to film in the Nicobars seems unlikely, so perhaps the real first sunrise of the new millennium will shine down on Katchall, observed only by the dugongs, leatherback turtles and saltwater crocodiles who live around its shoreline – and maybe that's as it should be.

"The millennium is freighted with immense historical symbolism and psychological power. It does not depend on objective calculation, but entirely on what people bring to it – their hopes, their anxieties, the metaphysical focus of their attention. The millennium is essentially an event of the imagination."

Time, Fall, 1992.

Is there any copyright on the word 'millennium'?

As the year 2000 approaches the world is about to overdose on millennium hype, with hundreds of products and services bearing the 'millennium' label. Information technology companies were amongst the first to jump on the bandwagon, either because they wanted to project a futuristic image or because they were involved in solving millennium time bomb problems. But now the marketing frenzy has reached absurd proportions. The US Patent and Trademark Office has already awarded 117 trademarks that include 'millennium' and more than 1500 with '2000' in the title, and thousands more are pending.

In Britain hundreds of companies have registered similar trademarks. Curiously, the first registration was made nearly a century ago: an application by the Royal Botanic Gardens at Kew to use 'millennium' for seeds and plants was made in 1902.

Few of the products being marketed bear any relation to the millennium. In the US, millennium merchandise includes chocolates, champagne, beer, floor wax, golf balls, motor oil, power saw blades, pest control products, gas masks, underwear, vacuum cleaners, electric light fixtures, and even wind chimes.

In Britain you can already buy the Millennium Kettle and fairly soon there'll be Millennium Ale, a Millennium Chair, Millennium Marmalade, Millennium Jewellery, and Next Millennium Kitchens. An environmentally friendly fuel treatment 'for the next century' almost justifies the millennium tag and a Millennium Cocktail sounds like a winner, but what of millennium car tyres, industrial lubricants, fishing tackle, beds, electric showers, herbicides, tea, bicycles, and artificial limbs?

Britain's Design Council has also jumped on board with a campaign to promote 2000 'Millennium Products', the top 200 of which will be on display at the millennium exhibition.

But the generic branding of the millennium has other implications. A New York company, Planet Marketing, holds the rights to use 'Year 2000' on clothing, footwear and novelties, and even has a full-time worker searching the Internet for anyone who might have the temerity to attempt to use the slogan. A computer analyst from Maine, David Bettinger, discovered this to his cost when he started selling 'Year 2000' T-shirts and found himself on the receiving end of a cease-and-desist letter from the company's lawyers. "I was astounded that they could even get a trademark on that term", Bettinger told the Associated Press. "It irks me that I can be receiving so much heat from people who are representing this generic term. How ludicrous is that?"

What is the millennium bug?

Also known as the Y2K (Year 2000) problem, or the millennium time bomb, it refers to the fact that computers all over the world may crash as their date systems roll 1999 over into 2000.

The problem originates with the design of early computer programs, when memory was at such a premium that programmers shortened commands to a minimum whenever they could. This included shortening the year to just two numbers (ie '56' instead of 1956) so that the date came to be represented as DD/MM/YY (08/03/56, for example). Although this seems like a tiny saving, dates occur so often in software systems that it saved memory space many times over, and programmers had no idea that these original computer languages would still be operating at the end of the century.

With the development of more powerful computers, the logic for this abbreviation has long since disappeared, but meanwhile it had become standard convention throughout the programming world.

As 1999 clicks over into 2000 the computer will register only '00', recognising the year as 1900 rather than 2000. It may then malfunction and possibly shut down altogether.

Some experts warn of disruption on a worldwide scale, as everything from cash dispensers to air traffic control systems and elevators begins to malfunction. Almost anything containing a microchip could be at risk. Some people predict that as dawn breaks over the Pacific and spreads across the globe, up to 50,000 mainframes will crash in succession, causing a wave of economic, political and social chaos.

The nightmare scenario could well result in a situation where databases that normally calculate taxes, pensions, mortgages and utility bills suddenly begin to churn out rubbish. Children might be sent pensions and pensioners might automatically be added to primary school intake lists; a hundred years of interest could be added to savings accounts, or vice versa, with massive amounts in interest debited to credit cards or bank balances. Everything from military hardware to civilian aircraft may be simultaneously scheduled for maintenance.

The problem is not simply confined to mainframe computers. Modern machinery is often constructed with built-in chips that control different functions. There are millions of these so-called 'embedded chips' located in places where removal and testing becomes a major technical operation.

It has already been called the biggest human-made disaster to hit the information technology industry. It's also an appropriately ironic apocalyptic scenario for millennial expectations in the age of the computer.

How expensive is the millennium bug?

Worldwide the cost is estimated at anything between £180–360 billion (US$300–600b). In the US alone the cost to the federal government is estimated at around US$7 billion (£4b).

The banking, insurance and telecommunications industries are most at risk since they are so heavily dependent on computers, although in countries like the US and UK they've spent millions on debugging their systems and are unlikely to be thrown into chaos. However, significant failures in the financial and telecommunications sectors elsewhere in the world could cause the whole system to unravel.

Many businesses have left it too late and will not be ready in time. Even if a company does manage to sort out its own systems, it could still be affected if its customers and suppliers don't do the same: if external systems aren't 'clean', they could infect the host computer. Some consultants estimate that up to 5 percent of all businesses will go bust if testing is not completed in time. Others are predicting a 70 percent chance of global recession brought on by the millennium bug.

Will the millennium time bomb really go off?

No one can accurately predict what is going to happen. Some

computer crashes have already taken place – a Swiss hospital, for instance, lost its systems for the first two days of 1999 due to the Y2K bug. Risk assessment analysts estimate that there might be around twenty to thirty major incidents worldwide as a result

of the millennium bug, ranging from accidents at industrial facilities to oil tankers running aground. Doomsday theorists claim that it will be the onset of worldwide Armageddon and cause the collapse of society.

The likeliest scenario is that in most countries it will cause a series of inconveniences, such as localised power or telecommunications failures. But the knock-on effects could be considerable, and there is the danger that computer crashes in less well-prepared countries could bring down global communications, banking and trading systems. As 2000 approaches it will become clearer what will and what won't work; as this information filters through there may well be mass panic in some countries, prompting a flight of capital into 'safe havens' from at-risk economies. A multinational business committee monitoring the millennium bug, Global 2000, suppressed a report in January 1999 which rated the Y2K compliance of the world's top 30 economies for fear that it would have a destabilising effect on developing countries.

Even in the developed world governments aren't taking any chances, and many have cancelled police and army leave as a contingency measure.

What is being done about the millennium bug globally?

Most of the advanced industrialised nations (such as the US, Canada, Britain, Australia and New Zealand) are spending billions to ensure that government systems and critical infrastructure can cope with the date change. Many other countries are less well-prepared. The Italian government, for instance, only set up a troubleshooting committee to deal with the problem in January 1999. The Kenyan government has set up a similar committee but it is not due to publish its results until April 2000, according to Nairobi's *Daily Nation*.

Central and Eastern Europe, Brazil, India, China and Russia are all high-risk areas. Many Asian countries – which may be amongst the first to experience the effects of the bug as midnight rolls over into 2000 – are simply ignoring the problem, partly because the region has so many local religious calendars. One Taiwanese company told the *Herald Tribune* they weren't worried about the bug because their computers run on the Chinese calendar – although when consultants checked they found that the operating system used the Julian calendar and would indeed crash. A report in February 1999 concluded that nearly 50 percent of Asian companies will suffer at least one mission critical system failure, and in some countries it could be as high as 65 percent. In China, 98 percent of all the software in use is pirated (including software used by government and state-owned enterprises), which will severely restrict the help they can get.

In many parts of the developing world it is unclear whether they have even heard of the problem, let alone taken steps to deal with it. A World Bank report in January 1999 warned that out of 139 developing countries only 21 are taking any concrete steps to safeguard their computer systems. The United Nations is considering setting up an emergency response system and crisis management centre to deal with major international disruptions to critical services.

Will the millennium bug affect my home?

Very few items in the home will be affected, simply because not many have date-related functions. Most household systems (such as central heating, air conditioning, and water heating) and normal domestic appliances will work normally. Most video recorders will be unaffected; those that fail to recognise the date change could have problems with time-related recordings but they will still function when manually controlled. Some fax machines might not recognise the year, but will still work even though the transmission date will be incorrect. The same applies to answer phones, camcorders, digital cameras and other items which use a date and time display. Most can be reset easily, however. Microprocessors used in the production of cars, motorbikes, and other vehicles are not date-dependent. If you're buying anything before the year 2000, make sure it comes with a written guarantee that it can cope with the date change.

Will the millennium bug affect my computer?

Quite possibly, yes, particularly if it is an older PC to which you have added programs and peripherals over the years. You need to test your PC and possibly upgrade some parts or programs. Apple Macs won't be affected, although some software might be. Most computer manufacturers have telephone support lines and Web sites with information on the millennium status of their products, and some provide free software fixes over the Internet.

For information on how to test your PC and advice on home appliances in the UK contact Action 2000 ℡ 0845/601 2000. Ⓦ http://www.bug2000.co.uk
See also pp.301–303 for other relevant Web sites.

Will the millennium bomb go off on January 1, 2000?

Not necessarily. It's thought that around 10 percent of all computer failures will occur on that date, with the rest spread over the following two years. For instance, a control circuit that fails to reset after 1999 may not show up this failure until a demand is placed on it, which could be days, weeks or even months afterwards. Other potential problem dates include:

- **August 22, 1999**: The world's network of GPS satellites, which provide precise timing signals for many energy management systems, are pre-programmed to reset themselves to zero on this day.
- **September 9, 1999**: Four nines are sometimes used by programmers to indicate that a stack of data has reached the end – a signal for the program to shut down.
- **February 29, 2000**: the year 2000 is a leap year, and will be the first turn-of-the-century leap year since 1600. Many programs will fail to recognise this.
- **October 10, 2000**: This will be the first time in the next century that computers will have to deal with an eight-digit date (10/10/2000).
- **December 31, 2000**: Some computers work by counting the days of the year, and if they haven't been programmed for the leap year they may wait until day 366 before failing.

What about nuclear weapons systems?

This is evidently an area of huge concern, since there is potential for more than just localised catastrophes. In the US, the Pentagon has spent US$2.5 billion (£1.5b) fixing its computer systems and claims that all 2300 systems critical to national defence, including those linked to nuclear weapons, will be free of bugs. Many weapons systems have already been tested on a 'dry run' which involved putting their clocks forward to December 31, 1999. This confidence is not shared by the British American Security Information Council, which says in a report, *The Bug in the Bomb*, that the Department of Defense has 'severe and recurring problems' in its Y2K programme and quotes the Deputy Secretary of Defense as saying that: "Everything is so interconnected, it's very hard to know with any precision that we've got it fixed." It recommends all nuclear weapons states should stand-down nuclear operations and uncouple warheads from missiles.

In the UK the Ministry of Defence is spending £200 million (US$336m) on bug-busting and says there is no possibility of accidental use of nuclear weapons. However, the Royal Navy is reputedly lagging behind even though it intends for all its ships to be bug-compliant by August 1999.

Faced with economic crisis, Russia is way behind other nations in preparing for the Y2K problem but it has agreed to co-operation with NATO in ensuring that its nuclear weapons don't pose a threat. It faces a race against time, however.

There is less certainty surrounding weapons systems in other parts of the world. Some analysts maintain that the risk is of complex programs crashing rather than of the accidental firing of missiles.

What about nuclear power plants?

Although there have been high-profile reassurances on the safety of nuclear weapons systems, the situation with nuclear power plants is less clear. The US Nuclear Regulatory Commission (NRC) says that there are unlikely to be problems with the operation of nuclear plants themselves, since most safety-related instrumentation and control systems are analogue hardwired. However, the computer-based control systems for turbines, security systems and radiation monitoring could still be subject to Y2K problems.

The NRC has adopted a contingency plan that steers a middle course between everything working as normal and a worst case scenario involving widespread loss of communications, a complete shut-down of the North American power grid, and several major incidents at nuclear power stations. Their assumption is that there will be localised power failures (but no national problems); local telecommunications failures; at least two nuclear plants affected directly or indirectly; and at least one nuclear plant outside the US being affected.

In the UK the Nuclear Installations Inspectorate says that all nuclear power plants will be Y2K compliant. British Nuclear Fuels (BNFL), which operates Sellafield, is planning to finalise its bug-busting project by September 1999 – just four months short of the deadline. France is said to be confident that its nuclear sites will be bug-free, but elsewhere in Europe little information has been released on Y2K problems.

In Russia one official from the Atomic Energy Ministry has been quoted as saying that "we don't have any problems yet. We'll deal with it in the year 2000". Russia itself has 29 reactors (eleven of which are similar to the one which exploded at Chernobyl), with a further 36 civilian reactors scattered throughout the former Soviet bloc countries. In early 1999 the Russian news agency Itar-Tass reported that Russia would need to find up to US$3 billion (£1.8b) to fix its millennium bug problems.

No information is available about the state of nuclear plants in Argentina, South Africa, the Philippines, Mexico, Cuba, Pakistan, Turkey, Iran, Spain, India, Korea, Taiwan or elsewhere.

Should I head for the hills?

The millennium bug has led to a huge growth in the survivalist movement in the US, with thousands of people stockpiling freeze-dried foods and other emergency supplies, purchasing generators and weapons, and buying up isolated plots of land to sit out what many consider will be a global crash triggering TEOTWAWKI – The End of the World As We Know It.

In Denver more than six thousand people attended Preparedness Expo '98 in late December, buying up everything from First-Aid kits to water purification systems, and even gas masks. In rural Ohio the country department store Lehman's, which usually supplies non-electrical goods to the local Amish community, has had a huge influx of shoppers snapping up items such as gas-powered fridges, wood stoves, hand-cranked food mills, and wind-up Baygen radios. One Los Angeles supplier has been inundated with orders for a US$3000 (£1800) 'family package' designed to keep a whole family alive for a year.

Other survivalists are buying land in the backwoods and arming themselves to ward off intruders who might come for their food supplies. Near Concho Lake, Arizona, survivalists have built a retreat known as the High 24 Ranch where they plan to live underground with power supplied by solar panels and wind generators. If you want to join you'll need to take along a year's supply of food and a weapon with 1000 rounds of ammunition.

Across the suburbs of America hundreds of thousands of people are reportedly enlisting in local suburban groups, preparing to mobilise themselves in the event of a national Y2K meltdown.

The upsurge in survivalism was partly sparked off by the so-called 'geek exodus', with reports of computer programmers moving their families out of the big cities because of their lack of confidence in the debugging process. And if the programmers – the latter-day high priests of the technological age – are panicking, what is everybody else supposed to do? The survivalist movement is a classic example of secular millenarianism, with believers tapping into ancient fears about the onset of Armageddon.

Ironically, as the rural survivalists hunker down to await Doomsday, it appears that urban dwellers might have the last laugh. If there are problems with electricity supply it's likely that the distribution companies would divert supplies to cities, which have a higher priority. So while city folk party away under the bright lights into the next millennium, the Y2K survivalists might be left sitting in their isolated cabins for several weeks waiting for the power to be restored.

Maybe I should stock up on supplies anyway?

In the UK the national task force, Action 2000, caused a furore when it suggested that people should stock up on tinned and dried food, grains, biscuits, long-life milk and 'sensible provisions in case of a potential emergency'. The government reacted swiftly and pointed out that the food and electricity industries are amongst the most prepared in the country and are investing heavily to ensure that there is no interruption in supplies. The supermarket chain Sainsbury's commented that everything would run as normal (refrigeration units with embedded chips and other equipment have been tested for problems) and that their main millennium preparations were now concentrated on the rental of an extra 400,000 sq ft of warehouse space to cope with the huge amounts of booze people will be consuming.

Crime Time

- Leave has been cancelled for the 1450 officers in Britain's National Crime Squad in order to combat a major crime wave over the millennium holiday. Police fear that organised criminal gangs are preparing raids and break-ins if computerised systems fail and blackouts occur.
- Prison chiefs in Scotland have expressed fears that the millennium bug may release inmates by unlocking computerised prison doors on December 31, 1999. Surveillance cameras and alarm systems could also go haywire, presenting the opportunity for mass break-outs.
- Banks are being targeted by fraudulent computer consultants who are overcharging by huge amounts for programming that will handle the year 2000 date change. In one case, consultants charged £20 million (US$34m) for work which should have cost just £6 million (US$10m).
- In New York the police discovered that the Mafia had set up a computer consultancy specialising in Y2K problems. It rewrote software for several corporations – and sent the clients' money straight into its own overseas accounts.

What are the chances of apocalypse in the year 2000?

Fairly low, but there may be a few surprises. On a cosmic scale, scientists claim that the earth is long overdue a collision with an asteroid or comet that would cause devastation similar to the event that is thought to have wiped out the dinosaurs 65 million years ago. Such an impact, thousands of times more powerful than the Hiroshima bomb, would send up a cloud of debris which would blot out the sun and send temperatures plummeting globally. It might happen in 2000 – but there again, it might not happen until 3000.

Another scenario which fits in neatly with millennium Doomsday scenarios is the predicted increase in sunspot activity in the year 2000. Sunspots follow an eleven year cycle, and the last major eruption was in 1989. The next major peak is expected to coincide with the millennium. Sunspots cause what are known as 'coronal mass ejections', whereby clouds of burning hot plasma stream out from the sun at speeds of up to two million miles per hour, buffeting the earth's magnetic field and generating huge amounts of electricity with the capacity to knock out entire national grids and disable satellites. In 1989, eight million homes in Canada lost power as a result of sun storms, some of them for up to eight days, and two crucial communications satellites malfunctioned, resulting in the loss of telephones and television to millions of people.

The 1989 sunstorms caused hundreds of millions of pounds worth of damage, but since then we have become even more vulnerable – thanks to increasing reliance on satellite telecommunications. The sunstorms predicted for 2000 could have catastrophic consequences.

"A millennial year has occurred only once before: fifty generations ago, in the year 1000, on what was a very different, more primitive planet earth. So this one has a strange, cosmic prestige, a quality almost of the unprecedented. The world approaches it in states of giddiness, expectation and, consciously or unconsciously, a certain anxiety."

Time, Fall 1992.

Is it safe to travel over the millennium?

Aircraft manufacturers are confident that there is absolutely no chance of planes falling from the sky, contrary to widespread belief that this might happen. A Boeing 747 contains 16,000 control chips but only a handful have been reported as having millennium-related problems, and these are easily fixed. Airbus has flown an A340 across the International Date Line with all its systems set forward to midnight on December 31, 1999 and reported no problems.

The risks lie elsewhere, particularly with airports, complex air traffic control systems, power systems and communications on the ground. The US Federal Aviation Administration (FAA) claims that all its systems will be fixed on time and is so confident that its head, Jane Garvey, has vowed to fly coast-to-coast on December 31, 1999 to demonstrate her faith in the preparations. Inside sources, however, claim that the FAA may shut down all US air traffic on December 31, 1999 and January 1, 2000 as a precautionary measure.

Several airlines have said that they won't fly into countries with problematic airports. The Geneva-based International Air Transport Association is auditing 150 air traffic control systems and 100 major 'critical' airports to determine whether or not they will be bug-free.

One possibility is that flights will be limited within western Europe, Canada, Australia, New Zealand and the United States. Black spots which are causing concern include much of Asia, Africa, South America, Russia and the Middle-East.

If you're planning to go abroad, be prepared for long delays at airports and don't plan to fly home on January 1 and 2, 2000. Find out what contingency plans your tour operator has made in the event of cancellation or other millennium bug problems. If you're planning a cruise, check with the operator that the ship is millennium bug compliant. You should also try to avoid high risk activities such as adventure sports, since hospitals are likely to be busy anyway. Above all, check your travel insurance – many policies include a clause excluding payouts arising from millennium bug problems.

Is it possible to celebrate the millennium more than once?

Indeed it is, by the simple expedient of celebrating New Year's Eve in a country to the west of the International Date Line and then catching a flight on January 1, 2000 eastwards, thereby losing a day and arriving in time to celebrate New Year's Eve all over again. Party destinations for two-timing travellers include Tonga, Kiribati, Sydney, Melbourne, Auckland and Fiji for the first night and Samoa, the Cook Islands, Tahiti or the US for the second night. There are some doubts, however, as to whether airline schedules will permit this kind of time travelling, and keen Pacific party-goers may need to charter their own planes. Additionally, the effect of the millennium bug on the aviation industry may well result in the grounding of aircraft, public and private.

Can Concorde beat the clock?

Yes. Concordes will play 'a major part in the New Year's Eve celebrations' say British Airways, which has seven in operation. Theoretically, you could celebrate the passing of midnight three times on a transatlantic Concorde trip: once in London, once in mid-air, and a third time in New York. However, the supersonic jet normally leaves London for its last transatlantic flight at 7.30pm, and special permission would be needed to allow it to take off after midnight. British Airways' plans would also depend on the level of preparation at airports to cope with the millennium bug (Concorde itself has been declared bug-free). BA say that plans for Concorde would involve a charity event alongside the strictly commercial possibilities.

Where can I go to avoid the millennium?

You could try taking an extended holiday in China, where it will be the year 4698.

Any Islamic country is probably a safe bet (in the Islamic calendar it will be the year 1420), as are remote areas of India and Asia. Large tracts of Africa and South America will be completely unaffected by the millennium, apart from areas with Catholic populations. According to other religious calendars 2000 will be the year 5760 (Jewish), 1716 (Coptic), 2544 (Buddhist), 1378 (Persian), 5119 (Mayan).

Forget about seeking sanctuary on a mountain top; every peak with spiritual connotations (and to some people, that's any peak at all) will probably be verging on the overcrowded. Fundamentalist Christians are already being urged to make their way to the mountain tops to await the Second Coming, and New Age believers hold that the only way to survive the forthcoming changes is to live in the mountains and prepare for the Dawning of the Age of Aquarius.

Who won't be celebrating the millennium?

Around 3.8 billion people, or the two-thirds of the world who live in predominantly non-Christian countries. That still leaves nearly two billion people who will be observing it in some form or other (even if only to dip into the worldwide telecasts on New Year's Eve 1999), making it the biggest mass celebration in the history of humanity. Other people who won't be celebrating the millennium are those staffing crisis helplines. Suicides run at record levels on New Year's Eve, and 1999 is expected to be a particularly bad year.

Is it okay to want to stay at home?

Exorbitant restaurant and hotel prices, skyrocketing rates for baby-sitters, as well as the anxiety about getting back from the celebrations (no taxis), means that a large proportion of people will be sticking close to home anyway. Ochlophobists – those with an aversion to crowds – will be staying well away from the big city centres and their million-strong revelling throngs, and the potential for millennium bug chaos will also put people off gravitating to mega-bashes unless they live locally.

Some of these factors have fed a growing millennial trend to organise a huge number of community festivals, neighbourhood get-togethers, street parties and other local events. As we enter the hi-tech world of the twenty-first century it seems a particularly appropriate way to celebrate.

Can't I ignore the millennium altogether?

Unlikely, since it will be impossible to avoid in the global media. Television, radio and print media will be awash with retrospective histories of civilisation and human achievements over the last 100, 1000 or 2000 years. Millennial cults, prophecies and apocalyptic expectations will also come under the media spotlight. On New Year's Eve 1999 most television channels will be screening versions of the celebrations taking place around the world, with 24-hour telecasts linking all the big parties in different time zones. There is also likely to be intense speculation about the effects of the millennium bug as midnight approaches, with any incidents being picked up quickly and flashed worldwide. All eyes will be on Australia, New Zealand and Asia for potential catastrophes. There will also be fierce competition amongst television crews to film the 'first' of everything, from millennium babies to bungee-jumpers.

But why try and ignore it in the first place? After all, a celebration of this kind only comes around every one thousand years and no one alive today will ever see anything like it ever again – well, not until 2001 anyway!

THE MILLENNIUM

GUIDE

ANTARCTICA

The first sunrise of the new millennium will take place over the **Dibble Glacier** on the edge of Antarctica. Previous calculations had placed the first sunrise over Antarctica's Balleny Islands, but it appears that in fact the sun doesn't set there in January, so no true sunrise is possible.

Unless someone out there is completely obsessed with getting into the record books, the Dibble Glacier is likely to remain deserted. However, quite a few teams will be hauling their way into the South Pole with sledges, which possibly qualifies as one of the least likely party destinations of the millennium.

One of these teams, the South Pole Millennium Expedition, aims to set off from Hercules Inlet in November 1999 to sledge-haul its way into the next millennium. The two month-long expedition, organised by the Polar Travel Company, aims to 'close the Pole' in the final hours of December 31, 1999 and witness the sun at its maximum elevation at the beginning of the next century.

Another expedition, Pole to Pole 2000, intends to set off from the North Pole in May 2000 on the start of an eight-month trek around the globe, with participants initiating environmental and humanitarian projects along the way, to arrive back in Antarctica again on December 31, 2000.

Finally, plans for a New Year's Eve party on the pack ice are on the cards for guests on the icebreaker *Kapitan Dranitsyn*, which will be off the northwestern coast of Antarctica searching for a suitable ice floe to moor up to on December 31, 1999.

TRAVEL BRIEF

No millennium bug problems are expected in Antarctica.

GETTING THERE Antarctica is connected to Chile and New Zealand by regular flights; some cruises depart from the port of Ushuaia at Chile's southernmost tip.

TOURS UK: The South Pole Millennium Expedition costs £55,000 (US$92,000) per person. Alternatively, you can cheat and fly in by Cessna for around £13,500 (US$22,750); the Polar Travel Company Ⓣ 01364/631470. US: Pole to Pole 2000 Ⓣ 212/586 7967. The icebreaker *Kapitan Dranitsyn* can be booked through Quark Expeditions Ⓣ 01494/464080. The eighteen-day trip costs from £9595 (US$16,000) per person, exclusive of flights.

TOURIST OFFICES n/a **COUNTRY CODE** n/a

AUSTRALIA

Australia is preparing for a massive influx during the year 2000 and beyond as the **Olympic Games** being held in **Sydney** generate worldwide publicity for the country. Tourism forecasts predict that as well as the 132,000 athletes, officials, judges, journalists and spectators who will descend on Sydney itself in 2000, a further 1.5 million people will visit the country up until 2004 thanks to the publicity generated by the Olympic Games.

Sydney is also gearing up for a mega New Year's Eve party on December 31, 1999, although one person who won't be joining in is Prime Minister John Howard. Answering a parliamentary question on the subject, he stated that "both the twenty-first century and the third millennium will begin on

Monday, 1 January, 2001", and festivities would therefore coincide with the Centenary of Federation on January 1, 2001. Technically he is right (see FAQs), but the statement shocked the hedonistic Aussies, who were looking forward to the biggest booze-up of the century.

The rest of the world is celebrating 2000 despite this, so it looks like the Aussies are going to have a party a year too late – or at least the prime minister will be the only one to miss the festivities on New Year's Eve, 1999.

Melbourne's Millennium Committee is promoting it as the 'City of the Third Millennium' thanks to the recent redevelopment of the city centre, and they are also planning a big New Year's Eve party with street performers and outdoor events in key locations such as Carlton Gardens, the Old Exhibition Building and the Museum of Victoria. They're hoping to keep the ball rolling with other events throughout 2000 and 2001, culminating in a special millennium edition of the Melbourne Festival in October 2001.

Adelaide is similarly planning a bigger and better Adelaide Arts Festival (March 3–19, 2000), 'focussing on new ways in which artists are choosing to collaborate and create in the next century'.

Perth is planning a **Millennium Bell Tower**. The A$5 million (£1.9m/US$3m) tower will house a set of bells donated by St Martin-in-the-Fields, London, as part of the 1988 Bicentennial celebrations. It was originally intended to represent a swan beneath a glass-and-steel tower, but the architects were sent back to the drawing board to redesign it after the State Cabinet rejected the plans as too controversial in early 1999.

In **Queensland** the Great Barrier Reef Visitor's Bureau has announced an exclusive (and expensive) **Great Barrier Reef Millennium Event**. Plans for the Planet Earth 2000 garden festival have been cancelled.

Australia has woken up late to the millennium bug: in early

1999 the National Australia Bank reported that 90 percent of companies are not ready and most expect it to affect their business.

Sydney

Sydney is busy preparing for the Games with a building bonanza, as over A\$2 billion (£800m/US\$1.3b) is being spent on sports and transport facilities in the city with construction taking place on over fifty sites. Many Sydney-siders are reportedly disenchanted with the Games already as a result of all the disruption, and one poll showed that almost 40 percent would leave the city during the Games themselves.

Sydney is ready to party, however. The city has been gearing up since 1996 to welcome the new millennium, and looks set to stage one of the most spectacular parties on the planet.

New Year's Eve, 1999

The city is planning a 24-hour party for residents and visitors, with most activities focused on the harbour. The celebrations will start in the afternoon and run right through until the dawn of the next century. More than a million people are expected to gather around the foreshores and a mass of spectator craft will also fill the harbour to witness a gigantic fireworks display, which will be launched from three major sites on either side of the harbour bridge and from the bridge itself, providing a total of seven synchronised firing platforms over a distance of 14km. Large video screens will be installed at a number of outdoor locations to provide close-up views and relay other events from around the world. Sydney-siders have also given their New Year's Eve party a masked theme in recent years, donning a unique 'Sydney mask' for the event – some of them even mask their boats.

Events planned include NYE Rock, a concert featuring headline international acts; NYE Carnaval, a programme of 'sophisticated dance music with a great dance floor' held in Hyde Park; NYE for Kids, a 'big concert for small people' with popular children's performers; the Lord Mayor's Picnic, which gives 1600 disadvantaged children and their families the chance to watch the spectacle from one of the best harbourside locations; and the Sydney Mask Party, which is hosted by the Lord Mayor at the Opera House Forecourt for local guests and celebrities. Street entertainers, magicians, Chinese dragons, jugglers and circus acts will also perform throughout the city.

Ⓔ publicaffairs@cityofsydney.nsw.gov.au

Ⓦ http://www.sydneycity.nsw.gov.au/whatson/millnnum.htm

Olympic Games 2000

The Olympic flame will be lit in Greece on May 8, 2000 and will then travel through twelve Pacific nations before arriving in Australia on June 8, where a relay of 10,000 torch-bearers will then carry it on one of the longest journeys (27,000km) in Olympic history. Starting at Uluru (Ayers Rock), the flame will travel by camel through Broome, by submersible over the Great Barrier Reef, and by surf boat across Bondi Beach before arriving in Homebush Bay for the opening ceremony on September 15, 2000.

More than 10,000 athletes from 171 nations are expected to compete in the Games of the XXVII Olympiad (September 15–October 1, 2000). The Games will be held in two zones. The Sydney Olympic Park, situated at Homebush Bay 14km from the city centre, will have venues for fourteen sports and will include the 110,000-seater Olympic Stadium as well as the 12,500-seater Sydney International Aquatic Centre, the Olympic Village, and a 440-hectare Millennium Park. The park will be bisected by a 1.5km-long strip, the Olympic Boulevard, where visitors can wander even if they don't have tickets to events. Olympic sailing will for the first time become a true spectator sport, with races set against the spectacular backdrop of the harbour, and the country's most famous beach, Bondi, will host the beach volleyball.

The **Paralympic Games** (October 18–29, 2000) will be the largest staged since the first one held in 1960, with over four thousand athletes taking part in eighteen sports (fourteen of which are Olympic sports).

The **Olympic Arts Festival** is a four-year programme of cultural events which started with the Festival of Dreaming (1997) and A Sea Change (1998). **Reaching the World** (throughout 1999) is a touring programme that takes top Australian artists and performers around the regions represented by the Olympic symbol (Europe, Africa, Asia, the Americas and Oceania). More than seventy events will take place in fifty countries and 150 cities and towns, involving exhibitions, films, literature, electronic and digital media, dance, theatre, and music. The **Harbour of Life** festival (August 1–October

Global Fireworks

● Scientists at the Moscow Space Institute want to create a millennium fireworks display in space by sending up decommissioned nuclear missiles loaded with metal strips and coils. The metal strips and coils would be lit up by the sun as they float back down, creating an 'illuminated cosmic cloud'. They've experimented with the concept in the past, but this time they want it to be a global public spectacle.

● Hundreds of cities and towns around the world are planning their 'biggest and best ever' fireworks displays but insiders predict that demand will outstrip supply. Chinese factories, where most of the world's fireworks are made, have already got full order books and some party organisers might be left with nothing but a damp squib.

● An eight minute-long fireworks spectacular can take up to 100 hours to plan, including writing a computer program to co-ordinate musical crescendos with concussions from shell flights of anything from 300 to 1000ft.

● It's estimated that around 400,000 tonnes of fireworks will be exploded globally over the millennium. Industry sources say that the environmental impact will be 'negligible'.

24, 2000) is billed as the 'final presentation of Australian culture at the dawn of the new millennium' and will embrace 'both the physical and imagined notions' of Sydney harbour. It will feature a series of spectacular concerts in the Domain, Centennial Park, the Olympic Park and around the foreshores of the harbour, as well as a comprehensive entertainment programme involving the performing, visual and decorative arts with the participation of Australia's leading theatre companies, orchestras, galleries, museums and dance companies.

Sydney Organising Committee for the Olympic Games (SOCOG),
PO Box 2000, Sydney, NSW 2001 Ⓣ 02/9297 2000 Ⓕ 9297 2020
Ⓦ http://www.sydney.olympic.org
Comprehensive and well-organised pages detailing every single aspect of the
Sydney 2000 Olympics.

Sydney Paralympic Games Organising Committee, PO Box 17, Broadway,
NSW 2008 Ⓣ 02/9297 2000 Ⓕ 9297 2355
Ⓦ http://www.sydney.paralympic.org

Olympic Arts Festival Ⓦ http://www.sydney.olympic.org/culture/

Mount Warning

The laid-back community of **Byron Bay** to the northeast of Sydney is popular with surfies, backpackers and hippies and is a popular spot to watch the sunrise since Cape Byron is the easternmost point on the Australian mainland. Inland, the 1157m peak of Mount Warning (or Wollumbin – meaning 'cloud-catcher' – to the Bandjalung Aborigines) is technically the first place where the sun's rays strike Australia. The **Caldera First Light Festival** will take place on December 31 at the foot of the mountain. This multicultural folk festival will feature a 'moonscapers' light show (designed to re-create the original form of Mount Warning), music on three stages on the floor of the valley, a children's festival, and a 'mini-festival at each light source, covering a diameter of around 40-50 kilometres'.

The Green Olympics?

As with any project of this size, the Sydney Olympics has attracted its fair share of controversy, most notably over fat-cat salaries for bureaucrats, cost over-runs and secrecy over contracting procedures. It also became embroiled in the scandal over Olympic bribery in 1999. Aboriginal groups campaigning on land rights are also threatening boycotts and protests.

Another aspect of the Games which has not escaped controversy is their environmental credentials. The Sydney Organising Committee for the Olympic Games (SOCOG) has set out a programme which it claims is 'the most comprehensive set of environmental commitments ever proposed by a bid city', and Greenpeace, which has been involved in developing these guidelines from the beginning, say they will be 'the world's first green Games'.

The Olympic Athlete's Village will be the world's largest solar suburb; all 665 homes will have solar-powered electricity and water heating (the homes will be sold to the public after the Games). Sydney 2000 will also be the world's first car-free Olympics, with almost all spectators using public transport; natural gas-powered vehicles will also be used.

But questions still remain over the presence of heavy metals and other contaminants at Homebush Bay: for decades chemical companies such as Union Carbide and ICI have left a 'toxic legacy of dangerous proportions' at this former industrial site. Although the Olympic site itself has been cleaned up, Greenpeace is calling for urgent decontamination of the surrounding area.

Queensland

One of the most extravagant galas taking place is the **Great Barrier Reef Millennium Event** (December 30, 1999– January 2, 2000). Aimed at the top end of the market, this five-day/four-night event is based at the *Sheraton Mirage* in Port Douglas and culminates in a trip aboard one of the Quicksilver catamarans to a huge platform moored on the Outer Reef 45 miles offshore, where tables will be set for a gourmet New Year's Eve dinner accompanied by spotlights, laser beams, a 'series of water sculptures bathed in ultraviolet light' and a giant reflective 'water screen' which will be hooked up to the world party. Space is limited to 240 people and packages cost from A$3180 (£1223/US$1960) to A$4060 (£1560/US$2500).

Great Barrier Reef Visitors Bureau ℡ 07/4099 4644
Ⓔ reservations@millenniumparty1999.com
Ⓦ http://www.MillenniumParty1999.com/

TRAVEL BRIEF

Australia and New Zealand together are undoubtedly *the* destination for the year 2000, and many people visiting one will also take the opportunity to visit the other. Expect difficulties with both flights and accommodation all year.

GETTING THERE Australia has two main airlines, Qantas and the largely domestic Ansett Australia, although many other major carriers also have services from around the world, most flying direct to Sydney. Ansett, the official carrier for the Olympic Games, is arranging extra domestic services to ensure full availability, but there are unlikely to be additional long-haul services owing to the difficulties of getting route licences. Book as far ahead as possible, and when in doubt try other Australian gateways. Fares are expected to rise by anything between 100–300 percent for December 1999.

ACCOMMODATION There are likely to be some accommodation shortages in Sydney during the Olympics, with around 50,000 beds currently available, an estimated 160,000 needed, and a 10 percent bed tax to help pay for the Games. As well as the new building currently underway, ships will be anchored in the harbour as floating hotels, and locals are being encouraged to open their doors for rentals and B&B. Expect to pay premium prices for apartment and house rentals. SOCOG has two official private home rental programmes, Homehost (B&B accommodation for athletes and their families) and Homestay, which will offer vacant, furnished houses and apartments. The official agent for Homestay is: Ray White Real Estate, PO Box 5200, Sydney, NSW 2001 ℡ 02/9262 3700 Ⓕ 9262 3737; within Australia: ℡ 1-800/646

766. Home exchanges are worth considering. Try home exchange bureaux in your home country or Web sites such as:

Ⓦ http://www.sydneycity.net//accomguide.htm

Ⓦ http://www.holi-swaps.com

Ⓦ http://www.sydney.auscape.net/accom.html

Olympic tickets: Official ticket agencies can provide a variety of packages to the Games. UK: Sportsworld, New Abbey Court, Stert Street, Abingdon, Oxon OX14 3JZ; Ⓣ 01235/554844 Ⓕ 554841

Ⓔ travel@sportsworld.co.uk Ⓦ http://www.sportsworld.co.uk

New Zealand: Sportsworld International Ⓣ 09/307 0770. South Africa: Sportsworld Events and Tours Ⓣ 11/646 4862.

TOURIST OFFICES National: Level 4, 80 William St, Woolloomooloo, Sydney, NSW 2011 Ⓣ 02/9360 1111 Ⓕ 9331 3385; New South Wales: 11–31 York St, Sydney, NSW 2000 Ⓣ 02/9132 077 Ⓕ 9224 4411. UK: London Ⓣ 0181/780 2229; Aussie Help-line Ⓣ 0990/561434. US: New York Ⓣ 212/687-6300; Los Angeles Ⓣ 310/229-4870.

Ⓦ http://www.aussie.net.au/ (tourism)

Ⓦ http://www.sydney.olympic.org/ (Olympics).

TOURS UK: Allways Pacific Ⓣ 01494/875757; Austravel Ⓣ 0171/734 7755; Jetset Ⓣ 0990/555757; Travel Portfolio Ⓣ 01284/762255. US: Ozdive Ⓣ 972/818-1575; Maupintours Ⓣ 800/255 4266; Travcoa Ⓣ 800/598-1001.

COUNTRY CODE Ⓣ 61

BELGIUM

B elgium has no official plans for the millennium beyond those revealed for the EC government-dominated city of Brussels. The city of **Gand** will be celebrating the 500-year anniversary of the birth of Emperor Charles V with festivities in the year 2000.

European Cities of Culture 2000

Brussels is one of nine European Cities of Culture in the year 2000, the others being Avignon, Bergen, Bologna, Kraków, Helsinki, Prague, Reykjavík and Santiago de Compostela.

Since the programme started in 1985 one European cultural capital has been selected each year, but to mark the millennium nine were selected: three from the north, three from the centre, and three from the south. Each city will present its own cultural programme, but they will also work together on a number of projects.

One example of this co-operation is the **ARCEUnet** project, a joint programme involving Bergen, Bologna, Kraków and Santiago de Compostela, which aims to link together by satellite all the main museums and cultural institutions in each city into a vast 'virtual museum', where visitors will be able to browse among art works, architecture, sculpture and other cultural treasures in any of the cities.

The nine cities will also be producing audiovisual **Self-Portraits** reflecting their individual identities and the diversity of Europe over the centuries. The self-portraits will then be combined into a CD-ROM creating a data bank of European cultural projects.

Another joint project is the **Transeuropean Literary Express**, a train packed with over a hundred writers from all over Europe which will leave Lisbon in May 2000 on a seven-week journey through twelve countries, winding up in Berlin. The participants will stop off for literary events en route and a book of their joint experiences will be published in 2001.

Brussels

As one of the **European Cities of Culture 2000**, Brussels is aiming to recast its stodgy image and to project a more dynamic, multicultural side to itself.

The theme of Brussels 2000 is 'The City'. The programme will include events such as a **Festival of Science** (April 1999–November 2000); a massive **Parade** along the course of the underground River Zenne (June 2000); the **Sablon Carousel**, an open-air festival of equestrian sports, dancing and brass band music in the Prince Albert Barracks (June 2000) and the renovation of the **Mont des Arts**. Other events and projects include an exhibition, **We Are So Happy**, featuring giant blow-ups of a hundred pictures taken by Magnum photographers from around the world which will be hung from public buildings and houses (Summer 2000); the **New Circus**, which will bring together top-class contemporary circuses for a series of guest performances and a huge circus festival (December 1999–Autumn 2000); a **Theatre Marathon**, with playwrights from abroad being invited to live in Brussels and stage a production; a **Bal Moderne**, which will build on the city's reputation for contemporary dance (September 2000); and the restoration of the **Garden of the House of Erasmus.**

Bruxelles/Brussels 2000, 50 rue de l'Ecuyer, 1000 Brussels ⓣ 02/214 2000 ⓕ 214 2020 ⓔ admin@brussels2000.be ⓦ http://www.tib.be

TRAVEL BRIEF

Most tourism in Belgium is centred on Brussels and the medieval cities of Bruges and Ghent. The pattern seems unlikely to change in 2000, with Brussels as one of Europe's many cultural capitals. Events are spread out over the year, from February onwards.

GETTING THERE Advance booking may be advisable, but there shouldn't be any major transport problems. There are numerous flights into Brussels from all major and many minor European airports as well as long-haul destinations, including several large US cities. There are frequent, fast rail links between Brussels and Paris, Amsterdam, London and other European cities.

ACCOMMODATION The presence of the EU, NATO and other major organisations means that Brussels has more than its fair share of expensive business hotels. There shouldn't ever be a crisis, but as ever, book well ahead for major public holidays in Brussels, Bruges and Ghent.

TOURIST OFFICES National: 63 Rue Marché-aux-Herbes (also known as Grasmarkt), B-1000 Brussels Ⓣ 02/504 0390 Ⓕ 513 0280; Brussels: Hôtel de Ville, Grand-Place Ⓣ 02/513 8940 Ⓕ 514 4538 Ⓦ http://www.tib.be Bruges: Ⓣ 050 448 686 Ⓕ 448 600; Ghent: Ⓣ 09/266 5232 Ⓕ 225 6288. UK: London Ⓣ 0891/887799 (premium rate) Ⓕ 0171/458 0045. US: New York Ⓣ 212/758-8130 Ⓕ 355-7675 Ⓔ info@visitbelgium.com Ⓦ http://www.visitbelgium.com (with links to many other sites operated by Belgian regions and cities).

TOURS UK: Allez France Ⓣ 01903/748100; Belgian Travel Service Ⓣ 01992/456101; Kirker Selected Cities Ⓣ 0171/231 3333; Page & Moy Ⓣ 0116/250 7979; Prospect Holidays Ⓣ 0181/995 2163; Travelscene Ⓣ 0181/427 8800. US: CIT Tours Ⓣ 212/697-2100; Euro Bike and Walk Tours Ⓣ 800/321-6060; Euroseven Ⓣ 800/890-3776; TravelBound Ⓣ 212/334-1350; Tti Travel Ⓣ 847/520-8087.

COUNTRY CODE Ⓣ 32

BRAZIL

Brazil has no national plans but **Rio de Janeiro** is likely to be a hot ticket for New Year's Eve 1999 – it was recently voted amongst the top five destinations in the world where people would like to party on that date, according to a survey by a German tour operator. Any celebration as big as Brazil's **Carnaval** is likely to be a popular option in 2000, and although Carnaval parades take place all over the country, the biggest draw is always Rio's spectacular parade.

In the year 2000 Brazil will also be celebrating the **500-year Anniversary** of its discovery by the Portuguese navigator

Pedro Alvares Cabral in April 1500. There is some debate as to where he actually landed but **Porto Seguro**, in the state of Bahia, probably has the best claim. This major beach resort will be the main focus of the '500 Anos' celebrations, and the stretch of coast near Porto Seguro has already been christened the 'Costa do Descobrimento'.

An **Encounter Memorial** is being built adjacent to the island of Coroa Vermelha in southern Bahia where the first mass was said in Brazil. It will feature a sculptural monument, an Encounter Museum, and a cultural centre for the Pataxo Indian community. National celebrations will include conferences, musical shows, films, publications, CD-ROMs, and creating a 500 Years Library. A replica of Cabral's ship *Capitania* is also being built and will sail from Lisbon in March 2000 for Salvador, Bahia, and then on to Rio de Janeiro in April 2000.

The **Sao Paulo Bienal** is one of the most important exhibitions of contemporary visual art in Latin America and is usually held later in the year. An especially grand exhibition is also being planned for April–June 2000 (in addition to the main event from October–December 2000), which has been provisionally named the 'Show dos 500 Anos'.

The mayor of **Brasilia** is planning celebrations in two hundred different venues across the capital, as well as a **Human Countdown Clock**. There will be a March of the Stars parade on December 31, 1999, followed by a hi-tech laser and fireworks display on the theme of the 500-year anniversary celebrations.

Ⓦ http://www.mre.gov.br/cnvc/entrada.html

Home pages of the National Commission for the Celebration of the 500-year Anniversary of the Discovery of Brazil (Portuguese only).

Ⓦ http://www.veracruz500.org.br/

The Ministry of Culture's 500 anos pages (Portuguese only).

Ⓦ http://www.brasil500.com.br/

Globo TV's pages on their 500 anos project (Portuguese only).

Rio de Janeiro

New Year's Eve in Rio de Janeiro is marked with special celebrations since the turning of the year is also the feast day of **Iemanjá**, the deity (*orixá*) of the Sea. People arrive from deep in the interior of Brazil to take part, but the event also attracts cariocas from all walks of life. The beach is bright with flickering candles and the sea sprinkled with offerings (mirrors, beads, combs, flowers) to **Iemanjá**, who is said to be incredibly vain. Everybody dresses in white, following the tradition that symbolises peace and honours **Oxalá**, the most powerful *orixá*.

This is primarily a religious event, but it has also become a massive party with some two million people descending on the 4km-long Copacabana beach. Three huge sound stages along the beach start belting out samba and Brazilian pop music from around 10pm onwards, keeping local cariocas and visitors dancing through until dawn. At midnight, a vast fireworks display is set off from five locations on the sand, an offshore barge, and the two forts at either end of the beach.

On New Year's Eve, 1999 a spectacular show will be transmitted from a 100m high resolution screen erected on the sands in front of the Copacabana Beach Hotel.

Many hotels and restaurants along the beach offer sumptuous buffets, dancing and samba shows in addition to the (free) public events on the beach itself, with grandstand views of the displays.

From New Year's Eve onwards preparations begin for **Carnaval**, building up to a week of intense revelry with numerous Carnaval balls (*bailes carnavalescos*) and culminating in the parade of samba schools for which Rio is famous. In 2000, Carnaval takes place in the week leading up to March 5, when the parade takes place.

TRAVEL BRIEF

Rio thrives on crowds and has always been known for its ability to party. The millennium promises to be the biggest party yet.

GETTING THERE Rio is served by 28 international airlines as well as the Brazilian carriers Varig, Vasp and Transbrasil. Between them they offer direct flights to eighty destinations around the globe, as well as a wide domestic network. Flight information ⓣ 021/398 4526/7. There are regular shuttles from Rio to São Paulo from Rio's Santos Dumont airport.

ACCOMMODATION Rio has over 256 hotels offering more than 21,000 beds but they are all likely to be heavily booked well in advance of New Year's Eve 1999 and Carnaval 2000. Other accommodation options include private house and apartment rentals. Some of the best views of the fireworks will be from parties on the 37th floor *St Honoré Restaurant* in *Le Méridien Copocabana* ⓣ 21/546 6447; the roof bar of the *Hotel Miramar Palace* ⓣ 21/521 1122; the roof bar of the *Rio Atlântica* ⓣ 21/548 6322; the *SkyLab Bar* of the *Rio Othon Palace Hotel* ⓣ 21/522 1522; and the *Sofitel Rio Palace* ⓣ 21/525 1232.

TOURIST OFFICES Embratur, Rua Uruguaiana 174, 8th floor, 20050-092 Rio de Janeiro ⓣ 021/509 6017 ⓕ 509 7381 ⓔ rio@embratur.gov.br ⓦ http://www.embratur.gov.br

Riotur, 9th floor, Rua da Assembléia 10, 20011-000 Rio de Janeiro ⓣ 021/217 7575 ⓕ 531 1872 ⓔ riotur@rio.gov.br ⓦ http://www.rio.rj.gov.br/riotur

Rio Convention and Visitors Bureau, Rua Visconde de Pirajá 547, 6th floor, 22415-900 Rio de Janeiro ⓣ 021/259 6165 ⓕ 511 2592 ⓔ rcvb@embratel.net.br ⓦ http://www.rioconventionbureau.com.br UK: London ⓣ 0171/341 0303 ⓕ 431 7920 ⓔ destinations@pwaxis.co.uk US: New York ⓣ 212/490-9350.

TOURS UK: Cox & Kings ⓣ 0171/873 5000; Journey Latin America ⓣ 0181/747 8315; Union-Castle Travel ⓣ 0171/229 1411. US: Amazon Explorers ⓣ 800/631-5650; Amazon Tours & Cruises ⓣ 818/246-4816; Frontiers ⓣ 800/245-1950; Grand Circle Travel ⓣ 800/221-2610.

COUNTRY CODE ⓣ 55

BRITAIN

B ritain is set for a millennium boom. No other country can match the huge range of new attractions and facilities, from state-of-the-art science and cultural centres to millennium forests, cycle tracks, stadiums, art galleries, public squares, bridges and environmental schemes springing up all over Britain. Many of these are intended to benefit local communities but numerous others are major leisure attractions in their own right. The British Tourist Authority has launched a massive overseas marketing campaign to attract potential visitors to 'the world's leading millennium destination' and hopes for an estimated 27 million tourists in 2000, generating £14.5 billion (US$24b) in revenue.

Marketing itself as 'The Millennium City', London in particular is hoping to capitalise on the year 2000, and is expecting fifteen million overseas tourists. Over £6 billion (US$10b) is being lavished on the capital's tourism facilities, which includes 55 new hotels as well as major projects such as the Tate Gallery of Modern Art, the British Airways London Eye, the Great Court at the British Museum, and the £758m (US$1.13b) Millennium Dome at Greenwich.

Britain's millennial bonanza is largely due to the success of the National Lottery, set up in 1993, which supports five 'good causes' including the **Millennium Commission**. The Commission's role is to 'assist communities in marking the close of the second Millennium and the start of the third Millennium' and will have distributed an estimated £2 billion (US$3.4b) by the year 2000 – a sum that dwarfs other national budgets.

As well as projects in **London** (see p.63–84) and the **Regions** (see p.86–108) the Millennium Commission has also supported a number of 'umbrella' projects covering the whole country. These include the creation of around three hundred **millennium greens** in local communities, the renovation of 122 miles of **canals and waterways**, one thousand new **woodland and forest areas**, one hundred new **town fountains**, and 250 new or renovated **village halls**.

One of the most extensive national projects is the creation of **Millennium Routes**, a network of over 3000 miles of cycle paths being co-ordinated by the Bristol-based Sustrans group. A combination of traffic-free paths on disused railways, towpaths and routes on minor or 'traffic-calmed' roads, the whole network is due to open on June 21, 2000. The Millennium Routes are part of a much larger National Cycle Network, planned to cover 6500 miles by the year 2005. The

Millennium in the Media

● The BBC's millennium programmes will include a definitive *History of Britain*; a ten-part series, *Millennium*, re-creating some of the great monuments of civilisation using computer graphics; a history of the twentieth century through the eyes of children called *Rewind*; and a series on religious art, *Seeing Salvation*. Preoccupations with the end of the world will come under the spotlight in *The Big End*, whilst *Dawn of Man* will portray our ancestors as they really lived. A five-day festival in May 2000, *Millennium Music Live*, will culminate in a 24-hour live musical broadcast from across the country, *The Perfect Day*. The BBC's national and local radio stations are producing *The Century Speaks*, based on interviews with over eight thousand people.

● ITV will be interweaving the cast of Coronation Street's millennium night celebrations with events taking place around Britain, anchored by Trevor MacDonald and Carol Vorderman, with Richard and Judy in the South Pacific. Channel Four's celebrations will probably be hosted by Chris Evans.

● Lion Television is stranding thirty volunteers on a remote Scottish island for a year for *Castaway 2000*. A New Year's Eve party on the island will be broadcast live on December 31, 1999, and will be followed by weekly updates over the following year.

● Channel 4 is transporting an average family back to a late Victorian terraced house in Greenwich in *1900 House*, where they will have to survive for three months without modern comforts.

● ITV is filming ten pregnant couples throughout 1999 in a series, *Birthrace 2000*, which will culminate in a race around the country's maternity wards on January 1, 2000 to locate the first birth.

● The new James Bond epic, *The World Is Not Enough*, will feature a spectacular opening sequence involving a high-speed boat chase down the Thames which ends with 007 (played by Pierce Brosnan) being dropped on to the Millennium Dome by balloon.

completion of the Millennium Routes will be celebrated with local, regional and national events during Ride the Net (June 17–25, 2000).

Other significant environmental projects for 2000 include the **Groundwork Foundation**'s transformation of wasteland sites into woodlands, wetlands or recreational facilities; **Woods on Your Doorstep**, a Woodland Trust programme to plant more than two hundred new community woods; and **Yews for the Millennium**, a programme to plant thousands of yews all over the country. Known as the tree of life to the Celts, yews can live for thousands of years, were often the focal point of pagan rituals and later became synonymous with parish churchyards.

On New Year's Eve, 1999 over four hundred churches will switch on new floodlights, a hundred others will ring new millennium bells, and some 2500 beacons will be illuminated all over the country – the biggest network of beacons lit in Britain since the reign of Elizabeth I.

Ⓦ http://www.visitbritain.com/millennium

The British Tourist Authority's millennium pages, with links to projects and events around the country.

LONDON

London has got millennium fever. Even taking big projects such as Sydney's Olympics 2000 and Hannover's Expo 2000 into acccount, no other city can equal the vast number of pro-

jects under construction or being planned in the capital. They may have little to do with the celebration of Christ's birth, but the city is about to acquire the Millennium Dome, a Millennium Bridge, a Millennium Village, and much more besides.

Part of the reason is, of course, that London includes the historic borough of **Greenwich**, the 'home of time' thanks to its status as the Prime Meridian of the World from where time all over the globe is measured. The sun might rise first in the South Pacific but the start of the new day, as the clock ticks past midnight on December 31, 1999 into the first millisecond of January 1, 2000, will most definitely be at Greenwich.

Greenwich

Celebrations at **Greenwich** will take place in two separate locations. The first of these is on the Greenwich Peninsula, 300 acres of derelict wasteland (formerly one of Europe's largest gas works) currently being transformed into Britain's national millennium exhibition, the **Millennium Experience**.

The second is in the historic centre of Greenwich itself, about a mile distant, which consists of **Greenwich Town** (where the tea clipper *Cutty Sark* is moored) and the adjacent Greenwich Park. Within the park are several famous listed buildings, including the **Royal Observatory Greenwich** (formerly the Old Royal Observatory), the **National Maritime Museum** and the **Queen's House**. The importance of the astronomical and maritime heritage of Greenwich was acknowledged with its elevation to World Heritage status in 1998.

Greenwich is promoting a series of millennium projects under the banner of **Greenwich Meridian 2000**, co-ordinated by the National Maritime Museum. Amongst these are a huge New Year's Eve party in the park (see p.80), a prestigious new exhibition on the theme of Time (see p.80), and sponsorship tie-ins with Guinness, Accurist and other corporations. The National Maritime Museum has recently been redeveloped at a cost of £20m (US$33m) and now boasts several new galleries and the largest free-span, glazed roof in Europe.

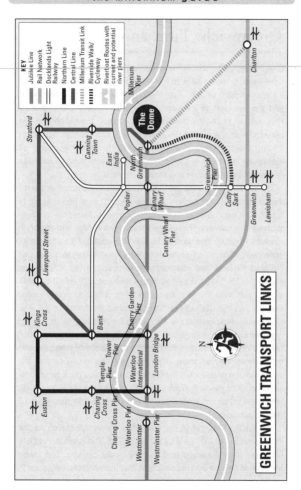

GREENWICH TRANSPORT LINKS

KEY

- Jubilee Line
- Rail Network
- Docklands Light Railway
- Northern Line
- Central Line
- Millenium Transit Link
- Riverside Walk/Cycleway
- Riverboat Routes with current and potential river piers

Charlton

Millenium Pier

The Dome

Stratford

Canning Town

East India

North Greenwich

Greenwich Pier

Greenwich

Lewisham

Poplar

Canary Wharf

Cutty Sark

Liverpool Street

Canary Wharf Pier

Kings Cross

Bank

Cherry Garden Pier

Euston

Charing Cross

Temple Pier

Tower Pier

Waterloo International

London Bridge

Charing Cross Pier

Waterloo Pier

Westminster

Westminster Pier

N

Greenwich, Time and the Meridian

Greenwich, the 'official home of world time', has associations with time-keeping dating back to the seventeenth century, with Charles II's appointment of John Flamsteed as the first Astronomer Royal and the founding of the famous Royal Observatory. Flamsteed's task was to study the positions of the stars, the moon and the planets, with the aim of discovering an astronomical method of finding the longitude of a ship at sea. This was becoming an increasingly urgent requirement, as maritime nations such as Britain set out to explore and map the oceans.

By the mid-nineteenth century it was also becoming apparent that an international system of time-keeping was needed, partly due to the expansion of communications and transport systems such as the railways. Previously, almost every town and region in the world kept its own time. In 1852 Britain adopted 'London time', essentially, Greenwich Mean Time (GMT), although this was not adopted formally by Parliament until August 2, 1880. At noon on November 18, 1883 the United States followed suit, adopting GMT and transmitting the time signal by telegraph to all major cities. Prior to this, the US had over three hundred local time zones. The Greenwich Meridian became a standard the following year.

A meridian is a north–south line used as a base point for astronomical observations, and thus for the calculation of longitude and time. There were so many different meridians in use around the world that the president of the United States called the International Meridian Conference in Washington, DC in October 1884 to decide where the prime meridian should be. Forty-one delegates from 25 nations attended.

During the conference the delegates chose Greenwich as the Prime Meridian of the World by a vote of 22–1. The International Date Line was then drawn up and 24 time zones created. The Prime Meridian is defined by the position of the 'Transit Circle' telescope in the Observatory's Meridian building; the cross-hairs in the eyepiece of the Transit Circle precisely define longitude 0° for the world.

Greenwich became the Prime Meridian for two reasons, the first of which was that the US had already adopted a system based on Greenwich Mean Time. The second was that by this period Greenwich's earlier expertise had ensured that 72 percent of the world's seafarers used charts based on the Greenwich meridian. Naming Greenwich as longitude 0° essentially solved the problem whilst inconveniencing the least number of people.

In the courtyard of the Old Royal Observatory at Greenwich a brass bar in the ground marks the Prime Meridian, 0° longitude. If there's one place in the world where you can be sure of knowing where you are, it should be here. And to the north of the Observatory, the New Millennium Experience is confidently planning a spire on Meridian Point in the Meridian Gardens to the west side of the Dome.

Unfortunately, the meridian has moved. Today, longitudes are defined by a differential Global Positioning Receiver, fed by a fleet of US military satellites, and this system places the meridian 336ft to the east of that brass strip at Greenwich. The WGS84 grid became the global standard for air navigation on January 1, 1988.

The New Millennium Experience is sticking with the Airy Meridian, although purists argue that this is a backward-looking approach which ignores advances in global mapping and the correct position as accepted by the international scientific community.

Ⓦ http://www.ast.cam.ac.uk/
The Royal Greenwich Observatory's pages contain a vast wealth of data on everything connected to astronomy and time.

Ⓦ http://www.greenwich2000co.uk/millennium/index.html
Describes plans for celebrations in historic Greenwich and sponsorship opportunities.

The compelling story of how the clockmaker John Harrison eventually solved the time-keeping problem is told in the best-selling book *Longitude* by Dava Sobel (Fourth Estate; Walker Pub. Co; 1995).

The Dome and the Millennium Experience

"This is Britain's opportunity to greet the world with a celebration that is so bold, so beautiful and so inspiring that it embodies at once the spirit of confidence and adventure in Britain and the spirit of the future in the world."

Prime Minister Tony Blair.

After seven years of planning, political wrangling and savagings by the media, Greenwich's **Millennium Dome** will finally open on December 31, 1999. Acting like a national lightning conductor for pre-millennial tensions, the Dome has attracted enormous criticism since architect Richard Rogers first unveiled his plan for what he described as 'an odyssey into the future, a twenty-first century Stonehenge'.

When Greenwich was first chosen as the exhibition site in 1996 fears were expressed that the peninsula, riddled with toxic chemicals from over a century of heavy industrial use, would never be cleaned up sufficiently. **Greenpeace** successfully campaigned against the Dome's PVC roof, claiming that it would create a 'toxic, plastic throwaway monster', and the government was forced to abandon it in favour of a glass-fibre and Teflon coating at an extra cost of £8 million (US$13.5m).

Despite an increasingly hostile press construction began, with the first of the 105-tonne steel masts hoisted into place in October 1997. The external structure of the Dome was completed in June 1998.

The Dome's translucent canopy, 1km in circumference, now glows in the Greenwich night sky, suspended by a web of steel from twelve vast, yellow masts. An unmissable statement of millennial confidence, Rogers' design is a visual triumph – and gratifyingly telegenic to boot. The interior, with its enormous 50m-high canopy creating a vast canvas for special effects, is breathtaking.

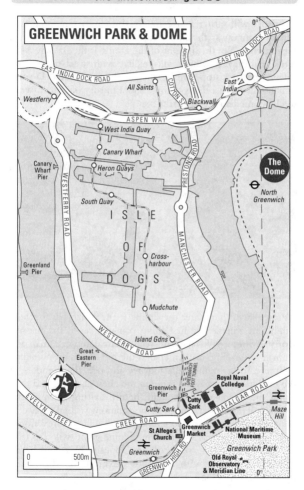

GREENWICH PARK & DOME

0°

East India Dock Road

Northern Approach

COTTON ST

EAST INDIA DOCK ROAD

Westferry

All Saints

Blackwall

East India

ASPEN WAY

West India Quay

Canary Wharf

Heron Quays

Canary Wharf Pier

WESTFERRY ROAD

South Quay

PRESTONS ROAD

The Dome

North Greenwich

I S L E

O F

D O G S

Crossharbour

Greenland Pier

MANCHESTER ROAD

Mudchute

WESTFERRY ROAD

Island Gdns

Great Eastern Pier

N

EVELYN STREET

Greenwich Pier

GREENWICH FOOT TUNNEL

Cutty Sark

Royal Naval Colledge

Cutty Sark

TRAFALGAR ROAD

Maze Hill

CREEK ROAD

St Alfege's Church

Greenwich Market

National Maritime Museum

Greenwich

Greenwich Park

GREENWICH HIGH RD

Old Royal Observatory & Meridian Line

0°

0   500m

Visitors will either arrive by riverbus from Greenwich or central London at the new **Millennium Pier** or by tube at **Greenwich North**. In front of the Dome is the 35-acre **Millennium Piazza**, which will be alive with street theatre and cafés. The first stop will be the 5000-seater **Baby Dome**, which will show a thirty-minute spoof history of Britain written by comedian Rowan Atkinson.

Visitors will then enter the Dome itself, which has fourteen exhibition zones. The first thing you will see is the massive **Body Zone**, a 90ft-tall, semi-recumbent statue of a man and woman embracing. You enter into the hip of this monumental sculpture for a 'multimedia journey through the wonders of the human body', passing through the chest chamber and then along the left arm of the man, before exiting through the woman's left foot. The main demonstrations will take place in the torso, where recorded sound effects will magnify noises made by our internal organs. The 'Dome giant' will also talk, and have a changing skin colour. Opposite here will be an Exploration Area, with interactive exhibits on the zone's theme of 'Look Good, Feel Good'.

The second most dramatic exhibit is the gravity-defying **Mind Zone**, a steel-and-plastic structure that is intended to challenge our perception to the limits, mixing science, art and technology to stimulate the senses, create new thoughts, and explore the boundaries of the human intellect. Visitors will be able to have their brains scanned, showing how different areas respond to different commands, and artificial intelligence will be explored in a 'robot zoo'.

In the other zones, **Transaction** will look at the power of finance and trade; **Global** examines the world 'from a different perspective, and what it means to be a global citizen'; **Communicate** is all about discovering different ways of talking to each other; **Learn** looks at creativity as the key to lifelong learning; **Mobility** probes into faster, cleaner, greener transport; **Living Island** challenges visitors with ways to protect and improve the environment around us; **Local** focuses on neighbourhoods and communities; **National Identity** explores what it means to be British; **Play** will have a digital playground and explores the future of play; **Rest** will give visitors a break in a 'magical sensory place'; **Spirit** delves into the spiritual and moral dimensions of humankind; and **Work** examines new ways of working in the future. There will also be a stage for **Our Town Story**, allowing communities around Britain to act out their respective histories.

At the centre of the Dome is a vast stage surrounded by a ring of multi-level viewing platforms where the **Millennium Show** will be performed up to five times a day. The show will fill the entire central space with 'light, colour and spectacle' and will be a cross between a rock show, a carnival and a musical. It will tell the story of man's fall from grace in the Garden of Eden and the search for redemption.

Within the Dome there will also be restaurants, bars, cafés, and rest areas. Surrounding it will be a landscaped riverside area with cycle- and walkways, lagoons and picnic areas.

Magic Mushroom 'Chill Out' Zone

Ever since the Millennium Dome was conceived the British press has been in a frenzy of speculation as to what it might contain, especially since final details for some zones were not revealed until well into 1999. But it didn't stop them guessing: 'The Dome for Druggies' trumpeted one *Daily Mail* headline, speculating that Dome chiefs planned to erect a 120ft-high 'magic mushroom' celebrating hippie culture as part of the New Age Rest Zone, with acid house music similar to that used in 'chill out rooms' in clubs to help ravers come down from a high. The 'massive fungus' story proved unfounded, although coincidentally London's Ministry of Sound nightclub launched a bid to take over the Dome's Spirit Zone using dance music to attract young people and rename it as 'High Trip', 'Beatbox' or 'DayClub'.

The Dome has attracted around £150 million (US$252m) in corporate sponsorship, with companies such as Boots, GEC, BAA, McDonalds, Tesco, BA, British Aerospace and British Telecom sponsoring zones relevant to their business. At the end of 2000 the Millennium Experience will close, and the Dome will be sold and redeveloped for leisure, hotel, exhibition or theme park use.

The **Millennium Village** is a separate development to create an environmentally and technically advanced urban village on the peninsula. The site will initially have around 250 homes (expanding later to 1400) built using state-of-the-art energy efficiency techniques. Work started in early 1999, with a Visitor Centre and show homes scheduled to open by 2000. The urban community is being designed as a model for six other similar schemes around the country and also incorporates the first of a new generation of Sainsbury's Ecostores. Designed to use 50 percent less energy, the store is half buried underground and incorporates solar- and wind-power energy generators, passive ventilation, natural lighting, and other innovations which may eventually be copied nationwide.

Ⓦ http://www.dome2000.co.uk

The official Millennium Experience Web site, with details on the National Programme as well as panoramic views from cameras inside the Dome.

GREENWICH TRAVEL BRIEF

TRANSPORT The Millennium Experience will have its own Jubilee Line tube station, North Greenwich (journey time from central London around twelve minutes). Designed by Sir Norman Foster, the tube station is the largest ever constructed in Europe. Nearly 40 percent of visitors are expected to arrive by tube, despite considerable delays in construction of the line which means that it may not open in time for the December 31 deadline. A proposed cable car across the river has been cancelled.

Because Greenwich has one of the worst records in London for traffic congestion, cars will not be able to park at or around the exhibition site (apart from pre-booked Orange badge holders).

The organisers are hoping that at least one million people will arrive by riverboat. Riverboat operators City Cruises are building four new luxury riverlines, each seating 520 passengers, to operate from the city centre to Greenwich, and Catamaran Cruises are adding a Hydrospace vessel to their fleet.

A Millennium Transit will operate from Charlton station on the North Kent Line. The site will be accessible from Greenwich Town Centre by bus, foot, bike and taxi.

Greenwich town centre can be reached by train from Charing Cross, Waterloo East or London Bridge (journey time around seventeen minutes). The Docklands Light Railway extension underneath the Thames to a new station at Cutty Sark (and on to Lewisham) is due to open in early 2000. Bus numbers 188 and 53 run from central London.

DOME TICKETS Timed tickets will be available through 20,000 National Lottery outlets, rail and bus stations, tour operators, and via the Dome's Web site from September 1999. Millennium Experience Information Line Ⓣ 0870/603 2000. City Cruises Ⓣ 0171/237 5134 Ⓕ 237 3498 is offering a combined 'Sail and Dome' package (return river travel and entrance) for £30 (US$50), or £55 (US$92) with champagne and smoked salmon en route.

TOURIST OFFICES Greenwich Tourist Information Centre, 46 Greenwich Church St, London SE10 9BL ℡ 0181/858 6376 Ⓕ 853 4607. The centre handles accommodation bookings and travel information.

VISITOR CENTRE The Millennium Experience Visitor Centre, Royal Naval College, Greenwich, London SE10 ℡ 0181/305 3456. Open 11am–7pm Monday–Friday, 10am–6pm weekends.

Millennium-on-Thames

The **River Thames** will undergo quite a revival for the millennium. An array of prestigious landmarks, from the Millennium Dome in Greenwich to the Tate Gallery of Modern Art at Bankside, are appearing on the river's banks; the old Battersea Power Station is to be converted into a new entertainment complex and the South Bank Centre is to be entirely revamped, forming part of a 'Millennium Mile' along the embankment. Plans are in hand to either restore or build new bridges and £530 million (US$890m) is being invested in 35 capital projects between London Bridge and Westminster Bridge.

In addition, transport on the river is being revived with the creation of new piers and the development of high-speed river bus services. The Millennium Commission is spending £6.83 million (US$11.5m) on two new piers at Blackfriars and Waterloo and enlarging existing piers at Westminster and the Tower of London.

The BA London Eye

Rivalling the Millennium Dome downstream at Greenwich as one of the capital's major millennium attractions, the **British Airways London Eye** (formerly known as the Millennium Wheel) will be sited in Jubilee Gardens on the South Bank, directly opposite the Houses of Parliament. The 135m-high structure will be the world's highest observation wheel and

London's fourth tallest structure. It will give passengers a bird's eye view of the capital and surrounding areas. The wheel features 32 fully enclosed capsules, each holding up to 25 people, and it will operate on a continuous rotation with the capacity to take 1500 people an hour; each rotation will take around thirty minutes and will be accompanied by a commentary on the scene below. It will open in early 2000.

The BA London Eye, Waterloo Millennium Pier. The wheel will be open in Winter (November–March) 10am–6pm, Summer (April–October) 9am–late evening. Tickets go on sale in Autumn 1999, priced at £6.95 (US$12) for adults, £4.70 (US$8) children.

The TS^{2}k Project

TS^{2}k (formerly Trafalgar Square 2000) is a project to help London's young unemployed find careers in the arts, media and entertainment industries by providing training at four creative enterprise centres in the capital. Its public centrepiece will be a spectacular programme of millennium celebrations integrating art, photography, video art, lasers and projections to showcase the creativity of those involved alongside international talents.

TS^{2}k, 8–14 Crinian St, London N1 9SQ ☎ 0171/833 0066.

The Millennium Bridge

By 2000 the eye-catching **Millennium Bridge** will span the Thames from below St Paul's Cathedral on the north bank to the new Tate Gallery of Modern Art at Bankside and the Globe Theatre on the south side. London's first new Thames crossing since Tower Bridge opened in 1894, it will also be the capital's first and only dedicated pedestrian bridge. The 4m-wide structure, with a central span of 240m, comprises an arc of stainless steel with a teak deck. Its minimalist horizontal lines won't be disrupted by lampposts or other paraphernalia, although it will have aerodynamically-designed handrails which will deflect wind high above pedestrians' heads. Designed by sculptor Anthony Caro in collaboration with Sir Norman Foster, the 350m-long bridge is expected to open in late 1999.

The South Bank

As part of the 'Millennial Mile' the **South Bank Centre** is to be redeveloped, with new galleries and concert halls replacing the Hayward complex and the restoration of the Royal Festival Hall. The oldest Gothic building in London, **Southwark Cathedral**, will also have a new visitor centre and extended parks to make it more accessible.

Two new footbridges are also being built alongside the current **Hungerford Bridge**, linking Charing Cross with Waterloo on the south side of the river. The two new pier-like walkways are intended to make the most of Brunel's original brick piers; there will also be pontoons for river boats and a floating restaurant.

The Tate Gallery of Modern Art

One of the most ambitious cultural attractions being created in London, the **Tate Gallery of Modern Art** is taking shape in Southwark, opposite St Paul's Cathedral. The £130 million (US$218m) redevelopment of the former Bankside Power Station will provide a permanent home for the Tate Gallery's collection from 1900 to the present day. The former turbine hall (an immense space 500ft long, 115ft high and 75ft wide) will become a 'covered street' displaying sculpture, and in addition there will be six gallery suites, 80,000 square feet of gallery space, a multimedia information centre, shops, cafés, and a rooftop restaurant. The gallery opens in May 2000 and is expecting 2.5 million visitors annually. The Tate's current premises at Millbank will be redeveloped at a cost of £32 million (US$54m) to become the **Tate Gallery of British Art**, for works from the sixteenth century onwards, and will be open in Spring 2001.

Elsewhere in London

The **British Museum**'s millennium project is the transformation of the 250-year-old building's central courtyard, the **Great Court**, into a covered square, providing a new cultural complex intended to rival the Louvre's glass pyramid.

Designed by Sir Norman Foster, the £94 million (US$158m) scheme involves the creation of a series of elliptical mezzanine floors around the Reading Room, with a 'spectacular walkway'

spiralling around the outside, linking the Great Court with the upper floors of the museum. On a lower level a new **Centre of Education** will offer a continuous programme of lectures, seminars and films, and a new suite of galleries for the museum's African collections. At the centre of the Great Court, the **Round Reading Room** is to house an information centre on the museum's collections and will be open to the general public for the first time in its history. The entire courtyard will be enclosed by a translucent roof. The scheme is due for completion in Autumn 2000.

Developers have announced a £20 million (US$34m) scheme to build a smaller version of the famous **Crystal Palace**, which was destroyed by fire in 1936. Situated in Blackheath, the project may be open by September 1999.

London Zoo's millennium project is a £4 million (US$6.7m) exhibit, the **Web of Life**. The three-storey glass building will house sixty of the world's most endangered species and will include a Micrariam, the tiniest zoo in the world, where visitors can observe insects normally hidden from view. They will also be able to visit a replica rainforest and a sea world with giant clams, jellyfish and other aquatic life. The project is scheduled to open in May 1999.

In the city's East End **Mile End Park** is being revitalised in a £33.5 million (US$56m) scheme that features a novel Green Bridge that will unite the two halves of the park currently separated by a busy road. The bridge will form a massive steel and earth archway over the road, planted with trees on top. It is due for completion in Autumn 2000.

In Wandsworth the **RENUE Initiative** (Renewable Energy in the Urban Environment) plans to demonstrate 'city living in the next millennium' with schemes including an environmental resource centre on the riverbank, wind turbines and photovoltaic systems for schools, and Britain's first solar-powered pub.

First Weekend Celebrations

● **Alexandra Palace**: The traditional New Year's Eve fireworks will be augmented by an ambitious plan to link Alexandra Palace with Crystal Palace by lasers, with 'flashing words and images meeting half-way over the Thames at Blackfriars Bridge'. ℡ 0181/365 2121.

● **Battersea Park**: The park will host a millennium fireworks and a free family extravaganza featuring street theatre, children's entertainment and music from 8pm–12.20am.

℡ 0181/871 7532.

Lighting the Skyline

A millennium project to illuminate the Croydon skyline, costing over £4 million (US$6.8m), will use new lighting technology to project artworks, videos, photographs, messages and other images onto high-rise buildings in the town centre. The data processing system will enable the buildings to change colour on a nightly basis, and people from around the world will be able to contribute ideas and images to be projected via the scheme's Web site. In 2000, for instance, the whole town will be temporarily draped in blood red colours during a campaign to collect 2000 pints of blood for the National Blood Bank. The illuminations will be launched on December 31, 1999 and will become a permanent feature.

Croydon Skyline Project ℡ 0181/667 6464 ⓦ http://www.skyline.org.uk

● **Church celebrations**: There will be a united act of worship at Westminster beginning at 7pm, with a gospel concert followed by a silent vigil at Westminster Abbey, a midnight mass at the Cathedral and a watchnight service at Central Hall; there will be services at all three venues from 11.30pm–12.10am. ℡ 0171/222 8010.

● **Greenwich Park**: The Old Royal Observatory and the National Maritime Museum are staging a party for around 50,000 people. The central event will be 'As Time Goes By', a spectacular multimedia show which will start with the Big Bang and use song, dance and narration to highlight the musical moments that have helped define humanity, from Mozart to McCartney, Schubert to Sinatra, and Gershwin to Gallagher. It will be broadcast live by the BBC. The top of Greenwich Hill and the Observatory is likely to be a crowded spot, offering a double vantage point over the park and the Dome. ℡ 0181/312 6745.

● **Millennium Dome**: The Gala opening night will be attended by 10,000 people including the Queen and Prince Phillip, VIPs and invited guests; competitions will be run for public tickets. The event will feature rock bands and classical orchestras, a special ninety-minute performance of the Millennium Show, plus lasers and fireworks over the Thames. The Royal Family and other VIPs will arrive on a flotilla of boats under police escort from Central London.

● **The Royal Parks**: Giant video screens may be erected in Regent's Park, Hyde Park, St James's Park, Green Park, and Kensington Gardens to alleviate the crush in central London. ⓣ 0181/298 2000.

● **The Thames**: Bridges on the Thames will be closed to traffic and used to stage a series of theatrical performances. Each bridge will provide a stage for a different performance or event on the theme of the river as the heart of London, and the river of time flowing down to the Dome at Greenwich. Fireworks will also be launched from barges and there may be grandstands in Battersea Park, Jubilee Gardens and elsewhere. Unfortunately, on millennium night the river will be at its lowest ebb and the extensive mud flats are not going to look good for the global broadcast. There is the possibility that the Thames Barrier might be closed for six hours to create an artifical high tide.

● **Trafalgar Square**: On Friday December 31, 1999 around 100,000 people are expected to crowd into London's biggest square and its surroundings, even though there is no entertainment (apart from a giant video screen) and alcohol is banned.

Saturday January 1, 2000

● **Celebration 2000**: Services will be held in churches, cathedrals and chapels to give thanks for the second millennium and seek a blessing on the third. The services will be preceeded by five minutes of nationwide bell-ringing at noon. ⓣ 0171/240 0880.

● **Millennium Dome**: Open to the public from 10am, with two sessions allowing 35,000 visitors in at a time.

● **New Year's Day Parade**: One of the world's biggest street parades is due to take place, with more than 10,000 performers. The three-hour jamboree will leave Parliament Square at noon and proceed via Trafalgar Square, Lower Regent Street and Picadilly to Berkeley Square. Two million spectators are anticipated.

Exhibitions and Festivals

● **Barbican Art Gallery**: 'Magnum: New Worlds' (January 1–March 31, 2000). An exhibition featuring the work of Magnum photographers worldwide, documenting the events of the last decade that raise global issues for the next millennium.

Barbican Art Gallery, Level 3, Barbican Centre, Silk Street, London EC2Y 8DS
Ⓣ 0171/638 5403.

● **British Museum**: 'Apocalypse and the Shape of Things to Come' (December 18, 1999–April 24, 2000). An exhibition on the demonic and apocalyptic artistic legacy of the Book of Revelation, featuring illuminated manuscripts, books, prints and drawings from the eleventh century to World War II.

British Museum, Great Russell Street, London WC1B 3DG Ⓣ 0171/636 1555.

● **Greenwich and Docklands International Festival**: (January 1–December 31, 2000). Numerous events with a millennium theme will take place throughout the year in Greenwich and surrounding areas.

Greenwich and Docklands International Festival, 6 College Approach,
Greenwich, London SE10 9HY Ⓣ 0181/305 1818 Ⓕ 305 1188.

● **National Gallery**: 'Botticelli: The Mystic Nativity' (November 17, 1999–December 31, 2000). An exhibition focusing on this famous and controversial work, exploring how the Florentine artist used the painting to contemplate the half-millennium in 1500 and the possible end of the world.

National Gallery, Trafalgar Square, London WC2N 5DN Ⓣ 0171/747 2885.

● **National Maritime Museum**: 'The Story of Time' (December 1, 1999–September 26, 2000). A large-scale exhibition with nearly three hundred artefacts from museums and galleries around the world illustrating our fascination with time and its symbols, from Father Time to the Apocalypse, from the Zodiac to immortality.

Queen's House, Romney Road, London SE10 9NF ⓣ 0181/312 6745.

● **National Portrait Gallery**: 'Faces of the Century' (October 22, 1999–January 30, 2000). An exhibition of one hundred photographic portraits illustrating diverse aspects of British life in the twentieth century.

National Portrait Gallery, 2 St Martin's Place, London WC2H OHE
ⓣ 0171/306 0055.

● **Royal National Theatre**: 'NT 2000' (January 1999–December 1999). Presentations from one hundred plays from the twentieth century, featuring readings, discussions with authors, directors and cast members. The programme runs chronologically through the year to demonstrate the progression of twentieth-century theatre.

National Theatre, South Bank, London SE1 9PX ⓣ 0171/452 3333.

● **The String of Pearls Millennium Festival**: (December 31, 1999–December 31, 2000). More than thirty 'national pearls' clustered along the banks of the Thames will be opening their doors in 2000, allowing access to many buildings normally closed to the public. These include Lambeth Palace, Westminster Hall, the Royal Courts of Justice, Custom House, and many other Establishment landmarks. Special events will also take place throughout the year at these and other locations.

String of Pearls Millennium Festival, 1 Hobhouse Court, Suffolk Street, London
SW1H 4HH ⓣ 0171/665 1540 ⓕ 665 1537 ⓦ http://www.stringofpearls.org.uk

● **Victoria and Albert Museum**: 'Art Nouveau 1890–1914' (April 6–July 30, 2000). A comprehensive exhibition on art and design at the turn of the century drawing on collections from a number of *fin-de-siècle* cities such as Brussels, Glasgow, Helsinki, Munci, Vienna and Paris.

Victoria and Albert Museum, Cromwell Rd, London SW7 2RL
Ⓣ 0171/938 8500.

LONDON TRAVEL BRIEF

TRANSPORT London Underground hopes to operate a free service on December 31, 1999 but there is uncertainty about how many of the 7000-strong workforce will turn up, or whether sponsors can be found to pay the £1000 (US$1700) bonuses being demanded. The police have asked for the whole network to be closed rather than run a partial service with the risk of dangerous overcrowding. There is also a risk of signal failures or ticket gates not working because of the millennium bug. There should be an extensive all-night bus service. Minicabs will be charging four times the normal rate, but black cabs must stick to fixed rates – so they will be scarce.

HOTELS Most of the capital's top hotels (such as the *Ritz*, the *Savoy*, the *Grosvenor*, the *Dorchester*) will be staging extravagant gala nights with prices to match; demand has been so high that ticket allocations will be based on a draw. More reasonably priced options include packages at the *Chelsea Village Hotel* Ⓣ 0171/565 1400, the *Radisson Edwardian* Ⓣ 0800/335588, the *Clarendon* Ⓣ 0181/318 4321 and Holiday Inns Ⓣ 0800/897121. Moderately-priced hotels can be booked for the Millennium period through the London Tourist Board Ⓣ 0171/932 2020, and good quality B&Bs through Uptown Reservations Ⓣ 0171/351 3445.

TOURIST OFFICES London Tourist Board, Glen House, Stag Place, London SW1E 5LT Ⓣ 0171/932 2000 Ⓕ 932 2067.

Millennium information is available on the Visitorcall line Ⓣ 0891/663344 or the Millennium Faxback service Ⓣ 0891/353717; calls cost 50p per minute. The millennium section of their Web site is at:

Ⓦ http://www.londontown.com/millennium

An (un)Dress Rehearsal for 2000

In the 1960s Timothy Leary had a vision that by the year 2000 cars would have vanished from Piccadilly to be replaced by grazing sheep and people strolling around naked. Impatience with the lack of progress towards this Arcadian vision led the group in this photograph to organise their own rehearsal in 1976, in the hope of popularising the concept. "The goats and cockerel were borrowed from the urban farm in Camden. It was early morning, and a few cars hooted. The police arrived just as the group was wrapped back in rugs", recalls one participant. No national paper would use the photo because of the naked men, but it did appear in the London magazine *Time Out*.

AROUND ENGLAND

As well as the numerous smaller projects taking shape in England, ten of the major Landmark Projects are being built at a total cost of over £600 million (US$980m).

Southern England

The first millennium sunrise in the country will occur over South Foreland, just to the east of the port of Dover. However, you won't be able to see it unless you live there: the residents of the village of **St Margarets-at-Cliffe** at South Foreland have asked the police to block off all access roads to the village, creating an exclusion zone for sunrise-watchers. The reason? They're worried that tipsy revellers will fall off the unprotected, sheer cliff face, and this remote location is very difficult for the emergency services to reach. The council is hoping instead that people will come to watch as sunrise strikes the **White Cliffs of Dover** just a few seconds later, and elaborate preparations are in hand for a **Torchlight Procession** on New Year's Eve, 1999 which will involve the lighting of hundreds of handmade lanterns from the Bethlehem Peace Lamp (an annual ritual) as street bands accompany the marchers to the seafront, where a huge sculptural bonfire, the 2nd Millennium Clock, will explode into a blaze of pyrotechnics. The first procession finishes at 7pm and another will take place at 11.30pm, culminating in the floodlighting of St Clements Church. On January 1, the **Carnival of the Planets**, with sculptural costumes, music and dance, will lead through the town to the Clock of the 3rd Millennium.

The **Isle of Wight** is famous for its palaeontological collections and at Sandown they're building a **Dinosaur Museum** in the shape of a pterodactyl which will be open by Autumn 2000.

One of the largest Landmark Projects in the south is the **Renaissance of Portsmouth Harbour**, an £86 million (US$144m) scheme which aims to make Portsmouth one of the great harbours of the world. The centrepiece is a 160m-high **Millennium Tower**, a maritime symbol in the shape of a billowing spinnaker where visitors will be able to ride up in lifts on the outside of the tower to a glass-floored viewing platform and then come back down again in a 'drop ride' with a 110m fall. The scheme also encompasses a 6km-long **Millennium Walkway** that will open up much of the Royal Navy harbour for the first time, a new footbridge, and a riverbus network to connect attractions on either side of the harbour. The historic dockyard (which includes the HMS *Victory*, the *Mary Rose* and the HMS *Warrior*) is being redeveloped into a hi-tech **Navy in Action** centre. On the Gosport side the former navy armaments depot, **Priddy's Hard**, is being redeveloped into a 20-acre Heritage Area with a new museum, **Explosion!**, and a redeveloped **Submarine Museum**. The entire project will be complete by Winter 2000.

Saving the world's most important plant seeds is an ambitious conservation programme being realised with the creation of the Royal Botanic Garden's **Millennium Seed Bank** at their facility at **Wakehurst Place** in West Sussex. The £75 million (US$126m) scheme aims to harvest over a thousand flowering plants native to the UK as well as 25,000 species of plants worldwide (10 percent of the world's flora) by 2010. The Seed Bank's public education centre is due to open in Autumn 2000.

Renaissance of Portsmouth Harbour, Civic Offices, Guildhall Square, Portsmouth PO1 2BG Ⓣ 01705/834812 Ⓕ 834975.
Ⓔ sjeffery@portsmouthcc.gov.uk
Ⓦ http://www.gosport.gov.uk/development/millennium/index.htm

Southwest England

The Georgian city of **Bath** will be hosting **Bath Ball 2000** on New Year's Eve, 1999. The privately-run event will be held in the city's recreation ground with eight thousand party-goers bopping through the night to DJs and three live bands. Bath is also planning a major refurbishment of its historic Roman baths as well as the creation of state-of-the-art spa facilities as part of the **Bath Spa Project**, due to open in Autumn 2000.

Bristol will be celebrating **First Weekend** with a major New Year's Eve event in the city centre at College Green and others in satellite districts. Over the weekend there will be street entertainment, beacon lighting, events at Colston Hall and the Council House, and a service in the Cathedral on January 1, 2000, culminating in bell-ringing at 12 noon.

Cornwall will be swamped by millions of visitors in August 1999 arriving for the **Solar Eclipse** (see box). To mark the occasion the Tate Gallery in St Ives is staging a special exhibition of new work, **Dark as Light** (May 1–November 30, 1999).

In the millennium year **Glastonbury Abbey** in Somerset will stage **Voices of Glastonbury** (Sept 13–17, 2000), a five-day programme celebrating the Abbey's history with dramatic performances of key events and a choral festival.

The port of **Plymouth** will be celebrating **First Weekend** with a live satellite link to Plymouth, New Zealand, the sealing of a time capsule, a premiere of New Music for the Millennium, fireworks and a series of beacons in a 'ring of fire' stretching into Cornwall.

One of the region's two Landmark Projects is **@Bristol**, which is at the centrepiece of a £400 million (US$672m) inner-city regeneration project in Bristol's Docklands – one of the largest in Europe. @Bristol will offer visitors an imaginative, hi-tech insight into the worlds of nature and science amidst stunning architecture and new public spaces.

The £97 million (US$163m) scheme covers eleven acres and has two main elements: **Explore@Bristol** is a hands-on science and technology centre where visitors will be able to take part in experiments, connect to telescopes, undersea rovers and science projects elsewhere in the world. It will also include a fully-equipped TV studio, a smaller TV studio for children and a planetarium. **Wildscreen@Bristol** is a completely new concept in wildlife centres, focusing on the insects and other small creatures which make up 95 percent of animal life on the planet. On-demand video, 'magic' observatories, and interactive exhibits will further the journey of discovery through the natural world. The centre will also include a **Botanical House** and an **IMAX theatre** for showing wildlife films and will act as the headquarters of ARKive, the

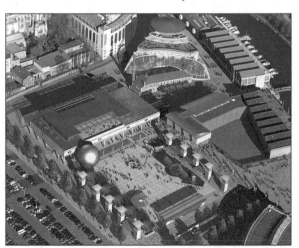

world's first globally accessible library of wildlife and natural history films, photographs and sound recordings. The development is expected to open in Spring 2000.

The region's other Landmark visitor attraction is the £74 million (US$124m) **Eden Project**, an ambitious scheme to transform a clay pit near **St Austell**, Cornwall, into one of the biggest greenhouses in the world containing two Biomes – miniature ecosystems showcasing the usefulness of plants and our dependence on them.

The larger of the two greenhouses will re-create the climate of the Humid Tropics and will rise to 50m in height to accommodate rainforest trees. The second Biome will re-create a Warm Temperate climate and house plants from regions such as the Mediterranean, Southern Africa and Southwestern America. Outside, 30 acres of grounds will display and interpret plants from temperate climates.

The project's energy will come from biomass and photo-voltaic cells, which will use sunlight to inflate the hexagonal Teflon panels covering the Biomes. The visitor centre will be open for Easter 2000, and the entire project by Easter 2001.

Bath Ball 2000, The Foundry, Walcot Street, Bath, Somerset BA1 5BD
Ⓣ 01225/310085 Ⓕ 319221. Tickets cost £220.

@Bristol, Deanery Road, Harbourside, Bristol BS1 5DB Ⓣ 0117/909 2000
Ⓕ 909 9920 Ⓔ information@at-bristol.org.uk Ⓦ http://www.at-bristol.org.uk

Eden Project, Watering Lane Nursery, Pentewan, St Austell, Cornwall PL26
6BE Ⓣ 01726/222900 Ⓕ 222901 Ⓦ http://www.edenproject.com

Glastonbury Abbey Ⓣ 01458/832267.

Tate Gallery St Ives, Porthmeor Beach, St Ives, Cornwall TR26 1TG
Ⓣ 01736/796226 Ⓕ 794480.

The East

Communities throughout **Essex** are participating in the **Essex Millennium Festival**, which has numerous events and activities planned. They're asking employers to donate £1 for each of their employees and for employees to donate £1 each to raise **A Million for the Millennium**. The project will focus on celebrations for young people, improving the local environment, and helping people in the developing world. The town of **Basildon** is building the world's first fully-glazed **Bell Tower**.

The resort of **Lowestoft** is the most easterly point in the British Isles and has grand plans for millennium celebrations despite the fact that South Foreland in Kent will see the dawn first because of the tilt of the earth's axis.

Norwich will be celebrating with a **City of Lights** spectacular and street theatre performances on New Year's Eve, 1999. On the **First Weekend** two temporary domes will be erected, a Dome of Science and Light, and a Multimedia Dome, which will house temporary displays on science, technology, and youth culture.

Kid's Millennium

● Said to be the UK's largest ever fund-raising campaign, the Children's Promise aims to persuade as many employees in the country as possible to donate the value of their final hour's earnings in 1999 to help the children of the next millennium. The campaign will help fund seven major charities working with children, and has been kick-started with a £1 million (US$1.7m) donation from Marks & Spencer.

● Channel Four has linked up with Oxfam, WWF-UK (Worldwide Fund for Nature) and VSO (Voluntary Service Overseas) to produce a series celebrating life around the world on the zero degree meridian. On The Line is an educational project for schools which aims to make the millennium meaningful for children.

Children's Promise, Bristol BS38 7ER ⓣ 0870/607 1999 ⓕ 609 1999
ⓔ childrens.promise@newmill.co.uk
ⓦ http://www.marks-and-spencer.co.uk/promise.

The **Norfolk and Norwich Millennium Project** is also taking shape in the city centre on the site of the old library opposite the cathedral. The facility will include a Millennium Library, a multimedia auditorium, business and learning centre, visitor centre, cafés and restaurants and is due for completion in March 2001.

In **Peterborough** work is underway on the **Green Wheel**, a 50-mile network of cycleways, footpaths and bridleways encircling the city which will link tourist attractions, nature reserves, picnic sites, sculpture trails, and parks. Phase II opens in September 1999, with completion of Phase III in September 2000.

Festival Co-ordinator, Essex Millennium Festival, Chelmsford Borough Council, Civic Centre, Chelmsford CM1 1JE ⓣ 01245/606901
ⓔ millennium@essexcc.gov.uk ⓦ http://millennium.essexcc.gov.uk
Norfolk and Norwich Millennium Project, 2nd floor, Blackburn House, 1 Theatre St, Norwich NR2 1RG ⓣ 01603/610524 ⓕ 610150.

The Midlands

Birmingham is staging **Towards the Millennium 2000**, a year-long festival of newly-commissioned work celebrating innovation and invention. It begins on New Year's Eve, 1999 with music and dance on two outdoor stages (Centenary and Victoria squares).

The city's Digbeth area is the site of **Millennium Point**, a Landmark project which aims to bring together 'education, leisure and technology in a centre dedicated to meet the challenges of the twenty-first century'. Construction on the £112 million (US$188m) project began in 1999, with completion due in late 2001.

The gateway to Millennium Point is the **Hub**, a series of linked public concourses with restaurants, cafés, exhibition and meeting areas and a 400-seater IMAX cinema. A key component is the **Discovery Centre**, which will integrate new technologies, historic and modern artefacts, interactive exhibits and multimedia displays in a three-dimensional network where you can move through the exhibits vertically as well as horizontally. Its exhibits will span three time frames: The Workshop of the World (1700–1900); Global Village (1900–2001); and Our Futures. Alongside this is the **Technology Innovation Centre**, where laboratories and workshops will show research and development in action. Millennium Point will also house the **University of the First Age**, which will include a young people's parliament, a library of educational futures, and facilities for young people to run their own local TV and radio channels.

Coventry is regenerating the northeast section of the city centre through the **Phoenix Initiative**, which will include the building of a Millennium Boulevard to link the Cathedral and Priory Place at one end with a new public square, Millennium Place, at the other.

Staffordshire's famous pottery industry will be celebrated in a major new visitor attraction, **Ceramica**, which opens in Burslem in September 1999.

Millennium Point, 1 Curzon St, Digbeth, Birmingham B4 7XG
Ⓣ 0121/303 2361 Ⓕ 303 4317
Ⓦ http://www.birmingham.gov.uk/millennium/

East Midlands

The city of **Nottingham** is staging the **Spirit of Notting-ham** festival over four days, starting with a street fair and sound and light spectacular on New Year's Eve, 1999; on January 1 local churches and community groups will stage a parade into the Old Market Square, an open-air service, and light a Flame of Hope, and on January 3 there will be a street theatre celebration.

The region's Landmark Project is the **National Space Sci-ence Centre** in **Leicester**, a dramatic, futuristic structure sited at Abbey Meadows, close to the city centre. Much of the building is below ground, housed inside disused stormwater tanks, but it is topped by a 38m-high tower housing rockets and satellites that will change colour and vary in opacity depending on the seasons and the viewpoint. The centre will comprise five core elements: the **Electric Sky Planetarium**, the largest outside London; a **Visitor Centre**, which will combine real space hardware with interactive exhibits and direct output from satellites; the **Challenger Learning Cen-tre**, where people can take part in simulated space flights; the **CATSAT** facility, where students can build their own satellite; and a **Research Centre**, housing one of Europe's largest University space research programmes. Construction started on the £46m (US$77m) project in 1999 and it is due to open in February 2001; the **Challenger Learning Centre** opens at a temporary location in Leicester in Autumn 1999.

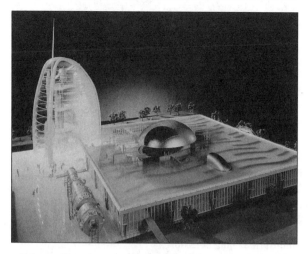

Other millennium projects include the National Forest's **Millennium Discovery Centre** and the construction of an **Aerial Walkway** in the Torrs Gorge.

National Space Science Centre, Mansion House, 41 Guildhall Lane, Leicester LE1 5FQ Ⓣ 0116/253 0811 Ⓕ 261 6800 Ⓔ info@nssc.co.uk Ⓦ http://www.nssc.co.uk

The Northwest

Liverpool will be staging the **River of Light** on New Year's Eve 1999, with the main event at Pier Head, with top bands and lighting and laser displays, linked to other locations in the city by widescreen broadcasts. Across the Wirral there will be live musical performances in Hamilton Square, with huge video walls on either side of the stage. The River of Light project will also illuminate buildings on both river banks, create light and water bridges across the Mersey, and stage light spectaculars with water screens in the docks. Other events planned include children's lighting shows on the river and a light ship with water screen that will travel along the Mersey and Manchester Ship Canal, connecting with community-based festivals and the Millennium Waterfronts celebration. The city's *Cream* club will be staging a New Year's Eve rave for three thousand people at its home base, as well as Manchester and London, with top DJs flying between venues.

Manchester will be staging a multi-cultural event which will climax with a **First Weekend Parade** on January 2, 2000. The famous *Cream* club will be staging a **Millennium Rave** for eight thousand people at the Manchester Evening News Arena on New Year's Eve. The city will also be staging **Streets Ahead**, a massive outdoor spectacle with parades, street theatre, music and fireworks (April 25–May 31, 1999 and April 23–June 3, 2000)

The Millennium Quarter and Manchester and Salford Cathedrals will be linked to Salford Quays and Trafford Wharf in a two-day **Millennium Waterfronts** celebration that will feature fire, light and laser displays, street entertainment and funfairs on New Year's Eve, 1999, followed by a waterborne pageant and community festival over the First Weekend.

Liverpool is building a **National Discovery Park** on Merseyside's Albert Docks which will focus on the history of exploration, as well as a £3.3 million (US$5.5m) **National Wildflower Centre** on the outskirts at Court Hey Park.

Manchester is to have a new £41 million (US$69m) cultural zone, the **Millennium Quarter**, which will include **Urbis** (a major visitor attraction exploring the past, present and future of cities), a city park, a visitor centre for the Cathedral, and Exchange Square with a 'sculpted river' which follows the medieval boundary of the city.

The region's Landmark Project is **The Lowry**, a £170 million (US$285m) waterfront arts complex in **Salford** that will include two galleries (one housing LS Lowry's work, the other for temporary exhibitions), two theatres, Artworks (a public creative centre), and the Digital World Centre (a showcase for digital technologies and virtual environments that will provide facilities for the community, education and business). The scheme also includes shops, cafés, restaurants, an open-air plaza and a footbridge spanning the Manchester Ship Canal to the new Imperial War Museum-North. The Lowry will open in Spring 2000, the Digital World Centre in Autumn 2000.

The Lowry Centre Trust, West Pavilion, Harbour City, Salford Quays M5 2BH
Ⓣ 0161/955 2020 Ⓕ 955 2021 Ⓔ info@thelowry.org,uk
Ⓦ http://www.thelowry.org.uk

Manchester Streets Ahead Hotline Ⓣ 0161/953 4238

Yorkshire and Humberside

Leeds will be staging a two-day **Millennium Overture** on the First Weekend of 2000. The project invites schools and community groups to create lighting designs that will be switched on all over the city on New Year's Eve, 1999, complemented by fireworks and a ring of bonfire beacons encircling the city. A special celebration concert will be relayed on loudspeakers throughout the city on January 1, 2000 as a prelude to a year-long programme of events under the title of **Absolute Millennium**.

The region's Landmark project, the **Earth Centre,** is currently taking shape on 400 acres of former coal-mining works in the Dearne Valley near **Doncaster,** South Yorkshire. Most of the attractions in this £40 million (US$67m) project are focused on a core 20-acre site which offers insight into futuristic technologies through exhibitions, shows, interactive features, outdoor play and adventure areas and gardens.

At the entrance to the Earth Centre is a vast solar canopy, the largest horizontal array of solar cells in Europe, providing up to 35 percent of the Earth Centre's energy requirements. At the heart of the centre is the **Planet Earth Gallery**, an underground gallery that uses lights, projections, mirrors and theatrical effects to explore the universe, planet earth, and the future. **Action Stations** offers ideas for energy-saving at home, and in the **Future Child Gallery** children can use their imaginations to see into the future and whisper a message for children a century from now. There is a **Japanese Sensory Garden**; a **Twenty-first Century Terraced Garden**, demonstrating organic techniques; **Nature Works**, an aquatic, hands-on exploratory area; and the **Wilderness Theatre**, a play cave. The centre also has a shop, café, its own radio station, and an Earth Arena with a full events programme. The first phase opened on April 2, 1999.

On **Humberside** the European Maritime Institute of Hull is building **The Deep**, a £40 million (US$67m) project that will house an aquarium, research centre, business facilities and an education centre. It's due to open in April, 2001. Other schemes within the region include the 714km **Trans Pennine Trail**, a route for walkers and cyclists linking Merseyside and Humberside; the restoration of the **Huddersfield Narrow Canal**; and the creation of a **Millennium Square** in Leeds.

During 2000 **York** is staging the **York Millennium Mystery Plays**, a high-profile production of Britain's oldest cycle of mystery plays, which date back to the eleventh century. For the first time ever they will be staged inside York Minster, and will involve two hundred actors and 2500 local schoolchildren (June 22–July 22, 2000).

The Earth Centre, Kilner's Bridge, Doncaster Rd, Denaby Main, South Yorks DN12 4DY ⓣ 01709/512000 ⓕ 512010 ⓔ info@earthcentre.demon.co.uk Tickets cost £8.95 (US$15) adults, £6.95 (US$12) children under 14, family ticket £30 (US$50). If you arrive by bike or rail (Conisbrough train station), entrance costs £4.95 (US$8).

York Millennium Mystery Plays, York Minster ⓣ 01904/635444 ⓦ http://www.mysteryplays2000.org

The North

Newcastle will be welcoming the millennium with **Countdown 2000**, featuring a lantern procession involving one thousand local school children, the French street theatre company Plasticiens Volants on parade with large inflatables of bizarre animals, and spectacular light and fireworks displays over the Tyne. Throughout the weekend ice artists will be creating large-scale sculptures all over the city. The city will also be throwing a £16,000 party (US$27,000) for 35,000 clubbers.

Carlisle is hoping to spend £6 million (US$10m) on its **Millennium Gateway** project to build a bridge and an underground gallery to reunite the city centre with its famous

The Millennium Party

● Friday December 31, 1999 has been declared a public holiday. Since Christmas Day and Boxing Day fall on a weekend, Monday 27 and Tuesday 28 December will also be holidays. The New Year's Day holiday will be taken on Monday January 3 because January 1 is a Saturday. There will only be two working days between December 25 and January 4, and many businesses are expected to close down for ten days.

● The public is expected to withdraw around £13.5 billion (US$22b) in cash before the ten-day long millennium holiday. The Bank of England will be issuing £8 billion (US$13b) of extra banknotes to cope with demand.

● Pubs will be allowed to stay open all night on December 31, 1999 (probably until 4am and possibly until 11am) so that revellers won't be forced to leave their local pub and pay to go to a night-club to celebrate midnight.

● Good rates of pay for working on party night are expected for baby-sitters (up to £50/US$85 per hour), top DJs (£4000/

Norman castle on the other side of a dual carriageway; however the scheme's centrepiece, a glass pyramid, has raised considerable local opposition.

In **Cumbria** the **Renaissance of Whitehaven** includes the Hub (event centre), the Quest (history centre), and Crow's Nest (an observation tower).

Durham is spending £25 million (US$42m) on its **Millennium City** project to reconnect the ancient peninsula with the rest of the city; the scheme includes a riverside walkway, Millennium Square, and a 500-seater Millennium Hall.

Newcastle's Landmark Project is the **International Centre for Life**, a multipurpose complex that combines a research institute, commercial biotechnology centre and visitor centre

US$7000 per gig), bar staff (up to £40/US$70 per hour) and waiters at top restaurants (£1000/US$1700 for the night). Most big-name bands and performers will be charging three to four times their normal rate, and minicab drivers will be picking up between £30–£50 (US$50–85) per journey.

● Computer staff are being offered 'golden handcuff' deals of a year's salary as a bonus if they remain on the job throughout the night, worth anything from £20,000–50,000 (US$34,000–84,000). Freelance programmers on standby are expecting at least £1000 an hour, or £10,000 (US$17,000) for the night.

● The party could cost the National Health Service £500 million (US$840m) in overtime and bonus payments to staff Accident and Emergency Departments which might be swamped with revellers who have had drink-related accidents or victims of millennium bug disasters.

● Some people who won't be partying include some civil servants (who will have to remain on duty all night in order to cope with millennium bug problems); police and army personnel; many junior doctors and nurses; engineers in the electricity industry; and security staff.

dedicated to the genetics revolution. The heart of the £55 million (US$92m) scheme is the **Helix Discovery Centre**, which aims to explain genetics via a futuristic Gene Dome in which visitors will be 'shrunk' so they can journey through the human body to witness genes in action. The centre will also include a **Timeline** spanning four billion years of genetic evolution and a **Health Quest** area. It opens in March 2000. Newcastle will be linked to Gateshead by the new **Baltic Millennium Bridge** for pedestrians and cyclists.

The 1999 total solar Eclipse

On the morning of Wednesday August 11, 1999 large swaths of the northern hemisphere will experience a spectacular total eclipse. The path of totality starts at sunrise in Nova Scotia and crosses Europe, the Middle East and India before ending at sunset over the Bay of Bengal. A partial eclipse will be seen in countries from Greenland to Thailand.

In Britain the eclipse will be visible as a totality in a 100km-wide strip encompassing Cornwall, western Devon, the Scilly Isles and Alderney in the Channel Islands; elsewhere in the UK the skies will darken measurably. The last total eclipse in Britain was in 1927 and the next is not due until 2090. The full experience of the eclipse will last from 9.57am to around 12.30pm, with the total eclipse occurring at 11.11am for two minutes. Approx 1.5 million extra visitors are expected to descend on Cornwall. Extra campsites are in preparation; don't set off without confirmed accommodation.

● Campsites can be booked through Total Eclipse of the Sun Ltd, PO Box 21, Penzance, Cornwall TR20 8ZL ℗ 01736/332189. Alternatively, travel in Pullman style on a private dining train to Penzance and back with the Train Chartering Company ℗ 01293/783347. Further information, Cornwall Tourist Board ℗ 01872/274057.

● France may be less crowded. Eurocamp ℗ 01606/787878 is offering tented holidays with astronomy lectures, or book a rural gîte through Brittany Ferries ℗ 0990/360360.

● See it from the sea with P&O European Ferries ℗ 0990/980555 who will have two ferries in the path of totality, or on board the cruise ship *Norwegian Sky* ℗ 0800/188-1560.

● Useful sites include Ⓦ http://ww.eclipse.org.uk or Ⓦ http://www.thisistheeclipse.co.uk

Sunrise times in the UK, January 1, 2000

	GMT
South Foreland	0758
Dover	0759
Hastings	0800
Eastbourne	0801
Southend	0803
Harwich	0803
Lowestoft	0804

F★ck the Millennium

Anarchic pranksters Jimmy Cauty and Bill Drummond (known in a previous incarnation as the band KLF, famous for burning £1 million (US$1.63m) in cash from their music earnings,) have floated the idea of the Great Northern Pyramid of the People. Designed to stand 150ft high on a 300ft square base, the pyramid will be built from 'eighty-seven million, two hundred and fifty thousand bricks (roughly)'. This represents around one brick for every person born in the UK during the twentieth century.

The 'People's Pyramid' will be open 365 days a year, 24 hours a day, free of charge. "You'll be able to do what you want with it. Climb it, paint it, polish it, eat your sandwiches on it, or chip it away", they say. "It will stand for as long as any of it is left. It will promote nothing, be sponsored by nobody, and be owned by everybody." It won't, of course, ever be built, but it's a nice spoof on what many consider to be the over-hyped Millennium Dome.

Ⓦ http://www.k2planthire.ltd.uk/

SCOTLAND

New Year's Eve **Hogmanay** celebrations take place all over Scotland and in 1999 several cities are vying to throw the biggest and best parties. The tradition dates back to the sixteenth century, when Protestant church leaders insisted on downplaying the importance of Christmas because of its associations with Catholicism. New Year's Eve thus became a more important celebration (the New Year's resolution, signifying a clean break with the past and a new beginning, is also rooted in Hogmanay traditions).

In recent years **Edinburgh** has gained a reputation as the party capital of the country with its massive Hogmanay celebration lasting several days. The official celebration has snowballed since it was inaugurated in 1993 and on New Year's Eve, 1999 the city centre will be cordoned off to prevent over-crowding, with entrance to the main Virgin and McEwans street party limited to 180,000 people with free passes. The event will run over a week (December 28, 1999–January

2, 2000) and feature a fire festival, torchlit processions, street theatre, live bands, a Hogmanay carnival and children's events.

Glasgow has a long-standing rivalry with Edinburgh and plans to try and beat the competition with its own massive Hogmanay celebration in 1999. Large-scale arts and entertainment events will take place on outdoor stages at several sites across the city. The programme will continue through January 1, 2000 and include street entertainers, Celtic performers, ceilidh bands and rock bands.

Aberdeen is also planning to beef up its Hogmanay parties, with live music and a torchlit procession in the lead-up to midnight as part of Aberdeen 2000. In **Dundee** they're staging **Millennium Dawn**, a laser-lit son et lumière performance on the theme of the city's heritage, accompanied by live performances and a week-long extravaganza of music, arts and drama. **Inverness** is planning a large-scale Hogmanay built on strong Highland themes. On New Year's Eve, 1999 there will be a torchlit procession from Inverness Castle, followed by an outdoor celebration in the city centre, with traditional and contemporary Celtic music, and twelve ceilidhs in community centres. Over the First Weekend there will be family-based entertainments, traditional dancing, massed pipe bands, street theatre, and river-based activities on the Ness.

Scotland's Landmark Project is the rebuilding of Glasgow's **Hampden Park Stadium** in a £46 million (US$77m) scheme to raise the National Stadium to international standards with the provision of a new South Stand. It will also include a new Museum of Football, which opens in Autumn 1999. Glasgow is also building **X-Site**, a new national science centre costing £71.5 million (US$120m) which is part of the Pacific Quay docklands redevelopment; it opens in Spring 2001.

In Edinburgh they have transformed a disused brewery into the city's first purpose-built visitor attraction, the **Dynamic Earth**, a striking building set against the backdrop of the Salisbury Crags. The first gallery, State of the Earth, introduces the planet as it is today, with video screens showing footage of natural phenomena as they occur. Visitors then descend in a Time Machine 'video lift' and emerge on the bridge of a starship to watch the formation of the solar system. Subsequent galleries focus on the Restless Earth, Glaciation, the Evolution of Life, Oceans, Polar Regions and Tropical Rainforests. The £16 million (US$27m) scheme opens in May 1999.

In Ayrshire **The Big Idea** will be the UK's first visitor centre devoted to invention and discovery. The Ardeer peninsula was the location of Alfred Noble's laboratory and chemicals company, and it is this connection which has led to the £10.6 million (US$18m) scheme. The centre will focus on the history of explosions – from the Big Bang to Space Exploration – and is due to open in Spring 2000.

Scotland's colleges and research institutions are to be linked via the **University of the Highlands and Islands**, and its history and culture made more widely available thanks to **SCRAN: The Scottish Cultural Resource Access Network**, which aims to digitise 1.5 million text records of historic monuments and artefacts held in museums and galleries, as well as a further 100,000 related archives and make them available to schools, colleges and libraries throughout Scotland on CD-ROM, the Internet and cable TV.

The **Millennium Link** is a project to reopen navigation on the Firth & Clyde and the Union canals linking Glasgow and Edinburgh.

Edinburgh and Scotland Information Centre, 3 Princes St, Edinburgh EH2 2QP Ⓣ 0131/473 3800. Millennium Hogmanay hotline Ⓣ 0131/473 1999. The 180,000 passes for 1999 will be issued on a first come, first served basis. For information send a stamped, self-addressed A4 envelope to: Edinburgh's Millennium Hogmanay, PO Box 12000, Edinburgh EH1 1XE.

Glasgow Hogmanay, UK Events, 40a High St, Glasgow G1 1NL Ⓣ 0141/552 6027 Ⓕ 552 6048 Ⓦ http://www.hogmanay.co.uk Ⓦ http://www.hogmanay.net Excellent resource with up-to-date listings on Hogmanay events throughout Scotland and practical travel information.

The Dynamic Earth, PO Box 23086, Edinburgh EH8 8ZH ⓣ 0131/550 7800
ⓕ 550 7801 ⓔ enquiries@dynamicearth.co.uk
ⓦ http://www.dynamicearth.co.uk
The centre is open daily from 10am–6pm (April–Oct), 10am–5pm (November–
March). Admission is £5.95 (US$10) adults, £3.50 (US$6) children, £16.50
(US$27) family ticket.

WALES

Cardiff plans to welcome the millennium with a three-day
event entitled **Calennig** (from a Welsh tradition of 'giving gifts'). It will bring people together from four landmarks
around the city and will feature outdoor stages, fireworks, funfair rides, fire sculptures, children's performances and lantern
processions. Calenigg will also light up the city with illuminations designed by communities from across Wales.

The **Swansea Millennium 2000 Festival** will feature a
Biodiversity Carnival as part of a Green Futures Eco Festival:
costumes, masks and giant puppets representing animals, plants
and different habitats will be made by local communities and
schools with the help of local artists, culminating in a massive
procession on New Year's Eve, 1999. Other community events
will take place throughout the First Weekend.

Wales's sole Landmark Project is Cardiff's **Millennium Stadium** at Cardiff Arms Park. The £144 million (US$242m)
project will have a retractable roof for all-weather use and will
also feature a Rugby Experience museum.

The city's **Millennium Waterfront** on **Cardiff Bay** will
feature two other major projects, the new **Welsh Assembly**
and the **Wales Millennium Centre**, a multipurpose arts centre which will include a lyric theatre, exhibition galleries, and
an IMAX cinema. Public piazzas and a new avenue will link
the waterfront area with the city centre.

In Carmarthenshire the 568-acre Regency park of Middleton Hall Estate is being transformed into the **National**

Botanic Gardens of Wales. The first national botanic garden to be built in the UK for two hundred years, the project features a **Great Glasshouse** with a spectacular interior landscape, gardens with medicinal herbs from around the world, an aquatic garden, woodlands from New Zealand and China, and a meandering broadwalk. The £44 million (US$74m) scheme will be dedicated to the protection of threatened plant species and is scheduled to open in Spring 2000.

At **Llanelli** there will be a new **Millennium Coastal Park**, a 20km-long area of wetland habitats, harbour developments and other leisure facilities linked together by a network of footpaths and cycle tracks. The park will host the **Welsh National Eisteddfod** in 2000 (August 5–12).

National Botanic Garden of Wales, Middleton Hall, Llanarthne, Carmarthenshire SA32 8HW Ⓣ 01558/668768 Ⓕ 668933
Ⓦ http://www.gardenofwales.org.uk

Millennium Stadium, St David's House, 1st floor, West Wing, Wood Street, Cardiff CF1 1EF Ⓣ 01222/232661.

COUNTRY CODE Ⓣ 44

CANADA

The Canadian government has allocated CDN$160 million (£62m/US$103m) for the millennium celebrations. Events are being co-ordinated through the **Millennium Bureau of Canada**, which will provide assistance for initiatives that will 'encourage Canadians to explore our heritage, celebrate our achievements, and build our future' under the slogan 'Sharing the Memory – Shaping the Dream'. Many of the projects being supported are community-based programmes designed to leave a legacy for future generations.

"Canadians don't want a big millennium blow-out with nothing to show for it the morning after but a hangover and a lot of bills", said Prime Minister Jean Chretien.

Under the **Millennium Partnership Programme** dozens of initiatives are underway, including the **Great Canadian Millennium Celebration Roadshow**, which will go on display at fifty venues across the country, celebrating the country's achievements; an International **Children's Games Millennium Festival**, with participants from forty cities; **Together 2000**, an exchange programme for three hundred families who will swap homes for a year; and a consortium of four leading conservation organisations, **Natural Legacy 2000**, which is planning a series of Canada-wide conservation measures.

2000
Canada

One project which is already in place is the **Canada Tree**, a 10m-high sculpture composed of over six hundred wooden artefacts donated by people across the country, including rare mementos and historic artefacts. Launched at the Canadian Museum of Civilization in June 1998, the tree will tour the country in 1999 and 2000.

Another national project is the creation of the **Trans Canada Trail**, covering 15,000km from coast to coast. When completed in 2000 it will be the longest recreational trail in the world.

Every government department (even Immigration, Statistics, and the Justice Department) has a millennium programme. Amongst the initiatives are an interactive **Discovery Centre** at the National Archives; a 24-hour **play-writing contest** at the National Arts Centre; a **Trek Fest** for young people across the country in Ottawa; a major exhibition to mark the 75th birthday of jazz pianist **Oscar Peterson** at the National Library; a series of **Millennium Awards** for citizens whose hundredth birthday falls in 2000; and the designation of a genetically-modified white spruce as the **Millennium Tree**, with thousands of cloned seedlings planted across the country.

Drums of the Global Village brings together drummers, choreographers and lighting effect specialists to create 'an innovative musical experience' with a cast of sixty performing artists. The show will start in Ottawa and then tour nationally. New work will also be commissioned for **Music Canada 2000**, which will bring together artists, composers and performers for a festival that will tour the country.

The government has also provided CDN$10 million (£4m/US$6.5m) for the creation of a **Millennium Arts Fund**, which is administered by the Canada Council for the Arts. Amongst projects they are sponsoring are **2000 Voices, 2000 Dreams**, an interdisciplinary event celebrating children and their visions of the millennium; a Chinese–Canadian opera, **Iron Road**, about the building of the Canadian Pacific

Railway; and a **Millennium Pole**, which is being created for the Museum of Anthropology by a Haida artist.

On New Year's Eve, 1999 there will be a **Millennium Continuum Concert**, co-ordinated by the National Arts Centre, which will span the country's five time zones and begin at 10pm in each time zone at cultural centres across the country. **Beacon Millennium Canada** plan to have 2000 communities linked up in a chain of beacons, fires, candlelit parades, fireworks and light shows across the country for New Year's Eve, 1999.

Canadians are also hoping for Friday, December 31, 1999 to be declared a national holiday, as in Britain and the US. But the Mounties are one group who won't be partying. Along with some city police forces, the Royal Canadian Mounted Police have cancelled all leave for two weeks in order to deal with potential Y2K catastrophes. The government has also activated emergency powers and troops will be on stand-by in an operation (code–named Abacus) to deal with civil unrest.

The biggest regional events and projects are listed below by province: for other provinces see the Millennium Bureau's Web site.

Millennium Bureau of Canada, 255 Albert St, 10th floor, PO Box 2000, Postal Station D, Ottawa, Ontario K1P 1E5 ⓣ 888/774-9999 (toll free) ⓕ 613/995-2766 ⓔ millennium@ic.gc.ca ⓦ http://www.millennium.gc.ca An excellent site with comprehensive information on hundreds of projects and events nationwide.

Millennium Foundation of Canada, 11th floor, East Tower, Toronto City Hall, 100 Queen St W, Toronto, Ontario M5H 2N2 ⓣ 416/392-1290 ⓕ 392-1289 ⓔ grtmill@direct.com ⓦ http://www.2000cdn.com/ The Millennium Foundation is an independent, non-profit body which has been working since 1996 to co-ordinate Canadian projects and initiatives. Their Web site has comprehensive links to projects in Canada and worldwide.

Alberta

The city of **Calgary** is planning a number of 'legacy projects', including the building of a **Millennium Clock Tower**, which

CALGARY
2000
IT'S TIME

Time to count down to a
new Century and a new Millennium

10 months, 17 days, 10 hours, 56 minutes, 20 secs until

will house 'one of the most accurate clocks in North America'; the creation of a **Millennium Park** in the heart of the city; a **Millennium Banner** programme; and the re-creation of the original 1885 **Calgary Town Hall**, where they will stage re-enactments of turn-of-the-century civic meetings.

Half a million people visit the town of **Drumheller** every year to see their exceptional dinosaur collection, so naturally they decided to build the **World's Largest Dinosaur**. It will sit on top of the town's tourist information centre, and you'll be able to climb up inside it and look out of the mouth.

The **i human: International Arts Society**, based in Edmonton, hopes to build a sculpture made from deactivated firearms, which will tour Canada as a symbol of the country's role in peacekeeping. Elsewhere, ice sculptures will be created as part of an international competition, Ice Magic, at Lake Louise (January 14–16, 2000).

Calgary 2000, PO Box 2100, Stn. M, Calgary, Alberta T2P 2M5
Ⓣ 403/268-2000 Ⓕ 268-5245 Ⓔ istime@cadvision.com
Ⓦ http://www.intervisual.com/calgary2000/

British Columbia

The city of **Vancouver,** which has one of the world's great harbour settings, will provide a stunning background to New Year's Eve, 1999. Festivities are being co-ordinated by **Millennium Vancouver 2000!** (MV2000!), a consortium of arts, business and civic leaders. Amongst their projects are a **Time Capsule**, which will be sealed on December 31, 1999; a **Countdown Clock**; an educational contest, **New Music for the Millennium**; and a **Millennium Medallion of Merit**, which will be awarded to two hundred people (alive or dead) for their contributions to Vancouver in the last two hundred years.

Dozens of boats, decorated with Christmas lights, cruise the harbour waters during the annual **Christmas Carolships Parade**. New Year's Eve, 1999 will be marked by a multicultural entertainment extravaganza, a black-tie gala, family events, a rock/pop concert and two midnight fireworks displays. A multifaith celebration will be held on January 3, 2000.

During the millennium year Vancouver will be hosting a **Futurists Festival** (Spring 2000) and a **Times Festival** (Summer 2000).

MV2000! PO Box 48381, 595 Burrard St, Bentall Centre, Vancouver, BC V7X 1A2 Ⓣ 604/878-7400 Ⓕ 646-2001.
Ⓔ millennium@vancouver2000.bc.ca Ⓦ http://www.vancouver2000.bc.ca

Newfoundland and Labrador

Cape Spear, the most easterly point in the province, is the first location to witness the millennium dawn on the North American continent. Nordic explorers arrived at L'Anse aux Meadows in Newfoundland around 1000 AD, and to commemorate the anniversary there will be a **Viking Millennium Exhibition** at the Newfoundland Museum, which will tell the story of the voyages, and of the indigenous people of the region at the period. The exhibits will form part of the **Viking Millennium Celebrations** (August 13–22, 2000), linked to those in Iceland (see p.148).

Millennium Council of Newfoundland and Labrador, 8 Appledore Place, St John's, Newfoundland A1B 2W9 Ⓣ 709/722-4003

Ontario

Ottawa 2000

The capital of **Ottawa** will be the main national focus on New Year's Eve, 1999, with a series of celebrations on and around Parliament Hill. **Ottawa**

Millennium Miscellania

● The Canadian Broadcasting Corporation is making *A People's History of Canada*, a major documentary series which will cover Canada's past from the arrival of the first inhabitants more than 12,000 years ago to the last decades of the twentieth century. The 32-hour series, produced in English and French, will be broadcast over 1999–2000.

● The Canadian Millennium Partnership Programme is sponsoring *The Scattering of Seeds*, a series of thirteen documentaries that will explore the hopes, dreams and determination of the country's first immigrants. The series draws on a rich archive of home movies, photographs, letters and oral history.

● The 125-year Anniversary of the Royal Canadian Mounted Police will be marked by several projects including the filming of the *North West Mounted Police March West*, a two-hour documentary on an historic march by the Mounties into Canada's uncharted western frontier in 1874.

● The Royal Canadian Mint is issuing 24 new 25-cent coins to mark the millennium. The first twelve, commemorating the past 1000 years, are being issued in 1999, and the second set will be issued in 2000 with designs representing Canada's hopes for the future. Canada Post is also issuing special Millennium Stamps.

2000 is co-ordinating events which will include cultural performances, a mega-party on the hill itself with several exterior stages, spectacular snow and ice carvings, and a special Christmas Lights programme.

The vibrant metropolis of **Toronto** is hoping for a major New Year's Eve bash, although the council's millennium task force is at odds with an independent group who have registered the name **Toronto 2000**. This non-profit organisation is planning an 'Urban Odyssey' with cultural, sporting and community events culminating in a New Year's Eve gala on December 31, 1999; there will also be an Exposition of the Future in 2000. The city will have an alcohol-free **First Night** event. An 'explosion of lights' will turn Niagara Falls into a 'fairy-tale image' during the **Winter Festival of Lights** (November 1999–January 2000).

Various projects are taking place throughout the province, including a **Millennium Celebration** in Brockville with a choir of two thousand drawn from all age groups in the community; the creation of a **Millennium Forest** and a **Children's Peace Park** in Bocaygeon; a new **Baseball Hall of Fame** in St Mary's; and a **Festival of the Visual Arts** in Stratford and Toronto during which the Royal Canadian Academy of Arts will host its first national arts exhibition for 27 years (Spring 2000).

Ottawa 2000, Room 2000, 111 Lisgar St, Ottawa, Ontario K2P 2L7
Ⓣ 613/560-2000 Ⓕ 560-2124 Ⓔ ottawa2000@rmoc.on.ca
Ⓦ http://www.ottawa2000.org
Toronto 2000 – An Urban Odyssey, 1 Yonge St, Suite 2000, Toronto, Ontario M5E 1N4 Ⓣ 416/777-2000 Ⓕ 862-8111 Ⓔ mjadpr2@inforamp.net

Quebec

The city of **Quebec** will hold a millennium edition of its annual **Winter Carnival** (January 28–February 13, 2000), with an ice sculpture competition, canoe races on the river, and other events. **Montréal** is famous for its jazz festival (June–July), and jazz will feature prominently in the celebrations; singer Celine Dion will perform a farewell show in the city on New Year's Eve.

One of the most unusual projects taking place is the **Year 2000 Art Monument** in the city of La Baie. The area was devastated by floods in 1996 and the course of the river Ha! Ha! altered to prevent a recurrence. Artist Jean-Jules Soucy is installing a gigantic lattice on the former riverbed composed of 30,000 multicoloured aluminium triangles and, on the old riverbank, building a 21m-high pyramid composed entirely of reflective triangular road signs, with an observation post at the top. The monument will be unveiled at midnight on December 31, 1999. Elsewhere in the province a giant figure of **St John the Baptist** will be built at L'Anse-Saint-Jean.

Ⓦ http://www.tourisme.gouv.qc.ca
The official Quebec tourism Web pages.

Ⓦ http://www.restuarationdaa.com/
Detailed description of the Year 2000 Art Monument.

TRAVEL BRIEF

Many families are likely to take the opportunity to stage big reunions at the millennium, and with large numbers of people from the US, Europe and Asia flocking into Canada to visit relatives flights may fill up fast.

GETTING THERE Book sensibly over peak holiday periods.

ACCOMMODATION Accommodation in Vancouver and Toronto may be in short supply and, as everywhere, the better hotels nationwide are laying on their own celebration packages. Canadian Pacific, who own 27 of the country's finest landmark hotels, are currently running waiting lists while they work out the fine points of their individual programmes.

Central booking for Canada and the US Ⓣ 800/441-1414.
UK: Ⓣ 0500/303030.

TOURIST OFFICES There is no national tourist office; each province has its own headquarters in the state capital. Amongst these are: Alberta: 3rd Floor, 10155 102nd St, Edmonton, Alberta T31 4L6 Ⓣ 800/661-8888. British Columbia: Parliament Building, Victoria, British Columbia V8V 1X4 Ⓣ 800/663-6000; Ontario: Queen's Park, Toronto, Ontario M7A 2E5 Ⓣ 800/668-2746; Quebec: Tour de la Place Victoria, Bureau 260, Montréal, Quebec H4Z 1C3 Ⓣ 514/873-7977 or 800/363-7777. UK: London Ⓣ 0891/715000 (premium rate). US: the toll-free numbers quoted for the provincial offices can be dialled from anywhere within North America. Ⓦ http://www.canadatourism.com
Home pages of the Canada Tourism Commission.

COUNTRY CODE Ⓣ 1

CHINA

F or people wanting to escape millennium fever China might be a good destination. The Republic uses the Gregorian calendar for all administrative purposes but the traditional Chinese calendar is still used for domestic purposes and for setting the dates of holidays and festivals.

Despite the fact that there are no official plans for celebrations the Chinese government has erected a **Countdown Clock** on the **Great Wall**. Located at the busy Badaling section of the wall, the white clock with red digital display exhorts the nation to 'seize the moment to build up the motherland'.

There are rumours that parties might be staged at the wall – at Badaling (around 70km from Beijing), Mutianyu (90km from Beijing) or Simatai (110km from Bejing). The Hong Kong Cancer Fund (HKCF) has plans to illuminate the Great Wall with lasers from space, but it is more than likely just another case of wishful thinking. And don't be fooled by another countdown clock in Beijing's **Tiananmen Square**: rather than ticking over the days until the millennium it is in fact counting down to the handover of the Portuguese colony of Macau on December 20, 1999.

The Vatican has requested that Chinese Catholics should be allowed to visit Rome during the Jubilee year. There are an estimated four million members of the authorised Catholic Church in China, and a further ten million who worship unofficially, according to the Holy See.

More than 20,000 couples have been invited to attend millennium weddings throughout China, starting with a 2000 couple marital extravaganza in Beijing on December 31, 1999.

The event sponsors said that the idea was to initiate 'a more wholesome, civilised and scientific lifestyle among young couples in the next century'.

China has adopted a novel approach to sorting out the millennium bug in the country's aviation industry. The head of the Ministry of Information Industries, Zhao Bo, has ordered all its airline executives to take a flight on January 1, 2000, as the ultimate proof of safety.

In **Hong Kong** there are no official plans for celebrations, although New Year's Eve is usually marked by spectacular fireworks over the harbour and lavish parties in the former colony's top hotels.

TRAVEL BRIEF

China might be a high-risk country for millennium bug problems. Avoid travelling immediately after January 1, 2000 and make sure your tour operator has contingency plans if travelling on a package holiday.

GETTING THERE The most important international gateways are Beijing and Hong Kong, with regular scheduled flights from London, Los Angeles, Detroit, Vancouver and Asian cities.

ACCOMMODATION There are unlikely to be any problems with hotel bookings over the millennium. The Millennial Foundation will be staging a charity party in the ballroom of the *Regent Hotel*, Hong Kong.

TOURIST OFFICES UK: London ☏ 0171/935 9787. US: New York ☏ 212/760-1710. Australia: Sydney ☏ 02/9299 4057.

TOURS UK: Asiaworld ☏ 01923/211300; China Travel Services ☏ 0171/836 9911; Hayes and Jarvis ☏ 0181/748 5050; Kuoni Worldwide ☏ 01306/740888. US/Canada: Asian Pacific Adventures ☏ 213/935-3156; Cathay Pacific Holidays ☏ 800/661-8881; China Air Tours ☏ 212/371-9899; United Air Vacations ☏ 800/328-2794.

COUNTRY CODE ☏ 86

EGYPT

The **Pyramids** at Giza are bound to be one of the prime targets for organisations planning multi-zone millennium parties around the world, not to mention all those mystics and prophets who venerate the ancient stones. The custodian of the pyramids, Zahi Hawass, wants to make the Great Pyramid whole again. Although it is not evident from the ground, the pyramid has lost its top 30ft and the plan is to cover most of the missing area with a steel frame, topping it off with a small capstone wrapped in thin gold foil.

The Egyptians hope to create a ceremony for the millennium to mirror the pomp and ceremony that accompanied the completion of the Pharaonic monument some 4600 years ago.

As we went to press no firm plans had been announced for celebrations at the pyramids, partly due to disputes between different Ministries as to who actually controls the monument. The Ministry of Culture has been negotiating with Jean-Michel Jarre to create a twelve-hour, multimedia spectacular called Twelve Dreams of the Sun, which would start at 6pm on December 31, 1999 and last through until dawn. The US-

based Millennium Society and the American Council for the United Nations University have been in talks with the Ministry of Antiquities with the idea of staging a televised extravaganza.

Independent travellers will discover vantage points on the hills overlooking the site, and one tour operator is planning a camel safari into the desert to watch the dawn.

In **Alexandria** the French couturier Pierre Cardin is planning to build an obelisk-shaped glass lighthouse to replace the port's ancient lighthouse (one of the seven wonders of the world until destroyed by an earthquake in 1349).

Cardin hopes to raise the £45 million (US$75m) needed to build the 500ft tower by selling shares to the public, and the Alexandria governor has agreed to donate land for the project near the city's eastern harbour. The designer describes the monument as an 'obelisk of light', with beams radiating from the top onto Alexandria's principal monuments.

TRAVEL BRIEF

Although it appears that there will be something happening at the Pyramids, no one can yet advise on travel plans. As a general rule Egypt is a difficult destination for the independent traveller and it is usually easier and cheaper to join up with a package tour operator.

GETTING THERE There are regular scheduled flights to Cairo from many places in Europe and Africa, and more limited options from the US. Mid-winter is high season and flights are often full over Christmas and the New Year.

ACCOMMODATION The major cities have a good range of luxury hotels, but any spare rooms will be filled up with celebrating locals, so book in advance. Good mid-range and cheap hotels are hard to find in Egypt at the best of times.

TOURIST OFFICES Cairo: 5 Adly St, Cairo Ⓣ 02/391 3454. Also at the airport, railway station, and opposite the *Mena House Hotel*, Giza. UK: London Ⓣ 0171/493 5282. US: New York Ⓣ 212/332-2570; Los Angeles Ⓣ 213/653-8815; Chicago Ⓣ 312/280-4666 Ⓦ http://touregypt.net/

TOURS UK: Abercrombie & Kent Ⓣ 0171/730 9600; The Imaginative Traveller Ⓣ 0181/742 8612. US: CostaTravel Ⓣ 800/598-1001; Maupintour Ⓣ 800/255-4266.

COUNTRY CODE Ⓣ 20

FINLAND

R ecent scientific research on the increased activity of sunspots seems to indicate that during the year 2000 we will witness some of the most spectacular manifestations of the Northern Lights ever seen. One of the best places to watch the Aurora Borealis is Lapland, but elsewhere in Finland they have devised their own way of illuminating the dark, five-month-long winter.

Helsinki

Inaugurated in 1995, Helsinki's **Festival of Light**, or Valon Voimat (which translates as 'the forces of light'), builds on existing Finnish traditions (such as placing lighted candles in windows on December 6, Independence Day) and features creations of light and sound performances by artists through-out the city, illuminations of buildings, and a Light Fair. The Festival of Light, 'which draws its power from darkness', is developing spectacular displays for 1999 and 2000. It will be open between November and December.

 Helsinki is also one of the nine European Cities of Culture 2000, with the theme of 'Knowledge, Technology, and the Future'. Nearly 300 million Finnish marks (£34m/US$56m) is being invested in the programme. **Heureka!**, the Finnish Science Centre, is producing an interactive exhibition on communication, in co-operation with the other eight partner cities. New Finnish glass technology will be represented by the **Magic Crystal**, a shimmering crystal structure that changes colour at the touch of a hand; in 1999 the Crystal will be

Helsinki's Virtual Reality Dream

In the biggest experiment of its kind in the world, 100,000 people in Helsinki are being wired into a virtual city which will allow them to see plays and concerts, go shopping, attend university lectures, meet the bank manager, visit friends for a chat and much more besides – all with real-time video links.

The project, **Helsinki Arena 2000**, involves creating a 3-D model (VRML) of the city detailing all its streets, shopping areas, cultural institutions, businesses and Government offices, which will then be linked via telephone, broadband and Internet networks to an integrated package easily accessible from home PCs. Whilst strolling around the virtual city, it will be possible to simply click on a shop or business and be connected via a normal telephone.

"By 2000 all of the city centre will be modelled, although not all of the suburbs", says Risto Linturi, the project's originator. "One of the best applications we've had yet is a GPS-taxi: you can see where all the taxis are and which are free – you pick the closest taxi by clicking on it with your mouse, and watch it turn in your direction until it is close enough for you to step out of the door." Virtual meeting points, Internet-telephony and video telephone services are already up and running in 1999.

The background to the project is available at:
Ⓦ http://www.helsinkiarena2000.fi/english.html

If you have the appropriate VRML plug-ins you can also see a demonstration of Helsinki's 3-D phone book at:
Ⓦ http://www.helsinkiarena2000.fi/summary/demos.html

divided into separate parts and will tour the other eight cities, connected by a real-time video link-up. Before 2000 its constituent parts will be brought back to Helsinki where they will be reassembled into a 3m-high, 18m-long tunnel of light.

FIND is another touring project, representing the best of Finnish design in furniture, arts and crafts; it will open simultaneously in all nine cities in February 2000. In May **Fish & Ships** will bring old wooden sailing ships into Helsinki harbour; there will be folk music and dancing on the quays, along with smoked fish and beer. A **Snow Church** will be built in Senate Square, and can be visited from February 7–March 7, 2000. New and renovated cultural centres in the city that will be staging special programmes in 2000 include **Kiasma**, the Museum of Contemporary Art, the **Lasipalatsi** (Glass Palace) Film and Media Centre, and the **Museum of Cultures** in the Tennispalatsi (former Tennis Palace). Wagner's immense Nibelung Ring series will be performed in its entirety at the **Finnish National Opera** in May and June 2000. The **Cutty Sark Tall Ships Race** will bring 120 sailing ships into the city in July 2000. The year 2000 also marks the 450-year anniversary of the founding of the city and 125-year anniversary of the birth of Jean Sibelius.

Festival of Light, Fredrikinkatu 61a, 00100 Helsinki, Finland
Ⓣ 09/686 6810 Ⓕ 605 297 Ⓔ info@mail.festivals.fi
Ⓦ http://www.hel.fi/valonvoimat

Helsinki 2000, Eteläranta 16, 00130 Helsinki
Ⓣ 09/169 3209 Ⓕ 169 3204 Ⓔ info@2000.hel.fi Ⓦ http://www.2000.hel.fi

TRAVEL BRIEF

Beautiful, bleak, chilly Finland is not usually high on the list of holiday hotspots, except over Christmas and New Year when the lure of Lapland, Santa Claus, reindeer rides, skiing and dog-sleds creates a mini-boom. In 2000, Helsinki is also a European cultural capital, but no one event threatens to overwhelm either the transport or accommodation.

GETTING THERE Finnair and British Airways each operate four–five flights a day from the UK, and Finnair has daily flights from New York (with onward links to many other US destinations). Although Helsinki is Finland's only major international airport, air travel is popular and convenient inside the country, with a tightly packed schedule of domestic services between 22 cities, and reasonably priced airpasses. There are good rail services between all major towns as well as links to neighbouring countries.

ACCOMMODATION Much of Finland's tourist accommodation is geared to winter sports and summer lakes, with small country hotels and cottages. Helsinki does have a number of larger hotels, but advance booking over the Christmas and millennium period is strongly recommended; hotels in Lapland are expected to be full by the autumn.

TOURIST OFFICES National: Matkailun edistämiskeskus/Keskusyksikkö, Töölönkatu 11, PL 625, 00101 Helsinki ⊤ 09/417 6911 Ⓕ 4176 9399 Ⓔ mek@mek.fi Ⓦ http://www.mek.fi and Ⓦ http://finland-tourism.com Helsinki: Pohjoisesplanadi 19, FIN-00100, Helsinki ⊤ 09/169 3757 Ⓕ 169 3839 Ⓔ tourist.info@hel.fi Ⓦ http://www.hel.fi UK: London ⊤ 0171/839 4048 Ⓕ 321 0696 Ⓔ meklon@mek.fi US: New York ⊤ 212/370-5540 Ⓕ 885-9710 Ⓔ fininfol@mail.idt.net Ⓦ http://www.travelfile.com/get/finninfo

TOURS UK: Aeroscope ⊤ 01608/650103; Finman Travel International ⊤ 01942/262662; Norvista ⊤ 0171/409 7334; Scantours ⊤ 0171/839 2927. US: Five Stars of Scandinavia ⊤ 800/722-4126; Finnway ⊤ 201/535-1610; Special Expeditions ⊤ 212/765-7740; Tursem Tours ⊤ 212/935-9210.

COUNTRY CODE ⊤ 358

FRANCE

The French were slow on the uptake for celebrating the approaching millennium, shrugging off the idea with typical Gallic insouciance until it was almost too late to do anything. The idea is "not particularly French", said one official. But the feverish activity in other European countries touched a raw nerve and, not

wanting to be left behind, the French government unveiled its own master plan, the **Mission for the Celebration of the Year 2000**.

In collaboration with numerous partners (including community organisations, cultural institutions and government bodies), the Mission has come up with a comprehensive programme covering the period from Autumn 1999 through to early 2001. The programme comes under three different rubrics.

A Time for Festivities invites every citizen to take part in 'new ways of being and living together' and focuses on three key celebrations: New Year's Eve, 1999; the annual Music Festival (June 21, 2000), which will be dedicated to 'doing away with borders – between cities and suburbs, and between different countries'; and around Bastille Day (July 14, 2000).

As well as national festivities, there will also be local initiatives such as a **Neighbourhood Festival** (Marseille), **Colours of the World** (Amiens), **Casa Musicale** (Perpignan), and touring events such as the **Hip-Hop Caravan** (the best of new urban music and dance on tour) and the **Children's Village** (a travelling community which will allow child musicians from all over the world to meet young audiences throughout France). Other programmes in the scheme include **Young People's Europe**, which will enable two thousand French youngsters turning twenty in the year 2000 to tour significant cultural sites on the Continent, and the **Trans European Literary Express** (see p.54).

A Time for Reflection is the second leg of this triumvirate, involving a series of **Forums for the Year 2000** inviting the public to discuss issues that will affect them in the next millennium. The first was held in Lyons in October 1997 and the last, on the topic of 'France's Identity', will be held in Paris in May 2000. Cities and towns throughout France, including Paris, are also staging various projects. This process of reflection will culminate in **The University of World Knowledge**, during which academics and researchers from all over the world will conduct 365 seminars in three host institutions in Paris, all of them open to the general public, which will eventually result in a book, a 'living encyclopedia of the present day'. Three major exhibitions will also be held: **Portraits of France** (Paris), **The French Language** (Lyons), and **Beauty** (Avignon).

A Time for Creation is the third part, involving French and foreign artists in the performing and visual arts, as well as architecture and urban design. Projects announced so far include **The Children's Pavilion** (one of the largest works of public arts ever carried out in France); the illumination of the **Pont du Gard**; **The Life of Jesus** (a photographic study); and a landscape project on the island of **Reunion**. Documentaries, films and various publications will also be produced.

One of the most spectacular national projects is the creation of **La Méridienne Verte** (The Green Meridian). Essentially, this 'woodland monument' involves the planting of a chain of trees corresponding to the Paris meridian running from north to south across the country. This huge project will extend 1200km, will cross 337 districts in eight regions of France, and will cost 40 million francs (£4.2m/US$7m). Evidently, it will pose challenges when obstacles such as cities are encountered, but the first trees were planted by the French Minister of Culture near St-Martin-du-Tertre (Val d'Oise) on November 25, 1998. The project will really take off on November 25, 1999, when school children from all over the country will plant a further 10,000 young trees.

By June 2000, they plan to have a walking path alongside the Green Meridian, inviting anyone to take a stroll across France. And on the day of France's biggest celebration in 2000, Bastille Day (July 14), everybody will be invited to a giant picnic along the line, with an aerial flypast overhead featuring every kind of flying machine from helicopters to microlights, hot-air balloons and Concorde. The Mission is also an official partner in **The Millennium Race/La Course du Millenaire**, which has been conceived by navigator Bruno Peyron as a spur to technological innovation in yachting. There are no restrictions on yachts taking part, so numerous experimental boats are expected to compete for the £1.2 million (US$2m) prize money. Live images will be broadcast from the boats as they circle the globe via three capes (Horn, Leeuwin and Good Hope). Fifteen challengers have so far entered for the race, which departs on December 31, 2000, finishing in March/April 2001.

A new scientific theme park, **Vulcania**, will open in the heart of the Auvergne region in 2000. This ambitious project, costing 420 million francs (£44m/US$75m), is the brainchild of former President Giscard d'Estaing but it drew considerable opposition from environment groups concerned about its impact on the surrounding natural volcanic landscapes. However, most of the park will be buried underground and it is now scheduled to open in November 2000.

Many provincial cities have announced plans for events and exhibitions in 1999 and 2000, including **Avignon**, which is to be one of nine European Cities of Culture 2000.

Mission for the Celebration of the Year 2000, 8 avenue de l'Opera, 75001 Paris Ⓣ 01.55.04.20.00 Ⓕ 01.55.04.20.01 Ⓔ etudes@celebration2000.gouv.fr

Ⓦ http://www.celebration2000.gouv.fr A bilingual site that includes details of how to get involved in the Forums for the Year 2000.

The Millennium Race, 4 place de Saverne, La Défense, 92 971 Paris Ⓣ 01.41. 16.16.96 Ⓕ 01.41.16.16.97 Ⓔ office@therace.org Ⓦ http://www.therace.org

Ⓦ http://www.tour-eiffel.fr/teiffel/an2000_uk/
From the top of the Eiffel Tower, an overview of the year 2000 and its history and future. Bilingual French and English.

Paris

At the launch of **Mission Paris 2000** its president, Yves Morousi, said that the city should take its part in the "international competition which the Year 2000 has created between the capitals of the world", adding that "we have to try and

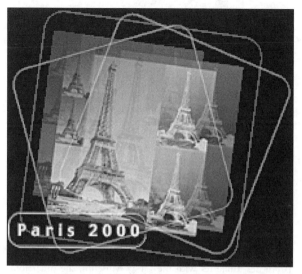

Paris 2000

recapture the spirit of the City of Light which, in 1900, led the world on the occasion of the Universal Exhibition."

Spurred on by a light-hearted rivalry with London, the French announced a millennium ferris wheel that would be 'bigger and better' than the BA London Eye – and twice as expensive. The designer of the project said that "if necessary, we will just go one metre higher" in order to beat their 500ft-high London rival.

Nothing has been heard of the wheel since, although the French announced a shortlist of lavish and fairly bizarre gestures that will include the Eiffel Tower laying a giant luminous egg, the perfuming of the Seine, and a new wooden tower rising up 650ft on the banks of the river. "From today, we are a length ahead of the rest of the world", said Morousi.

The French press begged to disagree, pouring scorn on the

dramatic and controversial plan to turn the Eiffel Tower into a hi-tech chicken for a night. The plan was eventually scrapped, as was the giant wooden tower.

But at least one project has received the enthusiastic approval of Parisians, and that is the plan to top the twin towers of **Notre Dame Cathedral** with two futuristic spires. The 60m-high spires, built from laminated wood, carbon fibre and cables, will be an event 'symbolising the meaning and optimism of the new millennium', according to the architects behind the scheme. The spires, weighing up to 25 tonnes each, will be hoisted into place by cranes and helicopters. If approved by the church authorities, the work is expected to start in May 1999 and to be completed by September 1999.

Just as London will see a major revitalisation of the Thames as part of its millennium celebrations, so too Paris has chosen the **Seine** as the main focal point for the arrival of the year 2000. Provisional plans include the creation of a 12km-long **walkway** along the river from one end of the city to the other; the creation of two new **footbridges** (one linking the Jardin des Tuilleries with the Orsay Museum, the other joining the Parc de Bercy with the new National French Library); the icing over of the existing Ponts des Arts footbridge to create a skating rink; and the illumination of the Seine's bridges and important monuments on the riverbank. A floating concert is also proposed, with percussion orchestras on twenty barges drifting downstream on September 3, 1999.

There is also a plan to float two thousand **plastic fish** in the river, extending about 3m above the surface, individually or in schools. The press didn't think much of this either, although they failed to notice it is scheduled for April 1, 2000 (April Fool's Day).

Another idea which has been proposed is the creation of a **giant balloon** which would carry thirty passengers at a time up to heights of 300ft for a bird's-eye view of the city.

The **Georges Pompidou Centre** will reopen after extensive renovations on January 1, 2000, with a major exhibition on the theme of **Time**. The **Grand Palais** in the gardens of the Champs-Élysées will also be restored for the occasion, one hundred years after its construction for the Universal Exhibition of 1900. The **Chatelet Theatre** will also reopen in October 1999, with a world premiere of a new opera entitled *Nativity for the Third Millennium*.

Other plans that have been unveiled include the conversion of the **Place de la Concorde** into a giant sundial, using the Egyptian obelisk at its centre as a pointer, and turning the **Place Charles de Gaulle Etoile** into a giant clock, using powerful lights mounted on the **Arc de Triomphe** to count down to 2000 on the twelve avenues leading into the square. Outside the **Hôtel de Ville** there will also be a giant electronic book, 22m wide and 15m high, which will offer a different theme on French literature on a daily basis, allowing passersby to browse through 170 acres of prose during the year.

At the **Cité des Sciences** in Paris the overall theme in 1999 will be **The New Arts of Learning and Inventing**, focusing on communications technologies. In 2000 and 2001 exhibitions will revolve around two themes, **The Living** and **The Environment**.

The huge space inside the splendid nineteenth-century **Le Parc et la Grande Halle de la Villette** will be temporarily transformed into a **Planetary Garden**, a giant greenhouse which will combine botany, biology and the life sciences with art, imagination, myths and legends (September 14, 1999–January 2, 2000).

The annual **Recontres Urbain** festival (mid-September to mid-November 1999) will be staging a special millennium edition, with original works in dance, music, theatre, cinema and the audiovisual arts. In 2000 the exhibition theme is **Man and Conflict**, with debates, films and music. There will also be a special edition of the annual **Fireworks Festival** in the park, which will be held over two nights.

At **Les Galeries Nationales du Grand Palais** several major exhibtions will all focus on the theme of the **History of Time**. These include **Europe at the Time of Ulysses** (September 30, 1999–October 5, 2000), **The Year 1000 in France** (Autumn 2000), **Visions of the Future** (Autumn 2000), **Europe in 1900** (Autumn 2000).

Le Palais du Cinema will be inaugurated in late December 1999 in the former Palais du Tokyo, and throughout 2000 will host a film festival on the theme of **The Civilisation of the Cinema**.

There will also be an exhibition on **Utopias** at the National Library, an exhibition at the Carnavalet Museum on Paris as **The Capital of Photography**, and an audiovisual display, **ExpoTerrestre**, which will project thousands of works (photography, paintings, texts and so on) onto the Grande Arche at Defense from December 31, 1999 onwards.

At the **Longchamps racecourse** there will be a concert in homage to Jimi Hendrix, marking thirty years since Woodstock, and there are also plans to turn Paris's ring road, the boulevard périphérique, into a vast concert venue for New Year's Eve, with every type of music being performed on stages around its length.

Around half a million people will celebrate New Year's Eve, 1999 at the traditional street party on the 2.5km-long **Avenue des Champs-Élysées**.

Mission Paris 2000, 32 quai des Célestins, 75004 Paris ℡ 01.42.76.20.00 ⓦ http://www.paris-france.org (general Paris information).

AROUND FRANCE

The French are determined to celebrate the millennium, not just on New Year's Eve, but with more long-term projects nationwide.

Southern France

As a European Cultural Capital **Avignon**'s theme for the year 2000 is **Passages** – the passage from one millennium to the next, passage from one shore to another, and passages between neighbourhoods inside and outside the city's famous medieval ramparts. Its major exhibition for the year, produced in partnership with the Mission for the Celebration of the Year 2000, is **Beauty** (April 15–September 15, 2000). It will be presented in four parts: The Experience of Beauty (a visual spectacular at the Palace of the Popes); New Beauties (great beauties of the twentieth century, at twenty different locations); Natural Beauty (masterpieces of nature which have inspired artists); and Beauty in Our Daily Life (throughout the city).

The city will also be hosting a special edition of the **Avignon Festival** (July 2000), featuring extensive collaboration with artists from Eastern European countries. Another major project is **AvignoNumérique**, a multidisciplinary development project which aims to engage residents through living theatre, technology displays, interactive workshops and performances to create a 'new cultural space' for urban growth. There will also be a chance to see the four hundred works of contemporary art currently held privately by the **Yvon Lambert Foundation**. The city is creating new gardens on the Isle de Barthelasse and at the Petit Palais, and will feature a major exhibition on the **Arts de la Table** (September, 2000).

Mission Avignon 2000, 9 rue Rempart de l'Oulle, 84000 Avignon Ⓣ 04.90.86. 17.65 Ⓕ 04.90.86.92.49 Ⓔ avignon.2000@wanadoo.fr

Running out of Fizz?

- More champagne will be consumed on December 31, 1999 than at any other time in history. Corks will fly from around 300 million bottles at parties worldwide.

- Champagne will not run out. Production in the Champagne region varies between 230–330 million bottles annually, and as well as this the producers keep around one billion bottles in reserve which they can release if demand is high. In addition, sparkling Champagne-style wines are produced in many other areas of the world.

- Although there will be plenty of non-vintage champagne, top quality bubbly will be in short supply. Certain vintages have already sold out, and prices for those that are left are expected to rise by at least 25 percent.

- Canny investors should buy stocks in French companies that own prestigious brands such as Moet et Chandon, Dom Perignon and Veuve Cliquot, say analysts.

- The leading French labels will be producing special millennium jeroboams, the equivalent of four normal bottles. Those filled with finest vintage fizz are expected to sell for around £1200 (US$2000).

- California-based Korbel Champagne Cellars has created the world's largest champagne bottle. Hand-blown in Germany and standing nearly 5ft tall, the 120-litre bottle holds the equivalent of 1000 glasses of champagne. The bottle is touring US cities during 1999 on Korbel's Millennium Practice Party Tour, and will end up in New York for Times Square 2000. Korbel is also producing a special edition of 2000 twelve-litre bottles, with a commemorative Millennium label, which will cost US$2000 (£1200) each. Ⓦ http://www.korbel.com

- The best guide to buying celebratory bubbly is Tom Stevenson's *Millennium Champagne & Sparkling Wine Guide* (Dorling Kindersley £12.99). This superbly-produced guide describes more than 900 wines.

Southwest France

The city of **Bordeaux** is undergoing an urban renovation programme which will be linked to a major architectural exposition, **La Triennale**. Two other expositions, 'Les Horizons Chimique' and 'Château Bordeaux' will accentuate the city's links with Montaigne, Holderline, Odlfon Redon and local and worldwide winemaking.

The aeronautically oriented city of **Toulouse** is holding several exhibitions on the theme of **Sky and Space**. The newly-opened **Cité de l'Espace** will host a major programme with links to other space centres worldwide and an international convention on space law. Events at the **Musée de l'Aeronautique** revolve around the Conquest of the Skies; the **Musée d'Art Moderne** and the **Musée des Beaux-Arts** will jointly host an exhibition on Space in the Plastic Arts.

The East

Strasbourg's theme for the millennium is 'Links' – between the past and the future, between countries, and between people. There will be a special **Festival of Theatre** (end of September to Christmas 1999), a celebration of the Pont de l'Europe, and an exhibition on links between the past and the future through the art of divination.

The West and Northwest

In **Blois** several events will illustrate the theme of 'Wonderment and Enchantment', exploring the magic of childhood. 'Knowledge is Memory' is an invitation to follow in the footsteps of great historical figures associated with the city; 'Nature and Environment' will link visitors to the Castle with a house of magic; 'Language and Communication' is a conference on the languages of the world; and 'Daily Life and Imaginary Life' is apparently an exhibition of rubbish collections and household objects from around the world.

An important sea port, **Brest** will be one of the official departure points for **The Millennium Race**, and it will also be staging a massive **Regatta** (July 13–17, 2000), with over two thousand boats of all descriptions, from ancient ships to pleasure craft, sailing into the docks. They are also planning to open a huge new complex devoted to the ocean environment at the Oceanopolis centre.

The city of **Nantes** will be honouring its most celebrated citizen, Jules Verne, with a series of exhibitions in 2000, princi-pally at the **Jules Verne Museum**, the **Musée des Beaux-Arts**, and the **Château des Ducs de Brittany**. The utopia/science fiction theme is echoed in a Nantes-based project, the **Grenier du Siècle** (The Attic of the Century), an imaginary museum where people can 'deposit' everyday objects.

Located halfway between Paris and the sea on the banks of the Seine, **Rouen** will be hosting the **Armada of the Cen-tury** (July 9–18, 1999), with a flotilla of craft which will then sail down to the sea. The celebration will be combined with displays of maritime art in the city.

TRAVEL BRIEF

France is the world's largest tourism destination (with 70 million annual visitors) and it is always worth booking ahead over holiday periods but millennium celebrations are ongoing throughout the year and there are few large single events to overload the system.

GETTING THERE France has superb international travel connections by air, rail, road and boat. Air France: UK ☏ 0181/742 6600. US ☏ 212/237-2747 Rail Europe: UK: ☏ 0990/848 848. US: ☏ 800/4-EURAIL. Ferries: UK: Brittany Ferries ☏ 0990/360360; Hoverspeed ☏ 0990/240241; P&O-Stena Line ☏ 0990/980980; Sally Line ☏ 0990/595522; Seafrance ☏ 01304/212696.

ACCOMMODATION Expect Paris to be very busy over the millennium itself and book well ahead, especially if you want to stay anywhere romantic or within reach of the Champs-Élysées. The great palace hotels such as the *George V* and the *Crillon* are already full and the best little hotels have limited capacity. You need to book ahead everywhere in July and August and at least six months in advance for the Avignon Festival; the city has relatively few hotels and the best are small (alternatively Arles, St Remy de Provence and Les Baux are within easy commuting distance).

TOURIST OFFICES National: There is no national tourist office for France open to the general public. The country is broken into 26 regions, each with its own head office; some support offices in Paris and most have dedicated Web sites with hotlinks to the national site Ⓦ http://www.franceguide.com or Ⓦ http://www.tourisme.fr

Paris: 127 av. des Champs-Élysées Ⓣ 01.49.52.53.54 Ⓕ 01.49.52.53.00 Ⓦ http://www.paris-touristoffice.com or Ⓦ http://www.pariscope.com; Avignon: 41 cours Jean Jaures Ⓣ 04.90.82.65.11 Ⓕ 04.90.82.95.03 Ⓔ information@ot-avignon.fr Ⓦ http://www.avignon-tourisme.com UK: London; 0891/244123 (premium rate) Ⓔ infor@mdlf.co.uk Ⓦ http://www.fr-holidaystore.co.uk US: New York; Ⓣ 202/293-6173 (hotline) or 212/838-7800 Ⓕ 212/838-7855 Ⓦ http://francetourisme.com or Ⓦ http://www.ftgousa.org

TOURS UK: Allez France Ⓣ 01903/748128; Brittany Ferries Ⓣ 01752/227 941; Cresta Holidays Ⓣ 0161/926 9999; French Expressions Ⓣ 0171/431 1312; Paris Travel Service Ⓣ 01992/456000; VFB Holidays Ⓣ 01242/240 330/340/331/332/338. US: American Dream Vacations Ⓣ 201/729-1806; Distinctive Destinations Ⓣ 401/423-3730; Europe à la Carte Ⓣ 800/827-4635; The French Experience Ⓣ 212/986-1115; Tour de France Ⓣ 201/891-0076; Travcoa Ⓣ 800/992-2003; Travel Concepts Ⓣ 617/266-8450. The Savour of France Ⓣ 313/331-4568 is hosting a masquerade ball in Cannes for New Year's Eve, 1999.

COUNTRY CODE Ⓣ 33

GERMANY

T he biggest project taking shape in Germany is **Expo 2000** in **Hannover**, the twenty-seventh in a series of world fairs which began with the Great Exhibition in London's Crystal Palace in 1851. World expositions are often an uneasy hybrid of an industrial fair and an amusement park but Expo 2000 hopes to go beyond this by presenting practical solutions to the global problems which confront humanity as we enter the twenty-first century. It will also be a platform to promote the political and economic future of the European Union.

Political symbolism will also dominate events in **Berlin**. The city is due to be inaugurated in 1999 as the new capital of a reunified Germany with the federal parliament, the Bundestag, transferring from Bonn to the newly-renovated Reichstag. Berlin is also traditionally the venue for the country's biggest New Year's Eve parties, and plans are in hand for a spectacular finale to 1999.

Düsseldorf is staking its claim to fame with an attempt to hold **The Longest New Year's Eve Party in the World**, from December 31, 1999 through to January 2, 2000. Various galas, balls, concerts and parties are also planned for New Year's Eve, 1999 in **Bremen**, **Cologne**, **Dresden**, **Hamburg**, **Munich**, **Nuremberg**, **Potsdam** and **Wiesbaden**.

One of the hottest tickets in 2000 will be for the millennium edition of the famous **Passion Play** cycle in **Oberammergau**, which takes place between May and October. Another major cultural event is the 250-year anniversary of **Johann Sebastian Bach**, which will be celebrated principally in **Leipzig** during July 2000. **Mainz** will be celebrating the 600-

year Anniversary of **Guttenberg**; highlights will include a performance of the Guttenberg Oratorium and a major exhibition, **Guttenberg's Time** (April–Oct 2000). Finally, **Bremen** is planning to celebrate the millennium by building a Space Park which they say will feature 'huge numbers of extraterrestrials'.

Ⓦ http://www.deutschland2000.de

An independent site with good coverage of news and events in Germany (German only).

Berlin

A glass dome tops the newly-renovated **Reichstag**, the former parliament building which now houses the Bundestag, the German federal parliament. The transfer to Berlin is a symbolic event designed to mark the tenth anniversary of the fall of the Berlin Wall and German reunification, and is being accompanied by major renovations in the new capital to accommodate the 50,000 politicians, bureaucrats and diplomats who have moved from Bonn.

Berlin has around two thousand bars, restaurants, nightclubs and discos and most host their own **Silvester** (New Year's Eve) party, with the best booked out months in advance. If they're not out for the night, Berliners like to celebrate at home before streaming out on to the streets to greet neighbours, light fireworks and eat iced doughnuts washed down with sparkling wine.

Before the fall of the wall, West Berliners used to climb to the top of Teufelsberg, a hill outside the city centre, for a grandstand view of the pyrotechnics across the city. Since the wall was pulled down one of the biggest party venues has become the zone around the **Brandenburg Gate**, the city's most famous landmark, previously stranded in No Man's Land.

Plans are afoot for an hour-long fireworks display at the Gate, with over two hundred stages being set up on the boulevard that runs from the gate to the Tiergarten, featuring rock bands, street entertainers, performance art and dramatic reconstructions of the historical high-points of the last millennium. The Chancellor is expected to broadcast a speech to the nation live from the gate.

Berlin traditionally stages a series of special New Year's performances at the **Komische Opera** (usually, Strauss's *Die Fledermaus*), the **Friedrichstadpalast** (revue with dancing, acrobats and an orchestra), the **Varieté Wintergarten** (vaudeville), and the **Konzerthaus Berlin** (classical music).

The city is expecting an influx of visitors staying here as a base to visit Expo 2000 or making side-trips from the exposition in Hannover (1hr 40mins away by high speed train). They are hoping to open museums and galleries until late in the evening throughout the summer of 2000 to give returning Expo visitors the chance to look in. Berlin will also host **Urban Futures 2000** (June 26–30, 2000), an international city planning summit that is part of the official Expo programme.

The long-standing **Berliner Festspiele** (Berlin Festival), which features music, dance, theatre, film and literature, will be staging a special millennium festival, **2000: In Berlin**, which will run from May 14, 2000 to January 7, 2001.

Berlin Tourismus Marketing GmbH, AM Karlsbad 11, D-10785, Berlin
ⓣ 030/264 7480 ⓕ 264 74899. Hotels and tickets hotline ⓣ 030/250025
ⓦ http://www.berlin.de (most pages in German only).

Berlin Festival GmbH, Budapester Strasse 50, D-10787 Berlin ⓣ 030/254890
ⓕ 254 89111 ⓦ http://www.berlinerfestspiele.de (bilingual site).

Düsseldorf

The management of the Düsseldorf Fair have announced plans to hold **The Longest New Year's Eve Party in the World**, and are hoping to make it into the *Guinness Book of World Records*. The celebration will span the entire fairground, which will feature several new fantasy and dream worlds (covering multimedia, history, fashion, toys, sports, music and more), each hosting a countdown party related to its theme. On December 31, 1999 there will be a 24 TimeZones Party, linked to others worldwide via satellite, with rock and pop bands. The party ends at noon on January 1, 2000 with a concert by the Vienna Symphony Orchestra. On January 2, 2000 there will be a millennium family party.

24 TimeZones Party, the Düsseldorf Fair, Düsseldorf ℗ 07961/564 2000
Ⓕ 564 2030 Ⓔ info@millennium-office.de
Ⓦ http://www.countdown2000.de/duesseldorf (bilingual site).

Hannover

EXPO 2000
HANNOVER

The World Exposition
Germany

The first of its kind to take place in Germany, **Expo 2000** will be held at the refurbished Hannover Exhibition Ground and the adjacent Kronsberg area from June 1–October 31, 2000. The exposition has already broken all records, say the organisers, with 175 countries or international organisations attending. Somewhat incongruously, Expo 2000 tourism officials are co-operating with the Vatican to bring together 'two milestones on the road to the new millennium' in an advertising and marketing campaign to encourage those going to one to visit the other. Expo 2000 is hoping for 40 million visitors.

Debt-free Millennium

As 2000 approaches the total of developing countries' debts stands at a record US$2.2 trillion (£1.3t), a burden which many have called 'the new slavery', reducing millions of people to a state of poverty, hunger, illiteracy, disease and early death. Each year the Third World pays the West three times more in debt repayments than it receives in aid. The **Jubilee 2000 Coalition** is calling for the millennium to be celebrated with a one-off cancellation of the backlog of unpayable debt owed by the world's poorest countries, and the abolition of this twentieth-century version of slavery. Jubilee 2000 stepped up its efforts in 1999, enlisting former world boxing champion Muhammad Ali as its global ambassador and U2's Bono and other musicians to stage a star-studded event during a crucial G7 meeting in Cologne in June 1999. The indications are that Jubilee 2000's 'Drop the Debt' campaign may lead to significant reforms on debt repayment.

Jubilee 2000 is one of the most significant humanitarian campaigns of the millennium and its success could affect the lives of a billion people worldwide – a point worth remembering as we get ready to party.

Jubilee 2000. PO Box 100, London SE1 7RT ℡ 0171/401 9999 ℻ 401 3999 Ⓔ mail@jubilee2000uk.org Ⓦ http://www.jubilee2000uk.org

Expo's theme, 'Humankind–Nature–Technology', aims to promote a new kind of Expo where issues are considered in some depth and solutions proposed, in contrast to the usually superficial presentations at many world fairs. It will aim to implement the principles of Agenda 21, the programme for global action which was signed by 176 nations at the UN Earth Summit in Rio in 1992. The idea is to make tangible the concepts behind Agenda 21, creating a visual and interac-

tive experience which will be a 'laboratory for the future in the year 2000'.

Expo comes in four parts. The flagship is the **Theme Park**, a 100,000 square metre display which will be 'an adventure journey through an experiential landscape', under the supervision of French virtual reality wizard François Confino. Within this area different zones will focus on: The Twenty-first Century; Knowledge, Information and Communication; Energy; Nutrition; The Future of Work; Mobility; Basic Needs; The Future of the Past; Environment: Landscape and Climate; Health and the Future; and the central theme, Humankind.

The designers are promising journeys through a virtual body, virtual tours of the cities of the world, subterranean voyages

through energy systems, links to space, and many other hi-tech goodies. These will all be linked into scenarios exploring sustainable options for the next millennium.

The second leg, the **National Pavilions** zone, promises some unusual structures: the Japanese pavilion will be built entirely from rice paper and the six-floor Dutch pavilion features a different natural landscape on each level, topped off by a rooftop lake flanked by wind turbines. The German pavilion and the EU pavilion will be built flanking the entrance to the Europa Boulevard, which will feature the pavilions of EU member states in order to 'jointly present Europe in a way that will send a clear political signal'. All national participants will present their own solutions to twenty-first century problems.

The third strand is the **Culture Programme**, featuring an extensive array of international performances in music, opera, rock and pop, theatre, film, the plastic arts, multimedia and much more.

Finally, there are the **Worldwide Projects** that aim to extend Expo's principles on sustainable development globally – the first time that an exposition has reached outside its boundaries in this way to projects of ecological and social significance worldwide.

Expo 2000 Hannover GmbH, D-30510 Hannover ⓣ 0511/8404 136 ⓕ 8404 180. Tickets are on sale through appointed sales agents worldwide and offices of Deutsche Ban (German Railways) and the Expo Call Centre hotline ⓣ 0/2000.

ⓦ http://www.expo2000.de/ or ⓦ http://www.expo2000.de/index-e.html Excellent site with more than 300 pages covering EXPO 2000 (contents in English).

Leipzig

The city of Leipzig will be celebrating the 250-year anniversary of Johann Sebastian Bach during July, 2000. Events planned include a Bach Festival (July 24–30), the XII International Bach Competition (July 9–20), and lectures and exhibitions at the Bach Museum. The **Thomaskirche** (St Thomas' Church), where Bach served for the last 27 years of his life, is being renovated at a cost of DM20 million (£7m/US$11m).

Leipzig Tourist Service, Richard-Wagner-Strasse 1, 04109 Leipzig ⓣ 341/7104 260 ⓕ 7104 260 ⓔ lipsia@aol.com ⓦ http://www.leipzig.de (German only).

Oberammergau

Once every decade the citizens of the Bavarian village of Oberammergau perform a **Passion Play**, focusing on the life and death of Jesus. The event has its origins in the seventeenth century, when bubonic plague was sweeping across Europe. Oberammergau lost a fifth of its 1500 inhabitants and, with no end in sight, the village council vowed to perform the Passion Play every ten years if God would show them mercy. The first performance was in 1634 and the series has continued unbroken since then (apart from 1940, during World War II). The season starts on May 20, 2000, with the final performance on October 8; over 2200 villagers will be involved in the production, which runs daily from 9am–5.30pm (with a 3hr lunch break). There is covered seating for 4700 spectators.

But tickets will be hard to come by (in 1990 there were 1.5 million requests for the 500,000 allocations); a seat-only ticket DM165 (£60/US$100) is expected to sell for many times its value on the black market.

Verkehrs-und Reisebüro Gemeinde, Oberammergau OHG, Mitgesellschafter abr-Reisebüro, Eugen-Pabst-Strasse 9a 82487 Oberammergau
Ⓣ (0) 8822/ 92310 Ⓕ 923190 Ⓔ H.Rettelbach@gap.baynet.de
Ⓦ http://www.oberammergau.de/
Well-organised, bilingual site with full performance timetables and ticket ordering form (most official tickets include local accommodation, although a limited number are available without if you can travel there and back in the same day).

TRAVEL BRIEF

With several major events taking place in Germany during 2000, it will be a popular destination and it is advisable to book both transport and accommodation as early as possible.

GETTING THERE Over one hundred international airlines, including the national carrier, Lufthansa, operate flights into Germany from across the globe, with the main international gateways at Frankfurt, Munich and Berlin. There will be additional direct flights to Hannover during Expo, with a new, large terminal at Hannover airport. There are also excellent rail connections both within Germany and from surrounding countries. To cope with demand during Expo, there will be additional services to Hannover and a new railway station at Laatzen, next to the Expo site. Tickets for both Expo and Oberammergau are on sale at all Deutsche Bahn (German Railways) agencies worldwide.

ACCOMMODATION Within a two-hour radius of Hannover there will be some 500,000 beds available. Within the city itself however, the number drops to about 35,000 beds, 27,000 of them in private guesthouses. With some 40 million visitors expected, book early. Berlin will be crammed for New Year and the whole Oberammergau region will be full between May and September.

TOURIST OFFICES National: Deutsche Zentrale für Tourismus e.V. (DZT), Beethovenstrasse 69, D-60325 Frankfurt am Main ① 069/97 46 40 ⑤ 75 19 03 ⑩ http://www.germany-tourism.de Berlin: GmbH, Am Karlsbad 11, D-10785 Berlin ① 030/264 7480 ⑤ 2647 4899; Hannover: Theodor-Heuss-Platz 1-3, D-30175 Hannover ① 0511/811 3569 ⑤ 811 3549. UK: London ① 0891/600100 (brochure request, premium rate; 24 hrs) or ① 0171/317 0908 ⑤ 495 6129 ⑥ Germannationaltouristoffice@ compuserve.com US: New York ① 212/661-7200 ⑤ 661-7174 ⑥gntony@aol.com Los Angeles ① 310/575-9799.

TOURS UK: Bents Bicycle Tours ① 01568/780800; City Escapades ① 0990/437227 (brochures) or 0181/563 8959; Club Europe ① 0181/699 7788; Danube Travel ① 0171/493 0263; DER Travel Service ① 0171/290 1111; Moswin Tours ① 0116/271 9922 (brochures) or 271 4982. US: American Sightseeing International ① 800/225-4432; Der Tours ① 800/782-2424; Euro Bike and Walk Tours ① 800/321-6060; KD River Cruises ① 415/392-8817.

COUNTRY CODE ① 49

ICELAND

In the year 2000 Iceland will be commemorating the **Millennium Anniversary** of the Discovery of North America by the Icelandic voyager Leifur Eriksson (see box on p.149).

Reykjavík is one of the nine European Cities of Culture 2000, and the country will also be celebrating the anniversaries of various national cultural institutions such as the Icelandic

Symphony Orchestra, the National Theatre of Iceland, and the National Broadcasting Service. The country will also be marking a **Millennium of Christianity** with celebrations at Thingvellir, the historic meeting place for nearly nine hundred years of the Icelandic Parliament (June 30–July 2, 2000). In July 2000 there will also be an International Viking Festival, and in November 2000 a large-scale Nordic Cultural Festival, in conjunction with the meeting of the Nordic Council.

Reykjavík

The city's theme as one of the nine Cities of Culture is **Culture and Nature** and over two hundred events have been planned, many of them large-scale spectaculars, others more low-key and experimental. Major events include **Voices of Europe** (New Year's Eve, 1999), a performance by a youth choir comprising ten singers from each of the nine countries, performing in all nine languages, with music written by the Icelandic pop star Björk. The event will be broadcast globally and will then tour the other capitals. There will also be a unique production of the musical drama *Baldr*, written by the Icelandic composer Jón Leifs. Based on the Icelandic mythical saga of the ancient god Baldr, it will be premiered in August 2000 and then be performed in Bergen and Helsinki. Other events planned include a **Festival of Fire**; a **Children's Opera**; **A La Mode Eskimo** ('a fashion show in the Laugardalur swimming pool'); a **Festival of Wind Harps**; and an outdoor festival, **2000 Children**. The **Reykjavík Arts Festival**, a biennial programme of international artists and performers, will be staging a special programme in the summer of 2000 between May and June.

New Year's Eve is celebrated with considerable panache in the capital, with everyone turning out on the streets to witness the night sky become a blaze of colour as fireworks are launched. The city has also acquired a reputation as a hot nightspot, so expect all-night dancing and partying.

Reykjavík 2000, Aoalstræti 6, 101 Reykjavík Ⓣ 575 2000 Ⓕ 575 2099
Ⓔ reykjavik2000@domino.europe.is Ⓦ http://www.reykjavik2000.is

The Leifur Eriksson Millennium

Around 1000 AD an explorer named Bjarni Herjolfsson set off from Iceland to Greenland but lost his way and came to the coast of Labrador and Baffin Island, although he didn't step ashore. Inspired by this, Leifur Eriksson followed the same route and is said to have got as far as Quebec, where he found wild grapes and gave the country the name of Wineland, and then built houses at L'Anse aux Meadows. A new book charting these voyages, *Wineland Millennium*, is being published in English in time for the millen-nium celebrations and the Leifur Eriksson Millennium Commission is planning a series of events to coincide with the discoveries. These include the sailing of a replica Viking ship from Iceland to Greenland, Canada and the US to arrive in time for Leif Eriksson Day (October 9, 2000), documentaries on the voyages, exhibitions and concerts.

Leifur Eriksson Millennium Commission, Aoalstræti 6, 101 Reykjavík
Ⓣ 575 2000 Ⓕ 575 2005 Ⓔ millennium@for.stjeeeeer.is
Ⓦ http: www/leifur-eriksson.org/

TRAVEL BRIEF

With only four or five hours of winter time daylight, this may not be the most obvious place to welcome in the New Year, but think of wallowing in a steaming outdoor hot spring, under clear winter stars, a drink in one hand and the prospect of a day's snowmobiling and suddenly it all becomes very appealing. The real rush comes in mid-summer (June–August), with festivities added by Reykjavik's role as a European City of Culture.

GETTING THERE Several international airlines operate flights into Reykjavík, but the largest of the carriers is Icelandair, with seven departure cities in the US and two in the UK. It is worth booking ahead during peak season.

ACCOMMODATION Reykjavík has a reasonably large supply of comfortable hotels, most three-star or above. Elsewhere in the country there is a much more limited supply of accommodation. Book ahead in peak season.

TOURIST OFFICES National: Læjargötu 3, Reykjavík Ⓣ 552 7488 Ⓕ 552 4749 Ⓦ http://www.icetourist.ice; Reykjavík: Bankastræti 2, 101 Reykjavík Ⓣ 562 3045 Ⓕ 562 3057 Ⓔ tourinfo@mmedia.is Ⓦ http://www.reykjavik.is UK: London Ⓣ 0171/388 7550. US: New York Ⓣ 212/885-9747 or 9700 Ⓕ 885-9710.

TOURS UK: Arctic Experience Ⓣ 01737/218800; Cresta Holidays Ⓣ 0161/927 7000; Icelandair Ⓣ 0171/388 5346; Regent Holidays Ⓣ 0983/864212. US: Borton Overseas Ⓣ 800/843-0602; Destination Wilderness Ⓣ 800/423-8868; Icelandair Ⓣ 800/223-5500; Nordic Saga Tours Ⓣ 800/848-6449; Union Tours Ⓣ 800/451-9511.

COUNTRY CODE Ⓣ 354

INDIA

The Indian subcontinent is a good bet if you want to escape millennium fever, since the population is mostly either Hindu, Muslim, Buddhist or Sikh. Given its status as one of the Great Wonders of the World the **Taj Mahal** at Agra is an obviously millennial destination, although there are no official plans for celebrations at the moment.

The only organised public event so far is the **Khajuraho Millennium**, a year-long festival to commemorate the 1000-year anniversary of this famous temple complex in the state of Madhya Pradesh (March 1999–March 2000).

Major hotel chains such as the Taj Group and Oberoi are planning lavish New Year's Eve spectaculars in their flagship hotels. Beach resorts such as Goa and Kovalam are likely to be packed out with independent travellers making the most of the impromptu New Year's Eve beach parties.

Given India's position as a highly successful centre for software processing, it would be ironic if they neglected their own millennium bug problems. Since no information is available, travellers should assume there might be problems. Avoid cities (unless staying in major hotels), and don't plan to travel home too early in January. Having said that, if the infrastructure crashes whilst you are lazing on a tropical beach you won't suffer – there are always fish in the sea and coconuts ripening on the trees.

Khajuraho

Situated in the heart of northern Madhya Pradesh, the Khajuraho temple complex dates from the tenth century and is dedicated to the Hindu deities Shiva, Jagadamba and Vishnu. The Khajuraho Millennium is a year-long festival (March 1999–March 2000) that will feature an international sculpture meeting, a film festival, a dance festival, and a newly-inaugurated music festival.

There will also be a special New Year's Eve celebration at the temple complex which will feature classical Indian music, percussionists,

dancers, fireworks, 'horses, elephants and camels', and a dramatic representation of the ten great dynasties in India's history.

Khajuraho Millennium Committee, 168 Nehru Apartments, Kalkaji, New Delhi
Ⓣ 1/646 7291 Ⓕ 648 7320 Ⓔ roy@teamworkfilms.com
Ⓦ http://www.teamworkfilms.com/millennium

Madhya Pradesh Tourism Development Corp Ⓣ 755/778383 Ⓕ 774289
Ⓔ mail@mptourism.com Ⓦ http://www.mptourism.com/

Travel arrangements and accommodation can be booked by Orient Express
Travel and Tours Ⓣ11/3322142 Ⓕ 3325198
Ⓦ http://www.OrientExpressLtd.com/

TRAVEL BRIEF

GETTING THERE The main international gateways are Delhi and Bombay, with charter flights also available to Goa and Kovalam from Europe.

ACCOMMODATION There is unlikely to be a millennium rush to India, although the famous palace hotels in Rajasthan will be heavily in demand. You can hire a fully-staffed Indian palace for week through Western and Oriental

Travel ⓉT 0171/313 6611 over the millennium; prices vary from £8–18,000 (US$13-30,000), which sounds hugely expensive, but the biggest palaces can sleep thirty couples.

TOURIST OFFICES UK: London ⓉT 0171/437 3677. US: Los Angeles ⓉT 213/380-8855; New York ⓉT 212/586-4901. Australia: Sydney ⓉT 02/9232 1600.

TOURS UK: Abercrombie & Kent ⓉT 0171/730 9600; Bales ⓉT 01306/740048; Cox & Kings ⓉT 0171/873 5000; Exodus Expeditions ⓉT 0181/675 5550; Himalayan Kingdoms ⓉT 0117/923 7163; Mysteries of India ⓉT 0181/574 2727; Pettits India ⓉT 01892/515966; Steppes East ⓉT 01285/810267. US: Adventure Centre ⓉT 800/227-8747; Cox & Kings ⓉT 800/999-1758; Himalayan Travel ⓉT 800/225-2380 Journeyworld International ⓉT 800/635-3900; Worldwide Adventures ⓉT 800/387-1483.

COUNTRY CODE ⓉT 91

IRELAND

B illing itself as the 'Party Capital of the World' Ireland has been quick to catch on to the opportunity for a pro-longed celebration and began a year-long party with a five-day **St Patrick's Day Festival** in March 1999. The centrepiece of the country's millennium celebrations will be a specially selected programme of some of the best-established and most successful festivals, including the **Galway Arts Festival** (July), the **Kilkenny Arts Festival** (August) and the **Wexford Festival Opera** (October).

The Government has set up a **National Millennium Committee**, with a budget of around £30 million (US$50m) for events and projects in 1999 and 2000.

IRELAND'S
MILLENNIUM
CELEBRATION

Projects taking shape throughout the country focus on Ireland's religious heritage, such as the walking routes along various medieval **Pilgrim Paths** being proposed by the Heritage Council. Those put forward so far include the Saint's Road on the Dingle Peninsula; St Kevin's Way in Glendalough; Balintubber Abbey to Croagh Patrick; Lough Derg; the Turas around Glencolmcille; St Declan's Way; and Durrow to Clonmacnois. It is hoped that the Pilgrim Paths will be officially opened in June 2000. The Heritage Council is also planning a millennium project to identify and develop semi-natural woodlands around the country.

The Augustinian **Mayo Abbey** in the west of Ireland has been pooling local resources for the creation of the **Mayo Millennium Project**, an interpretive centre in a disused church on the site which will tell the story of the abbey's creation in the seventh century and its subsequent prominence in the region (it gave its name to County Mayo). The project will also involve links with Iona, Lindisfarne and the creation of the **Mayo Pilgrimage Trail**. The centre is due to open at Easter 2000.

Millennium Festivals Ltd, St Stephen's Green House, Earlsfort Terrace, Dublin 2, Ireland Ⓣ 01/676 4566 Ⓕ 676 3208 Ⓔ info@millennium-ireland.com Ⓦ http://www.millennium-ireland.com

National Millennium Committee, Millennium Office, Department of the Taoiseach, Upper Merrion Street, Dublin 2 Ⓣ 01/619 4071 Ⓕ 619 4270.

Dublin

Dublin's most prestigious project is the **Millennium Monument**, a soaring, stainless steel spire which is to be erected on the former site of Nelson's pillar in O'Connell Street. The £3 million (US$5m) design was selected after an international architectural competition and has been greeted with enthusiasm by Dubliners. The 120m-high spire tapers to an optical-

glass apex which will be illuminated to shine like a beacon above the city. Variously described as 'a symbol of optimism for the future' and 'a sensational structure which will redefine the city centre', the monument has also attracted its share of epithets from the city's legendary wits, who have nicknamed it 'the stiletto in the ghetto'. It should be completed by November 1999, and the city has already received offers of £1 million (US$1.6m) for the rights to franchise images of this dramatic spike.

Dublin's **Millennium Partnership**, Míle Átha Cliath, has unveiled plans for seven other projects following a public competition on the theme of 'Dream It for 21st Century Dublin'. These include a **Liffey Boardwalk**, which will run from O'Connell Bridge to Grattan Bridge on the North Quay: a **Millennium Footbridge**, which will link Eustace Street and Ormond Quay; a **Millennium Cycle Track**, which will run for 5km along the Grand Canal; a **Millennium Zone** on the banks of the Liffey; and a **Millennium Book Market** in a newly-pedestrianised space on the Grattan Bridge. Míle Átha Cliath is also planning to light the **Liffey Bridges** permanently, starting with a grand switching-on ceremony on December 31, 1999, and a **Millennium Kaleidoscope** arts festival, which will culminate in a major exhibition in the year 2000.

Dublin was one of the first cities to install a Millennium Clock, although it was removed just a few months after being installed in 1996 thanks to a basic design flaw – it was supposed to float just below the surface of the River Liffey, but no one could read it through the murky waters. The ill-fated 'time in the slime' cost £250,000 (US$400,000), according to *The Irish Times*.

Míle Átha Cliath – Dublin's Millennium Partnership, Huband House, 16 Upper Mount St, Dublin 2 ⓣ 01/661 6931 ⓕ 661 6932 ⓔ info@dublin-2000.com ⓦ http://www.dublin-2000.com

Northern Ireland

P yramids, domes, spires and arches are springing up elsewhere throughout the world, but Northern Ireland is the
only place that has the distinction of erecting a millennium
megalith, or large standing stone (see box on p.159). In a
thousand years' time it may well be the only millennium project from the year 2000 to remain standing.

The biggest investment is the creation of the £90 million
(US$149m) **Odyssey** complex in **Belfast**, which is one of the
UK's fourteen Landmark Projects.

Elsewhere, **Downpatrick** is building the **St Patrick Visitor Centre**, which will portray the life and legacy of St
Patrick, whose grave is in the town. The first of a series of
21st Century Halls has been opened, and a further 27 community centres are to benefit in the £6.8 million (US$11m)
scheme.

Belfast

The city will be celebrating the millennium with a three-day
festival, **Time to Make a Difference**. On New Year's Eve,
1999 there will be a funfair, jazz festival, a series of ice shows,
a parade of lights, and live entertainment at various venues
around the city centre. A tunnel under the Lagan River will
be transformed into a time tunnel and a street in the cathedral
quarter will re-enact life in the eighteenth century. The
evening will finish with fireworks and a gala ball. On New
Year's Day the Sculling Championships take place on the river,
and afterwards there will be a carnival, a street party, and a
series of candlelit concerts in the Cathedral of St Anne. On
January 2 there will be an interdenominational church service,
a 'people's concert' at Waterfront Hall, followed by an evening
of traditional Irish music and song in Belfast Castle.

Covering 23 acres around the Abercorn Basin in Belfast, the **Odyssey Complex** will be the biggest single structure of its kind ever to be built in Ireland. The complex will incorporate the first science and technology centre in Ireland, a 3-D IMAX theatre, and a multifunction pavilion with restaurants, bars, leisure and shopping facilities. It will also include a cinema complex and a 10,500-seater indoor stadium. Odyssey is scheduled to open in November 2000.

The Science Centre, under the direction of the Ulster Museum, will feature five zones with interactive displays focusing on 'Ourselves' (body, mind, health and sports); 'Energy and Movement' (electricity, magnetism, air and flight, water and boats); 'Communications'; the 'Changing Earth'; and a children's play area.

The Odyssey Trust, 2 Queen's Quay, Belfast BT3 9QQ ℗ 01232/451055 Ⓕ 451052.

Londonderry

The city council is planning various celebrations on the theme of **Derry-Londonderry 2000 Living Our Lives** which will include a Millennium Mile with stages and venues throughout the city featuring artists and musicians, and a community carnival, on New Year's Eve, 1999. Later, beacons will be lit and there will be a procession to Derry's famous seventeenth-century walls. The Guildhall will host a Millennium Ball and the River Foyle will be the setting for an extravagant 'triple site fire and laser show' incorporating giant moving set pieces.

The city is also building the £11 million (US$18.5m) **Derry Millennium Complex**, a multicultural community centre for cultural events, indoor sports, drama performances and exhibitions. The complex will include a Millennium Hall and Millennium Plaza.

Megalith for the Millennium

Northern Ireland's 'megalith for the millennium', the Strangford Stone, is a 12.4m-high granite monument which will stand in Delamont Country Park on a ridge overlooking Strangford Lough and the County Down countryside, with the Mountains of Mourne in the background. The brainchild of County Down resident Martyn Todd, the idea grew from the concept of raising a standing stone in the same way as they used to millennia ago, using sheer musclepower – and involving over one thousand young people in the country 'pulling together' as a symbol of co-operation for the future amongst previously divided communities. Teams underwent a series of training sessions all over the country (including practicing by pulling buses) in preparation for the big day and the five-hour long erection of the monolith by the Megateam. The 52-tonne stone will be the tallest megalith in Ireland or Britain, and is unadorned apart from a plaque showing the alignment of the planets on the day it will have been erected, Midsummer's Day (June 26) 1999.

Delamont Country Park is two miles south of the small town of Killyleagh, 25 miles from Belfast. There is a bus service from Downpatrick. Park information ☎ 01396/828333.

TRAVEL BRIEF

Ireland is more of a summer destination, but country cottages and other rural retreats are likely to be popular over Christmas and New Year's Eve, 1999.

GETTING THERE There are numerous airlines operating flights into Dublin, with twelve from the UK alone. Belfast is served by British Airways, British Midland and Aer Lingus (connecting to the US via Dublin). Regular ferries shuttle between Wales, Scotland and Ireland; connecting services with the ferries are operated by Irish Railways (Republic) and Translink (North).

ACCOMMODATION Dublin Tourism operates a central credit-card reservation service ☎ 01/605 7777. Accommodation in Belfast can be booked through the Tourist Information Centre ℡ 01223/246609.

TOURIST OFFICES (Republic) National: Baggot St Bridge, Dublin 2 ℡ 01/602 4000 or 602 4100; Dublin: Suffolk St, Dublin 2 ℡ 01/605 7700 Ⓕ 605 7749. UK: London ℡ 0171/493 3201. US: New York ℡ 212/418-0800 Ⓦ http://www.ireland.travel.ie/home/index.asp Ⓦ http://www.irelandvacations.com./

(North) Northern Ireland Tourist Board, St Anne's Court, 59 North St, Belfast BT1 1NB ℡ 01232/231221 Ⓕ 240960. UK: ℡ 0171/766 9920. US: ℡ 212/922-0101 Ⓦ http://www.ni-tourism.com

COUNTRY CODE (Republic) ℡ 353 (North) ℡ 44

ISRAEL, JORDAN AND PALESTINE

The ancient biblical sites of the **Holy Land** are likely to be the second busiest pilgrimage destination in the world (after Rome) in the year 2000. Millions of visitors are expected, thanks in part to an unprecedented papal decree encouraging pilgrimages to **Israel** and the **Palestinian territories**. **Jordan** is also hoping for its share of millennial visitors.

Pope John Paul II has expressed hopes for a mass gathering of spiritual leaders in the Holy Land at the end of 1999, but his own presence remains unconfirmed. Apart from his ailing health, another possible obstacle is the Vatican view on Jerusalem. Considered holy to Christianity, Judaism and Islam, the city is claimed by both Israel and Palestine. The Vatican believes that it should be a special 'international open city', a move which is firmly rejected by Israel. A papal visit would also depend on progress in the peace process.

Projections that up to eight million pilgrims would visit the Holy Land have now been downgraded to around four million. Catholic pilgrims are expected to comprise the largest group, with around two million arriving from Europe and the United States.

Around one million Eastern Orthodox pilgrims will arrive by sea and air routes from Greece, the Balkans and the former Soviet Republics. The Israeli airline El-Al will be operating charters in conjunction with Russian airlines, and the Russian President, the Mayor of Moscow, and the head of the Russian Orthodox Church, Patriarch Aleksiy II, have been invited to attend.

Remaining visitors will consist of around 500,000 Protestants, as well as Jewish and secular tourists. Around 350,000 visitors are expected from the UK.

The Israeli Ministry of Tourism has allocated £48 million (US$80m) to fund a massive promotional campaign overseas as well as producing special pilgrim brochures, videos, CD-ROMs, posters and films. The three main centres for pilgrimages will be **Jerusalem**, **Bethlehem** and **Nazareth**.

The Israelis are also trying to disperse pilgrims to other areas, such as the infamous **Golan Heights** (captured from Syria in 1967); a new *Golan Heights Pilgrims Companion* says that 'Jesus spent most of his ministry, not to mention the most exciting part of his life, in Galilee and on the Golan'.

On the shores of the Sea of Galilee a 2000-year-old fishing boat, known as the **Jesus Boat** lies in a special preservation tank at Kibbutz Ginossar, where it was discovered in 1986. A storm of protest erupted in 1999 when it emerged that the Antiquities Authority was planning to move the boat to Jerusalem and on to the Vatican as part of the millennium celebrations, with protestors claiming that the fragile relic would be irrevocably damaged in transit.

In February 1999 Israel's National Parks Authority announced a controversial plan to build a submerged bridge into the Sea of Galilee that would allow tourists to simulate Jesus's miraculous walk on water. The crescent-shaped bridge will be submerged two inches below the water, and will hold up to fifty people at a time.

Other events planned include the Jubillennium Great Embrace, a 'circle of life' around the Dead Sea with thousands of people joining hands to assert their dedication to peace.

The site of the **Battle of Armageddon** as portrayed in Revelation is also set to lure tourists. Forty-five miles north of Tel Aviv, the **Mount of Megiddo** (*megiddo* is Hebrew for Armageddon) will feature a hi-tech laser and hologram performance to transport visitors back through 6000 years of Holy Land history.

The Kingdom of **Jordan** is working jointly with tourism officials from Israel and the Palestinian territories to promote millennium pilgrimages. The country has more than fifty biblical sites, the most important of which is the area around Bethany on the east bank of the Jordan River,

where John the Baptist baptised Jesus Christ. Access to the baptism site, once a military zone, was made possible after Jordan signed the 1994 peace treaty with Israel.

The Jordanian Department of Antiquities is currently surveying and excavating some twenty sites in the area, and has uncovered monastic complexes, churches, caves and other structures from the Roman and Byzantine eras. It has also discovered an ancient pilgrimage route linking Bethany with Jerusalem, the Jordan River and Mt Nebo (where Moses was buried).

The Bethany site (with new facilities and infrastructure improvements) will be open to the public in mid-1999 and a **Worldwide Prayer Service** will be held there in December 1999. The **Bethabara Church**, located near Bethany and built by the Emperor Anastusius in honour of John the Baptist, will be open by 2000.

Jerusalem

Considered a holy city by Jews, Christians and Muslims alike, **Jerusalem**'s significance to the three monotheistic religions means that it is visited by thousands of pilgrims and tourists every day.

The city and surrounding areas contain a vast number of sites connected to Jesus's ministry in Jerusalem and his eventual crucifixion there. The **Temple Mount** was the site of the Jerusalem Temple, which played a key role in Jewish religious, political and economic life during the time of Jesus. Judaic tradition holds that the **Ark of the Covenant** (containing fragments of Moses' tablets) rested in the 'Holy of Holies' inside the temple.

The site is now dominated by a Muslim shrine, the **Dome of the Rock**, which was built after the Muslim conquest of Palestine in the seventh century. The original **Western Wall**, which was left standing when the temple was destroyed, is a holy site for Jews.

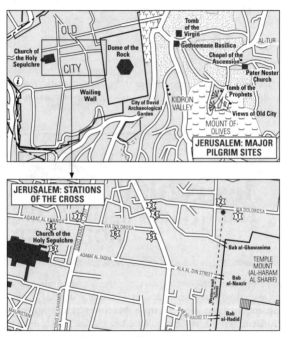

JERUSALEM: MAJOR PILGRIM SITES

JERUSALEM: STATIONS OF THE CROSS

STATIONS OF THE CROSS (shown as stars)			
Jesus is tried and condemned	1	Veronica wipes Jesus's face	6
Jesus takes up the cross	2	Jesus falls for the second time	7
Jesus falls for the first time	3	Jesus consoles the women of Jerusalem	8
Jesus meets his mother	4	Jesus falls for the third time	9
Simon the Cyrene takes the cross	5		

One of Jerusalem's most sacred places of pilgrimage is the **Church of the Holy Sepulchre**, believed to have been the resting place of the body of Jesus after his crucifixion.

The church is jointly administered by rival denominations, including the Greek Orthodox, Roman Catholic and Armenian Orthodox churches, a situation which for decades has prevented urgent renovations taking place. A new dome was installed in 1996, finally allowing natural light into the church, but the greatest challenge remains the restoration of The Tomb of Christ, currently a crumbling edifice held together by a steel framework. Scholars have recently revealed that the interior may indeed contain the original rock-cut tomb of Jesus, and there are hopes that it will be restored for the millennium.

His final path to **Calvary** from the **Garden of Gethsemani** is marked by the **Stations of the Cross**, locations that indicate incidents on the journey. The Christian tradition of devotion at the Stations of the Cross began with early Byzantine pilgrims, and by the eighteenth century the route had become known as the **Via Dolorosa**.

The Israeli government has spent US$40 million (£24m) on renovations in the city, including creating an impressive new **Valley of the Kings** archeological park.

One problem facing the Israelis is that New Year's Eve, 1999 falls on the Jewish Sabbath, and hotels, restaurants, cafés and bars that want to maintain their kosher certificates will not be able to hold any celebrations. The Ministry of Tourism is negotiating with the Orthodox rabbinate in the hope that a special arrangement can be made for millennial visitors. Arab hotels and restaurants in east Jerusalem and the Palestinian Territories will undoubtedly benefit if the restrictions stay in place.

Events planned in Jerusalem include an **International Choir Concert** (December 23), **Christmas Symphonic**

Concerts (December 24–25), a **Christmas Parade** and festive prayers (December 25), and a special production of Handel's *Messiah* (January 2, 2000).

Jerusalem is gearing up to cope with possible mass outbreaks of **Jerusalem Syndrome;** the city is also considered to be 'Ground Zero' by many millennial cults who are arriving to await the Apocalypse (see FAQs, p.13).

Bethlehem

In the Palestinian West Bank town of **Bethlehem** they are hoping that the millennium celebrations will bring in three million people to Jesus's birthplace on his 2000-year anniversary. Set up in 1997, the **Bethlehem 2000** project is headed by the Palestinian president Yasser Arafat who has ambitious plans for infrastructure developments that will hopefully serve to kick-start the Palestinian tourism industry. An international programme of events, **Follow the Star**, has been devised in collaboration with the British advertising agency, M&C Saatchi.

Like the citizens of Rome, the 30,000 residents of Bethlehem will spend 1999 surrounded by building works as telephone, electricity, sewerage, water and road systems are rebuilt. The town's famous **Manger Square** has been reconstructed, financed by Swedish donations, and other countries are helping to finance the preservation of the cultural heritage in the surrounding network of pedestrian alleyways, with its traditional *souk* (marketplace) and layers of Islamic, Byzantine, Turkish and Crusader-era history. There are also plans for the restoration of the cultural heritage in neighbouring **Beit Jala**

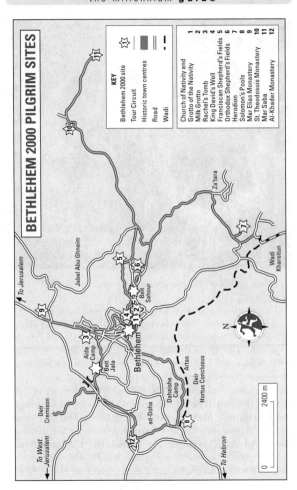

BETHLEHEM 2000 PILGRIM SITES

KEY

☆ Bethlehem 2000 site

▬ Tour Circuit

▬ Historic town centres

▬ Road

¦ Wadi

1 Church of Nativity and
  Grotto of the Nativity
2 Milk Grotto
3 Rachel's Tomb
4 King David's Well
5 Franciscan Shepherd's Fields
6 Orthodox Shepherd's Fields
7 Herodion
8 Solomon's Pools
9 Mar Elias Monastery
10 St. Theodosius Monastery
11 Mar Saba
12 Al-Khader Monastery

and **Beit Sahour** and the creation of an archeological park at **Solomon's Pools**.

The completion of the programme, however, is dependent on overseas contributions: by early 1999 only US$100 million (£60m) had been raised of the US$350 million (£208m) required. The United Nations held a two-day Bethlehem 2000 conference' in Rome in February 1999 to mobilize further international support for the project.

Celebrations will last from November 1999 through to Easter 2001. **Follow The Star** begins with the grand opening of the **Christmas Market** (November 27) in Manger Square and the illumination of the **Christmas Tree** on the first Sunday of Advent (November 28); an **Advent Concert Series** will take place on each subsequent Sunday featuring world-class orchestras and choirs and a performance of Bach's *Christ-*

mas Oratorio. There will be several **Festive Services** on Christmas Eve, culminating in Midnight Mass in the **Church of the Nativity**, where the opening of the Holy Door will be broadcast globally. A programme of Christmas traditions from around the world, **Catch the Star**, will take place in Manger Square (December 24–25).

The **Christmas Day Celebrations** will include a parade of crèche scenes and a candle-lit procession from the Orthodox Shepherds Field to the Greek Catholic Church. Christmas Day will also mark the start of **Thirteen Holy Nights** (December 25, 1999–January 7, 2000), a series of evenings of Western and oriental music and street parades. On New Year's Eve there will be a **Concert of Hope**, broadcast globally, and a party.

Events will continue throughout 2000, amongst them Christmas celebrations for the Eastern denominations (January 6), **Easter Processions** (April), an **International Choral Festival** (June 4–8), and the **Bethlehem 2000 Summer Festival** (July).

Bethlehem 2000, PO Box 2000, Bethlehem, Palestine ⓣ 02/274 22 24
ⓕ 274 22 27 ⓔ BL2000@palnet.com ⓦ http://www.bethlehem2000.org
Well-designed and comprehensive site with full details on the project, events, holy sites and hotels.

Nazareth

Nazareth has been a key pilgrim centre for most of the past two millennia. Half of all tourists to the Holy Land visit this celebrated Galilee city where the Annunciation took place and where Jesus spent most of his life. It is surrounded by numerous important sites including Cana of Galilee, Sephoris, Mount Tabor, the Mount of the Precipice, and Tiberias.

Within Nazareth itself key holy sites include the **Basilica of the Annunciation** and the **Grotto of the Annunciation**, **St Joseph's Church** (said to have been the site of his carpentry workshop), the Greek Catholic **Synagogue Church**, the Franciscan chapel of **Mensa Christi** (built around a large block said to be the table at which Jesus and the disciples sat after the Resurrection), and **Mary's Well**.

The largest Arab city in Israel with a population of 60,000 Christians and Muslims, Nazareth has suffered from a lack of investment over the years but has managed to secure US$100 million (£61m) to rejuvenate the city in preparation for the millennium. The programme for **Nazareth 2000** includes refurbishing parts of the **Old City**, resurfacing the streets with ancient-style paving, building new hotels, renovating the *souk* and creating a pedestrian walkway between the Basilica of the Annunciation and Mary's Well.

Around 1.2 million pilgrims are expected in 2000 and Christmas in Nazareth will rival the celebrations in Bethlehem. A colourful, lively parade takes place at 3pm on Christmas Eve, followed by a traditional Mass at 7.30pm in six churches in town. There will also be a **Festival of International Choirs** (December 26), and **Liturgical Concerts** (December 27–28).

Ⓦ http://www.inisrael.com/tour/nazareth/project.htm

Home pages of the Nazareth 2000 project Ⓦ http://www.jesus2000.com/

Based in Nazareth, this 'virtual pilgrimage to the Holy Land' has pictures, maps, audio and video, and the 'largest Christian souvenir mall on the Web'.

ISRAEL TRAVEL BRIEF

As the world's most popular Holy City with Bethlehem and Nazareth nearby, Jerusalem is expecting millions of pilgrims, so book well ahead.

GETTING THERE Most people visiting Israel arrive by air to Ben Gurion airport, between Tel Aviv (23km) and Jerusalem (46km), which is served by twenty international carriers. The airport will have new access roads, extra parking spaces for planes, and possibly a new temporary terminal to deal with the congestion. Eilat in the south also has scheduled and charter services. There are some internal flights, but distances are short and easily covered by road, with a superb bus system. El Al will put on extra flights to cater for the demand. There are ferries to Haifa from Greece and Cyprus.

ACCOMMODATION Israel will have around 55,000 rooms available, including hotels, rural accommodation, youth hostels and Christian hospices. To overcome bottlenecks at peak times during the millennium the tourist board is encouraging the establishment of rooms in rural areas within an hour's drive from the holy sites in Jerusalem and the Sea of Galilee. There are no central hotel reservation systems in Israel, but several major international chains such as Holiday Inn, Hilton and Sheraton have a number of hotels in the country for easy booking. Even though Jerusalem has a number of new hotels, booking over the millennium will be extremely heavy and luxury landmark hotels such as the *King David* are already full. Specialist pilgrim tours may have access to additional accommodation.

TOURIST OFFICES National: Tel Aviv: 5 Shalom 'Aleichem St
Ⓣ 03/660 259/60/61; Jerusalem: 24 King George St Ⓣ 02/675 4811
Ⓕ 625 3407; Jerusalem Municipal Information Office: 17 Jaffa Rd
Ⓣ 02/625 8844 Ⓦ http://www.infotour.co.il
UK: London Ⓣ 0171/299 1111 Ⓕ 299 1112 Ⓔ igto-uk@dircon.co.uk
US: New York Ⓣ 888/77-ISRAEL Ⓕ 212/499-5660
Ⓦ http://www.goisrael.com

TOURS UK: Andante Ⓣ 01980/610555; Longwood Holidays
Ⓣ 0181/551 4494; Mancunia Ⓣ 0161/228 2842; Peltours Ⓣ 0181/343 0590;
St Peter's Pilgrims Ⓣ 0181/244 8844; Superstar Ⓣ 01233/211203
(brochures) or 0171/957 4300; WST Charters Ⓣ 0171/224 0504.

US: Best of Israel Ⓣ 800/982-9783; Israel Revealed Ⓣ 800/272-7662 or
801/553-0183; Israel Tour Connection Ⓣ 201/535-2575; Pilgrimage Tours
and Travel Ⓣ 516/627-2636. Special events packages to Jerusalem in 2000
are available through International Millennium 2000
Ⓣ 800/477-2306 Ⓕ 278-8113.

THE PALESTINIAN
TERRITORIES TRAVEL BRIEF

Palestine is where it all started, 2000 years ago (or thereabouts). Bethlehem is a very different place these days, but with thousands of pilgrims flocking in, the local stables could be back in use.

A useful contact is PACE (Palestine Association for Cultural Exchange), PO Box 841, Ramallah, West Bank, Palestine Ⓣ/Ⓕ 02/998 6854
Ⓔ pace@planet.edu Ⓦ http://www/planet.edu-pace

GETTING THERE The Palestinian Authority does now have an international airport in Gaza, but it is much easier and cheaper at present to fly into Tel Aviv and travel from there. Security varies from time to time, so always double-check before setting out and again at the checkpoints en route. Preferably, take an organised tour. Advance booking will be necessary.

ACCOMMODATION It is estimated that Bethlehem will need about five times the number of beds that it actually has (around 1200). Many visitors will end up staying in nearby Jerusalem. Border crossing procedures between Jerusalem and Bethlehem will be simplified in order to allow people to move more freely between the two. Early booking is in any case essential.

TOURIST OFFICES Bethlehem: Ministry of Tourism and Antiquities, Manger Square, ⓣ 02/741 581 Ⓕ 743 753 Ⓦ http://www.visit-palestine.com There are small tourist offices in each of the main Palestinian towns; some information is also available from Israeli tourist offices.

TOURS See Israel

COUNTRY CODE (Israel and Palestine) ⓣ 972

ITALY

P lans are in full swing in **Rome** for the celebration of what Pope John Paul II has dubbed **The Great Jubilee** to mark the third millennium of Christianity. Estimates vary as to how many pilgrims will descend on the holy city, with city authorities predicting around thirty million and the Vatican (on the basis of previous jubilees in 1950 and 1975) expecting more like ten to fifteen million.

Bologna was the site of the first university in Europe a thousand years ago, and in 2000 it will be one of the nine European Cities of Culture.

The historic port of **Genoa** will be one of the starting points for the European leg of the **Tall Ships 2000** race, with a series of maritime events and exhibitions to celebrate (April 20–23, 2000).

In **Turin Cathedral** the **Holy Shroud**, the cloth that was wrapped round the body of the crucified Christ according to Catholic tradition, is to have a special showing for the millennium. The last time the shroud was put on display in September 1987, three million pilgrims made the journey to see it.

The Italian government has allocated US$30 million (£18m) for cultural events and projects for the millennium, which include four major art exhibitions in the renovated stables of Rome's Quirinale presidential palace. Funds are also going to the Rome Opera, young artists nationally, and opening new cultural sites.

Rome

The Pope will usher in the new millennium by banging on the Holy Door of St Peter's Basilica with the traditional silver hammer. Elsewhere, visitors may find that jackhammers rather than silver hammers will mark the holy pilgrimage: construction work for the jubilee is taking place on 86 building sites around the capital and, if the Holy Year in 1975 is anything to go by, much of it will still be going on as pilgrims start to arrive.

One of the most controversial construction projects was a proposed mile-long tunnel close to the Vatican near the Castel Sant'Angelo (a fortress built to house the tomb of Emperor Hadrian). Archeologists uncovered ancient Roman buildings which may contain a number of important tombs around Hadrian's burial site, and the tunnel has now been abandoned. A proposed widening of the motorway from the airport into the city has already been reduced from four lanes to three; a new ring road, which was meant to have doubled in size, is now only to be enlarged on sections near the Vatican. A new underground linking the Colosseum and the Vatican has already been abandoned.

One project that still looks feasible is the restoration of the **Colosseum**, which is undergoing a facelift paid for by the Banco di Roma. Additionally, the **Borghese Picture Gallery**, closed for the last twelve years due to stabilisation works on the building, reopened in 1997. The city also plans to reorganise access to areas that will be popular with pilgrims, including the **Basilica of St Peter, St Paul Outside the Walls, St John**

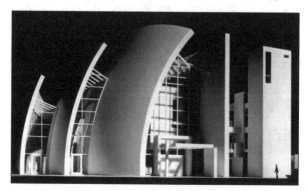

Lateran and **San Lorenzo**. One of the most prominent new churches in Rome will be the **Church of the Year 2000**, which has been designed by the distinguished New York architect Richard Meier. The church, which bears some resemblance to a cut-down version of the Sydney Opera House, is based on 'a series of displaced squares and four circles'.

The Vatican has also commissioned a **Mosaic for the Millennium** in the Holy See's Redemptoris Major chapel. Created by Russian artist Aleksandr Kornoukhov, the work is composed of over one hundred million mosaic pieces and has been described as 'one of the century's most ambitious works of art' and compared to Michelangelo's Sistine Chapel ceiling. However, the chapel lies in the heart of the Apostolic Palace, which houses the Pope's private apartments, and it is not known whether the public will be allowed in to view it. New glimpses of old Rome are also likely with the discovery of a stunning series of frescoes and mosaics under the Oppian Hill, which are to be opened up to the public in time for the millennium.

The Vatican will be issuing ten million hi-tech 'pilgrim cards' which will allow people to book visits to the Vatican and use telephone and transport services. The card's microchip will also carry information on the pilgrim's identity, hotel reservations, and travel plans; it has been designed to cut down on the need to carry cash in a city notorious for its pickpockets. Nearly 60,000 volunteers are to be recruited to help pilgrims around Rome.

The Vatican's millennium celebrations will last from December 24, 1999 to January 6, 2001. If he is fit enough, the Pope hopes to deliver a blessing every day to the crowds in St Peter's Square. The Vatican is also planning 29 Jubilee Days for different groups of people (artists, children, teachers, scientists, workers, politicians, etc). A significant date in the Vatican's calendar is March 8, 2000, the 'Day of Request for Pardon', when the Pope is expected to ask forgiveness for past errors including the Inquisition.

Great Jubilee 2000, Vatican City, 00129 Europe ⓣ 06/698 82828
ⓕ 698 81961 ⓦ http://www.vatican.va/
The official Vatican Web site; multilingual. Lists all Jubilee 2000 religious services.
ⓦ http://www.roma2000.it
Information on museums and monuments to visit in Rome, bilingual.
ⓦ http://www.jubilee2000com
An unofficial Jubilee Web site.

Bologna

The city's theme as a Cultural Capital 2000 is **Communication**. As part of its programme Bologna will be opening a number of new or refurbished museums and other cultural institutions at a cost of 150 billion lire (£54m/US$90m). These include the **Mediatheque**, which will be the largest library in Italy and will also house a multimedia project presided over by Umberto Eco; the opening of a new **Museum of Jewish Culture**; the restoration of the **Palace of King Enzo** and the **Podestà**; the creation of a **National Library and Documentation Centre for Women**; and the conversion of a derelict area around the former Tobacco Factory into a **Centre for the Visual Arts**. There will be numerous special shows and events throughout the year, including an art exhibition on the **European Spirit** (Spring 2000, Gallery of Modern Art), **The Etruscan Princes** (Autumn 2000), **Made in Bologna** (Autumn 2000), and a special programme of **Religious Art** for pilgrims on their way to Rome.

Bologna 2000, via Oberdan 24, 40126 Bologna ⓣ 51/204653 ⓕ 268636
ⓔ Bologna2000@comune.bologna.it
ⓦ http://www.comune.bologna.it/Bologna2000
Text-heavy and fairly dull site.

The Great Jubilee

The tradition of a Holy Year or Jubilee began when thousands of Christians travelled from all over Europe to pray at the tombs of the Apostles Peter and Paul at Christmas 1299. Having discovered why they were there Pope Boniface VII was so impressed by their faith that he declared 1300 'a year of forgiveness for all sins'.

A Jubilee can be ordinary if it falls after a set number of years and extraordinary if it marks some outstanding event. The year 2000 will be the 26th ordinary Jubilee (there have been two extraordinary Jubilees in this century, 1933 and 1983). John Paul II has issued a papal bull, *Incarnationis Mysterium*, setting out the dates for more than 140 religious events during 2000 and the terms under which believers can earn papal indulgence – which include doing good turns, giving to charity or giving up smoking, drinking and other forms of excessive consumption – if only for a day.

ROME TRAVEL BRIEF

Anywhere between ten to thirty million people are expected to visit Rome in 1999 and 2000. Rome's preparations for the influx include several new and improved roads, underground and tram lines, connecting the airport, Vatican and other places of pilgrimage. Work has fallen behind, however, and some may not be completed in time. Expect the city to be more chaotic than usual over Christmas and the New Year.

GETTING THERE There are direct scheduled services into most major Italian cities from destinations across Europe, including several major UK airports. Most long-haul flights, including those from the US, serve only Milan and Rome. There will be extra flights to cater for the increased traffic, but it is still advisable to book as early as possible. Italy has an excellent rail system with links to the European TGV network.

ACCOMMODATION Due to potentially severe shortages of accommodation, plans are in hand to open the local convents and monasteries to pilgrims (available via the church and specialist pilgrimage tour operators). Book as soon as possible.

TOURIST OFFICES National: ENIT, Via Marghera 2, 00185 Rome
Ⓣ 06/49 711 Ⓕ 446 3379 Ⓔ sedecentrale.enit@interbusiness.it
Ⓦ http://www.itwg.com *or* http://www.enit.it Rome: Via Parigi 11
Ⓣ 06/488 991; Vatican Information Office, St Peter's Square
Ⓣ 06/698 4466 or 4866. UK: London Ⓣ 0171/408 1254 Ⓕ 493 6695
Ⓔ enitlond@globalnet.co.uk US: New York Ⓣ 212/245-5095 Ⓕ 586-9249
Ⓔ enitny@bway.net; Chicago Ⓣ 312/644-0996 Ⓕ 644-3019; Los Angeles
Ⓣ 310/820-2977 Ⓕ 820-6357.

TOURS UK: Alternative Travel Group Ⓣ 01865/315678; Citalia Ⓣ 0181/686
5533; Italiatour Ⓣ 0171/605 7500; Magic of Italy Ⓣ 0990/462442 (brochures)
or 0181/748 7575; St Peter's Pilgrims Ⓣ 0181/244 8844. US: American
Sightseeing International Ⓣ 800/225-4432; Bendall International Ⓣ 216/238-
3711; CIT Tours Ⓣ 800/CIT-TOUR; Donna Franca Tours Ⓣ 800/225-6290;
Euroseven Ⓣ 800/890-3876; Maupintour Ⓣ 800/255-4266.

COUNTRY CODE Ⓣ 39

NETHERLANDS

T he Netherlands has no official millennium plans,
although the privately-run **Millennium Foundation**
(Stichting Millennium) founded in 1987 in Haarlem can jus-
tifiably claim to be one of the first millennium groups in the
world and, even if they only have two hundred members,
they have devoted considerable energy to artistic projects
since then. They have also managed to complete the world's
first millennium project, the grandly titled **Monument to
the Twentieth Century** in downtown Haarlem.

One of the most unusual events taking place is a massive
New Year's Eve party for around a thousand people in an old
coastal fortress at **Den Helder**. The city of **Utrecht** is creat-

ing an original art project, **Panorama 2000**, in 1999 and the town of **Fryslan** in the north of the country has big plans for a massive gathering in 2000.

Den Helder

Den Helder's **Fort Kijkduin** will be the setting for a New Year's Eve spectacular. The fort, built during the Napoleonic era, has a 360° view of the sea, beach and sand dunes from its upper level, which has room for several bands, and a labyrinth of tunnels below, each of which will have its own bar and entertainment. There will also be a small casino and a champagne fountain at midnight (sponsored by Heineken).

Stichting Entree-2000, Middelzand 2611, 1788 CK, Den Helder, Netherlands
Ⓣ 0223/642305 Ⓔ entree@tref.nl Ⓦ http://www.trefnet.nl/kvnh/entree-2000/
Bilingual site; tickets cost Dfl.200 (£63/US$106) which includes drinks, food and entertainment.

Fryslan

Simmer 2000 (Summer 2000) is a foundation in Fryslan planning a series of events based around the Frysk Festival (July 1–22, 2000). The festival will feature music, theatre, a special production of Gluck's opera *Orfeo* on the lake, outdoor art installations, ice skating and the local sport of Korfball.

Simmer 2000, PO Box 2000, 8901 JA Leeurwarden, Netherlands
Ⓣ 58/2925687 Ⓕ 2925124 Ⓔ fryslan@simmer2000.nl
Ⓦ http://www.simmer2000.nl
Bilingual site with an excellent links page to other events worldwide.

Haarlem

The **Millennium Foundation** was formed twelve years ago by five friends whose aim is to 'explore the future together with musicians, artists, architects, and others'. The five core members are supported by around two hundred donors, who each year give an annual contribution amounting to the same number of Dutch guilders as the last two digits of the year: in 1999, for instance, it will be 99 guilders (around £31/US$53) but in the year 2000 it will be zero. Donations are used to fund a stylishly-produced range of artworks, one for each year and all focusing on some aspect of time or the future, which are then given as gifts on the annual donors' day.

The foundation has also created a 'living sculpture' of trees in Haarlem city's woods, the Haarlemmerhout. The twin rows of trees, running along either side of a road through the woods, have been planted at angles and trained along steel cables to form a living arch, 'an *estafette* (a relay) through time'.

Their most ambitious project to date has been the **Monument to the Twentieth Century** in downtown Haarlem. The twin arcs of the monument house two 'clocks', neon ribbons which light up as time passes – one on an annual

cycle, the other on a daily cycle. A conventional clock and a digital countdown clock are also built into the monument. The project was inaugurated in 1995.

The foundation has also collaborated with the **Academy of Photography** in Haarlem to run an annual project for students, who have to provide a photographic vision of the millennium. The results of the ten-year programme will go on public display in 2000. Stichting Millennium will be involved in various other events in 2000 before being disbanded – but a museum has already shown an interest in archiving their art works, photos, videos and publications to put in a time capsule for the year 2100.

Stichting Millennium, PO Box 5467, 2000 GL Haarlem ⓣ 023/532 0217 ⓕ 532 0346 ⓔ millenum@xs4all.nl ⓦ http://www.xs4all.nl/~millenum/

Utrecht

Utrecht's Centraal Museum is organising an unusual millennium project, **Panorama 2000** (June 5–September 30, 1999). Twenty international artists will be contributing works which will be displayed not in the museum itself – but on the city's rooftops. The works in the exhibition, which will perch on top of houses, churches, car parks, and even in the air itself, are designed to be viewed from the Netherland's tallest church tower, the Domtoren. The Domtoren has three look-out points (at 40, 75 and 100m) and offers a panorama of the city and beyond to Amsterdam. The city's unique project is the only large-scale millennium exhibition currently scheduled for the Netherlands.

Panorama 2000, Centraal Museum, PO Box 2106, 3500 GC Utrecht, Netherlands ⓣ 30/236 2362 ⓕ 233 2006 ⓔ cmus@xs4all.nl

ⓦ http:// www.panorama2000.com
Bilingual, includes a 3-D simulation of the city from the top of the Domtoren.

TRAVEL BRIEF

The Netherlands is compact, well-organised and everything is accessible geographically from everywhere else.

GETTING THERE Amsterdam Schiphol is one of the largest and most efficient airports in Europe, with flights to and from destinations around the world, including many regional UK airports. The Dutch rail system is also excellent, as are its road and rail connections with neighbouring countries. There are no planned events large enough to disrupt normal service for long. As ever, it is worth pre-booking flights over peak periods.

ACCOMMODATION The Netherlands is small enough for you to stay in Amsterdam and commute to events, should you choose to do so. Amsterdam has a vast range of tourist accommodation at all prices.

TOURIST OFFICES National: De Ruyterkade 5, 1013 AA Amsterdam Ⓣ 020/551 2560 Ⓕ 020/421 2567 Ⓔ info@nbt.nl UK: Ⓣ 0906/871 7777 Ⓕ 0171/828 7941 Ⓔ information@nbt.org.uk Ⓦ http://www.goholland.co.uk/ US: Chicago Ⓣ (toll-free) 888/GO-HOLLAND (24 hr) or 312/819-1500 Ⓔ GO2Holland@aol.com Ⓦ http://www.goholland.com

TOURS UK: Anglo Dutch Sports Ⓣ 0181/289 2808; City Escapades Ⓣ 0990/437227 (brochures) or 0181/563 8959; Kirker Selected Cities Ⓣ 0171/231 3333; Travelscene Ⓣ 0181/427 8800. US: Butterfield and Robinson Ⓣ 800/387-1147; Der Tours Ⓣ 800/782-2424; Europe through the Back Door Ⓣ 425/771-8303; Euroseven Ⓣ 800/890-3876; Flying Wheels Travel Ⓣ 800/535-6790; Four Seasons Cycling Ⓣ 804/253-2985.

COUNTRY CODE Ⓣ 31

NEW ZEALAND

N ew Zealand is planning to make the most of its 'place in the sun' and is firmly resisting all claims from rival islands in the Pacific to the first dawn. "New Zealand is guaranteed to see the first light of the new millennium", say the Government-sponsored **Millennium Office**.

At present, the consensus is that the **Chatham Islands** are the first inhabited islands in the world to witness the new dawn. Wrangling between neighbouring landowners, however, has threatened to scupper plans to broadcast globally from this location.

Acrimonious disputes have also broken out between competing locations on the mainland, principally **Gisborne** and **Hastings** on the northeast coastline. Gisborne has always promoted itself as the first city to greet each new day and holds an annual First Light festival which attracts up to 40,000 visitors for a series of events between Christmas and New Year's Day. However, a survey released in 1997 by Terralink NZ claimed to show that Te Mata Peak, just outside Hastings, would see the sunrise before Gisborne's Kaiti Hill. Hastings was immediately galvanised into action and set about promoting 'Hastings – the Millennium 2000 City'. Gisborne refused to take this lying down and switched the focus instead to Mount Hikurangi, which is 1354m higher than Te Mata, although it is more than fifty miles north of the city. Gisborne's claims have now been backed by the Millennium Office and the Towards 2000 Taskforce.

The government is spending NZ\$18 million (£6m/US\$10m) on the celebrations, hoping to capitalise on the millennium as well as the **America's Cup** taking place in Auckland and the Sydney 2000 Olympics across the Tasman Sea.

The millennium taskforce has budgeted NZ$1.8 million (£600,000/US$1m) for official dawn events in the Chathams, Gisborne and at Mt Hikurangi, with a broadcast by TV3 on the theme of 'First to the Future'. Other projects granted funds include **Onward 2000: First Light, Last Post** involving army veterans and the Maori battalion in Wellington, and **Te Ngaru Matau: The Ancient Wave**, a series of ocean races for *waka* (canoes) using traditional voyaging techniques.

Projects still under consideration include the Millennium Bell ('the largest tuned bell in the world' – although they will have competition from Newport, US, which has already cast its bell); the creation of **Te Araroa**, one of the world's great walking tracks; **Highway 2000**, enhancing over 400km of coastal highway; the creation of a virtual reality **Canoe Voyage** at the Auckland Maritime Museum; and a **Millennium Train** which will travel the length and breadth of the country with 'time travellers' from the last century on board.

On the North Island the main events will take place in Gisborne and Hastings. The central town of **Rotorua**, famous for its volcanic hot springs, will be staging a special **Mardi Gras** on New Year's Eve, 1999. **Hamilton** is hosting a **Sunrise Marathon** around the city with a 6am start on January 1, 2000, plus an easier 10km race and a 5km walk for those who are too hungover to compete in the main 42km event.

The **Pacific Tall Ships Festival**, which will feature fourteen square-rigged and historic ships (including a replica of Captain Cook's *Endeavour*) arrives in Wellington on December 10, 1999. The ships will then sail to Gisborne for the millennium celebrations and onwards to Auckland for the first round of the America's Cup 2000.

In the South Island plans are well advanced in the **Canterbury** region, where Turning Point 2000 has numerous events planned. The country's most southerly city, Invercargill, is

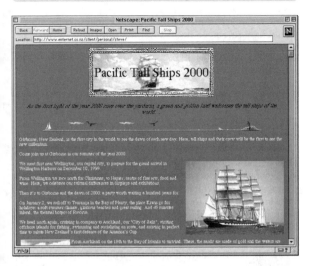

Pacific Tall Ships 2000

As the first light of the year 2000 rises over the eastern, a green and golden land welcomes the tall ships of the world.

Gisborne, New Zealand, is the first city in the world to see the dawn of each new day. Here, tall ships and their crew will be the first to see the new millennium.

Come join us at Gisborne in our summer of the year 2000.

We meet first near Wellington, our capital city, to prepare for the grand arrival in Wellington Harbour on December 10, 1999.

From Wellington we row north for Christmas, to Napier, centre of fine arts, food and wine. Here, we celebrate our cultural differences in displays and exhibitions.

Then it's to Gisborne and the dawn of 2000: a party worth waiting a hundred years for.

On January 2, we sail off to Tauranga in the Bay of Plenty, the place Kiwis go for holidays: a soft summer climate, glorious beaches and great sailing. And 45 minutes inland, the thermal hotpot of Rotorua.

We head north again, cruising in company to Auckland, our 'City of Sails', visiting offshore islands for fishing, swimming and socialising en route, and arriving in perfect time to salute New Zealand's first defence of the America's Cup.

From Auckland on the 18th to the Bay of Islands to unwind. There, the sands are made of gold and the waters are

making a bid for millennium revellers with the **Southland Millennium** programme, which is promoting remote Bluff Hill as a likely sunrise spot. The lively resort of **Queenstown** on the shores of Lake Wakatipu was New Zealand's first '24-hour city' and, as the acknowledged party capital of the South Island, it will be humming on New Year's Eve 1999 with parties spilling out onto the streets and around the lakeshore.

Finally, if the 'Land of the Long White Cloud' lives up to its name on the big day you could always hop on to an Air New Zealand sunchaser flight which will climb above the clouds to see the sunrise. The airline's plans are a demonstration of confidence, they say, that it has solved its millennium bug problems. The rest of the world, too, will be watching to see how the millennium bug affects the country in general: New Zealand will provide an early warning of glitches, according to the Ministry of Commerce, and if specific problems are encountered the United States, for example, would have seventeen hours to make contingency plans.

New Zealand Millennium Office, 46 Waring Taylor St, PO Box 805, Wellington
ⓣ 04/495 9337Ⓕ 494 0684 Ⓔ millennium@dia.govt.nz
Ⓦ http://www.millennium.govt.nz

Thin on content, and surprisingly contains no links to other NZ Web sites.

Auckland

The 'City of Sails' is gearing up to host the **America's Cup 2000** regatta. Competition for one of the oldest and most hotly-contested sailing prizes will be intense as sixteen crews, representing ten countries, prepare to take on the Kiwis (who won in 1995) to be the first winners of the new millennium. Auckland's Viaduct Harbour is being redeveloped at a cost of NZ$58 million (£22m/US$37m) to create the American Express New Zealand Cup Village, which will provide facilities for racing teams and visitors alike during the six-month cup festival, from the opening ceremonies in October 1999 through to the final matches in March 2000. Races will take place on the Hauraki Gulf, with spectators able to watch from charter boats or on live large-screen broadcasts back at the Cup Village.

Ⓦ http://www.americas-cup.co.nz
Home pages of the race, with news pages and video links.
Ⓦ http://www.aucklandnz.com Home pages of Tourism Auckland.

Canterbury

Turning Point 2000 aims to involve communities right across the province of **Canterbury** on South Island in a series of events to celebrate the millen-

nium as well as the 150-year anniversary since European settlement. The organisers are budgeting NZ$1.3 million (£500,000/US$850,000) for a New Year's Eve party and NZ$3.84 million (£1.5m/US$2.4m) for eleven other projects.

The celebrations begin with a 24-hour party, **New Year's Eve – Dawn 2000** in Christchurch's Hagley Park (around 200,000 people are expected), linked to other international parties. This will be followed by **Karanga at Dawn**, a Maori ceremony to greet the new day at Godley Heads, and a **Sunrise Breakfast** at Brighton Beach. Kites will also be launched at dawn on Brighton Beach to open the **Millennium Kite Festival** (January 1–4, 2000).

In the millennium year a major exhibition, **SciTec 2000**, will open at the Westpactrust Centre (Jan 22–February 18, 2000), featuring a 'world-class interactive exhibit' of science and technology; other events planned include a **Millennium Garden Competition** (February 2000), and a **Schools' Olympics** (March 2000).

Turning Point 2000, PO Box 237, 392 Moorhouse Ave, Christchurch
T 03/379 2008 F 379 7131 E turningpoint2000@ccc.govt.nz
W http://www.tp2000.org.nz

Chatham Islands

According to the Government, the new millennium's first rays will hit Mount Hapeka on **Pitt Island** in the Chathams at 3:59am local time (4:59 NZ Daylight Saving Time). But parts of Mount Hapeka are owned by separate farming families, the Lanauzes and the Moffats, both of whom have been trying to attract international broadcasters to their piece of the mountain. Huge fees have been bandied about, but because neither family can guarantee unique footage the result is a stalemate. Plans are now underway to broadcast from the main Chatham Island even though the sunrise there is a few seconds later than Pitt Island.

Ironically, it's quite likely that the dawn won't be visible anyway. The Chathams lie in the Roaring Forties and locals rate the chances of being able to see the sunrise on January 1, 2000 at around 50/50.

The 55 Pitt islanders are hoping to avoid a millennium invasion, and events will be low-key. The Millennium Adventure Company, one of the groups competing for the film rights, say that they will possibly host a gathering of young people to witness the event.

On Chatham Island they're hoping to get into the record books with the first sporting event of the millennium, a **horse race** which will start at 00:05am GMT on January 1, 2000. The event will take place at the Chatham Islands Racing Club, which will be floodlit for the occasion.

Time Capsules

● Creating time capsules or time vaults is one of the most obvious ways of commemorating the millennium. An 80-kilo stainless steel container has been buried beneath the foundations of Britain's Millennium Dome, containing objects chosen by viewers of the BBC children's programme *Blue Peter*. It is due to be unearthed in 2050 and contains items such as a Tamagochi, a Spice Girls CD, videos, photographs and drawings. Other time capsules are being planned for the US, Canada, and in space (see p.300).

● It may be easy enough to interpret a drawing, letter or other item of personal memorabilia in a hundred or a thousand years time, but what of CD-ROMs, tapes, videos, DVDs and other archive formats? Time vaults containing items like these will also need to contain the equipment to interpret them, as well as instructions on how to use them, since by then they will no doubt be antiquated. Time vaults designed to last for a thousand years or more will also need to be filled with an inert gas to preserve the contents.

● One of the most ambitious time capsule projects was Kiwi sculptor Denis Hall's plan for a Millennium Time Vault, a huge underground chamber which would have been topped off by a 15m-high pyramid. The team planning the Time Vault spent four years trying to persuade the New Zealand authorities to support the project, but they had no success and have now decided to go it alone. Denis has changed his design, too, and now wants to see his time vault topped off by an 85ft-high statue of a Golden Girl, her arms outstretched to catch the rising sun. In March 1999, Time Vault 2000 announced that they had secured the rights to build Golden Girl on the slopes of Mount Hikurangi, and are now offering time capsule space for sale worldwide.

Time Vault 2000, PO Box 27378, Wellington Ⓣ 06/855 8290 Ⓕ385 7470 Ⓔ office@timevault-2000.co.nz Ⓦ http://timevault-2000.co.nz

Gisborne

Gisborne is preparing for a millennial invasion that will swell its 35,000 population to 150,000 as revellers arrive. These include 10,000 Christians camping in a tented city outside the town for **Servant 2000** (December 27, 1999–January 5, 2000); hundreds of bikers arriving for their annual rally and **'Battle of the Streets'** race (January 2, 2000); two thousand athletes taking part in the **First Light Triathlon** (January 3, 2000); and two thousand cyclists taking part in the **2000 First to the Sun** ride from Auckland to Gisborne.

One of the biggest celebrations will be the **Gisborne 2000 Festival**, which will be staged over 24 hours (31 December, 1999–January 1, 2000) on a fifty-acre waterfront site looking towards the dawn horizon. The site encompasses an oval-shaped grass stadium and a park (which will become a tented village with bars, restaurants and other facilities) and the organisers, Odyssey's End Ltd, are promising top flight entertainment as well as a performing group of one thousand Maori warriors; David Bowie and Split Enz are apparently confirmed bookings.

Other events taking place on the same night include the **First Light Te Kowhai Music Festival 2000**, with World Music and Maori cultural entertainers (12 noon–7am, Brown's

Beach, Muriwai); the **Party of the Millennium** at Coops Beach, Young Nick's Head; and the **Town Clock New Year's Eve Party** with live entertainment.

The local Ngati Porou tribe will be holding the **Ngati Porou C2000 Festival** (January 1–3, 2000), with three days of sport and entertainment. The festival will include a **dawn ceremony** on Mount Hikurangi.

The fleet of the **Pacific Tall Ships Festival** will arrive in Gisborne for the festivities ashore on New Year's Eve. Passengers and crew will return to their vessels for a cannon-fire salute to greet the millennium dawn.

At the coastline the dawn will be greeted with a **Voyaging Canoes Pageant**, which will be a unique spectacle as *waka-hourua* (double-hulled voyaging canoes with sails), *wakatua* (war canoes) and *waka-ama* (racing canoes) from all over New Zealand converge offshore for the sunrise. There are also plans for a **Multicultural Festival** and a **Cultural Centre**, the centrepiece of which will be an enormous carving, **Whakairo Nunui**, which will be the biggest of its kind in the world.

On New Year's Day there will be a **First Light Family Festival** and millennium services in local churches.

One of Gisborne's millennium projects, **Eco 2000**, has been selected as part of the international programme for Expo 2000 in Hannover. Eco 2000, whose key theme is sustainable land management, will be holding a series of workshops, conferences and field days through the year (February–November, 2000).

Gisborne 2000, First Light Tourism, PO Box 2000, Gisborne Ⓣ 06/868 1568 Ⓕ 868 1368 Ⓔ events@firstlight.co.nz Ⓦ http://www.gisborne2000.org.nz/ Now much improved visually, Gisborne's pages contain full contact details for events.

Odyssey's End Tours Ltd, PO Box 90644, AMSC, Auckland Ⓣ 09/302 3384 Ⓕ 358 3386 Ⓦ http://www.gisborne2000.co.nz

Pacific Tall Ships Festival, First Light Tourism, PO Box 2000, Gisborne Ⓣ 06/868 1568 Ⓕ 868 1368 Ⓔ events@firstlight.co.nz

Hastings

The city of Hastings will hold a family-oriented, alcohol-free **First Night** event on New Year's Eve, 1999, with around twenty shows and performances suitable for all age groups taking place in the downtown area (admission is on purchase of a First Night 'button'). The main focus, however, will be on **Te Mata Peak**. From its 399m summit there are superb views across Hawke's Bay for the millennium sunrise. **Peak 2000**, a party for one thousand people, will start at 5pm with 'light entertainment and international cuisine' at the restaurant, whilst halfway up to the peak there will be a Kiwiana Area, with further entertainment later on, and finally you'll be able to climb to the ridgeline for the millennium sunrise. This is a popular spot for hang-gliding and paragliding, so dawn launches are likely.

Other events planned include a bigger than usual **Harvest Hawke's Bay** wine festival (February 2000) and **Tumeke**

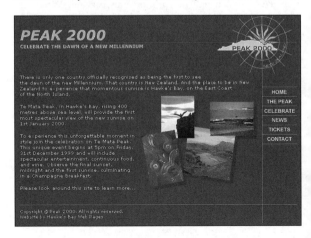

PEAK 2000
CELEBRATE THE DAWN OF A NEW MILLENNIUM

PEAK 2000

There is only one country officially recognised as being the first to see the dawn of the new Millennium. That country is New Zealand. And the place to be in New Zealand to experience that momentous sunrise is Hawke's Bay, on the East Coast of the North Island.

Te Mata Peak, in Hawke's Bay, rising 400 metres above sea level, will provide the first most spectacular view of the new sunrise on 1st January 2000.

To experience this unforgettable moment in style join the celebration on Te Mata Peak. This unique event begins at 5pm on Friday, 31st December 1999 and will include spectacular entertainment, continuous food, and wine. Observe the final sunset, midnight and the first sunrise, culminating in a Champagne Breakfast.

Please look around this site to learn more...

HOME
THE PEAK
CELEBRATE
NEWS
TICKETS
CONTACT

Copyright © Peak 2000. All rights reserved.
Website by Hawke's Bay Web Pages

('Too Much!'), an international children's festival which will feature 65 performances over seven days (March 20–26, 2000).

Hastings Millennium Committee, PO Box 000, Hastings ⓣ 06/877 1122 ⓕ 877 1123 ⓦ http://www.hawkesbay.com/millenn.html

Peak 2000, PO Box 8236, Havelock North ⓣ 06/877 8671 ⓕ 877 3942 ⓔ peak@clear.net.nz ⓦ http://www.peak2000.co.nz/
Tickets to the event cost NZ$700 (£270/US$450) including food, drinks, entertainment, champagne breakfast and transport from Havelock North village to Te Mata Peak.

TRAVEL BRIEF

New Zealand is always a popular Christmas and New Year destination. The North Island will be hosting numerous events on New Year's Eve 1999 and combined with the Tall Ships Race and the America's Cup fleet visiting in January, the country will be heaving. The Olympics in Australia will bring another tidal wave of visitors in September/October.

GETTING THERE There are regular direct services to Auckland from the UK, US, Australia and other world centres, but massive price hikes imposed by British Airways, Qantas and Air New Zealand for millennium flights are threatening to scupper a tourism boom and many Kiwis will be having to leave their jobs overseas as early as November in order to get home for Christmas 1999.

ACCOMMODATION Book as soon as possible if you're planning to be in Gisborne. The good news is that New Year is high summer in the southern hemisphere, so you could always camp outdoors.

TOURIST OFFICES New Zealand Tourism Board head office, PO Box 95, Wellington ⓣ 04/482 8860 ⓕ 478 1736 ⓦ http://www.nztb.govt.nz/ Auckland Visitor Centre, 299 Queen St, Auckland ⓣ 09/366 6888 ⓕ 366 6893. UK: London ⓣ 0171/930 1662. US: California ⓣ 310/395-7480 ⓕ 395-5453. Australia: Sydney ⓣ 02/9247 5222 ⓕ 9241 1136.

TOURS UK: Australian Pacific Tours ⓣ 0181/879 7444; Explore Worldwide ⓣ 01252/319448; First Light 2000 ⓣ 0171/289 1031; Kuoni Worldwide ⓣ 01306/741111; Mount Cook Line ⓣ 0181/741 5652. US: Collette Tours ⓣ 800/832-4656; Global Touring Inc. ⓣ 800/942-9399; Maupintour ⓣ 800/255-4266; Newmans South Pacific Vacations ⓣ 800/421-3326; Sunbeam Tours ⓣ 800/955-1818.

COUNTRY CODE ⓣ 64

NORWAY

I n 1998 the Norwegian government set up a limited company, **Millennium – Norway 2000**, to make plans for the celebrations and implement them all across the country. They will also be responsible for the centenary celebration in 2005 of the dissolution of the union between Norway and Sweden. The company's guidelines are 'optimism, solidarity, responsibility, openness and environmental awareness'; they have received ideas for 1200 projects to celebrate the millennium, although the only national project so far confirmed is the creation of **Millennium Halls** (*allmenningen* in Norwegian) all over the country. These meeting places have a long tradition in Norwegian life, and the intention is to create new or refurbished halls in 435 communities.

The millennium celebrations will take place over three days: **New Year's Eve, 1999** will focus on the nation and the people, with everyone receiving an invitation to take part, from children to pensioners, under the slogan 'no one shall be left alone'. Two minutes before midnight candles will be lit in silence and reflection, followed by public bonfires and fireworks in towns and villages everywhere. The most spectacular firework displays will be in the capital, Oslo, where 75 million kroner (£6m/US$10m) has been allocated for pyrotechnics. **New Year's Day, 2000** will focus on Oslo, as well as on the laying of the foundation stones for the 435 community halls. **January 2, 2000** will be devoted to international solidarity and interdenominational services.

Millennium – Norway 2000, Postboks 2000 Sentrum, 0104 Oslo ⓣ 22 32 2000 ⓕ 22 32 2033 ⓔ Tusenaarsskiftet@norge2000.no

Bergen

The city of **Bergen** is one of the nine European Cities of Culture in the year 2000, the first time Norway has been represented. The programme is still under development but will focus on three main themes: Dreams (Spring), Roaming (Summer), and Spaces (Autumn). Each season will contain art projects and 'spectacular folk festivals'. The Spring and Autumn programmes will be centred on Bergen itself, whilst the Summer season will embrace the whole of the western fjord region of Norway. The cultural year opens on February 17, 2000, with a special edition of the **Bergen International Festival** in May.

Bergen 2000, Vagsallmenningen 1, PO Box 434, 5001 Bergen Ⓣ 55 55 2000 Ⓕ 55 55 2001 Ⓔ bergen2000@bergen2000.no Ⓦ http://www.bergen2000.no (in Norwegian only).

TRAVEL BRIEF

Icy fjords, floodlit cross-country skiing, brightly painted wooden houses and throat-grabbing aquavit are amongst the possibilities for New Year in Norway. The downside is that it stays dark nearly all day – but during the summer the midnight sun will shine down on the festivities as Bergen celebrates its year as a European City of Culture 2000.

GETTING THERE Flights are always busy over Christmas and New Year and during the peak Summer holiday season (June–August). The year 2000 is unlikely to be any different. Several airlines fly out of both regional and London airports in the UK to Oslo and Bergen. SAS are the main carriers from the US, with many of their flights connecting via Copenhagen. There are direct ferries from the UK (Newcastle–Bergen) on Color Line.

ACCOMMODATION Both Bergen and Oslo have a good range of accommodation and no problems are anticipated. Bergen is ringed by country hotels and self-catering chalets within easy commuting distance.

TOURIST OFFICES National: PO Box 2893, Solli, Drammensvein 40, Oslo 0230 Ⓣ 22 03 44 00 Ⓕ 22 56 05 05 Ⓦ http://www.tourist.no
Bergen: Bryggen 7 Ⓣ 55 32 14 80 Ⓕ 55 31 56 82

Ⓦ http://www.bergen-travel.com Oslo: Vestbaneplassen 1 Ⓣ 22 83 00 50
(outside Norway), 82 06 01 00 (in Norway, premium rate) Ⓕ 22 83 81 50; Oslo
Use It – Youth Tourism Information Ⓣ 22 41 51 32 Ⓕ 22 42 63 71
Ⓔ webmaster@unginfo.oslo.no UK: London Ⓣ 0171/839 6255 Ⓕ 839 6014
Ⓔ norwaytourism@btinternet.com Ⓦ http://www.norway.org.uk/travel
US: New York Ⓣ 212/885-9700 Ⓕ 688-0554 Ⓦ http://www.norway.org

TOURS UK: Norsc Holidays Ⓣ 01297/560 0033; Norway Only
Ⓣ 01274/393480; Scandinavian Travel Service Ⓣ 0171/559 6666; Scantours
Ⓣ 0171/839 2927; Sovereign Scanscape Ⓣ 0161/742 2288.
US: Brekke Tours Ⓣ 800/437-5302; DER Travel Services Ⓣ 800/782-2424;
Five Stars of Scandinavia Ⓣ 800/722-4126.

COUNTRY CODE Ⓣ 47

POLAND

Poland's millennium plans revolve around the designation of
Kraków as a European City of Culture in 2000. Kraków
is a popular European short-break destination and a surge of
visitors is expected as its medieval beauty is highlighted
through cultural events in 2000.

Kraków

For centuries the spirituality of East and West have intermin-
gled in the former royal capital of Kraków, with three major
religions – Christianity, Judaism and Islam – coexisting peacefully. This unique spirit of tolerance has given the city its
theme for the year 2000: 'Thought – Spirituality – Creativity'.
One of the principal aims of the programme is to demonstrate

the significance of the sacred in the visual arts, as well as to highlight the 600-year anniversary of the founding of the University of Kraków.

Aspects of God is an event comprising three exhibitions: Gods of Ancient Egypt (Archaeological Museum, February 2000 onwards); Treasures of St Francis (Historical Museum, March–May 2000); and The Cradle of Slavic Christianity (Archaeological Museum, January–April 2000).

Throughout the month of July, a series of concerts of traditional European folk music, **Encounters 2000**, will be staged, including Armenian, Polish, Romany and Jewish music.

The Gothic – Shape and Light is a photographic exhibition that will run from August 10–November 30, 2000 in Kraków's Dominican cloister. The **Stanislaw Wyspianski Festival**, September–October, 2000, will feature performances, exhibitions, and a drama contest will focus on the life of this eminent Polish playwright. The **600-year Anniversary of the University** September 25–October 30, 2000, will include a celebratory exhibition on the University's role in European history.

Wawel 1000–2000, an exhibition of art masterpieces celebrating a thousand years since the establishment of the Cathedral on Wawel Hill, will take place between May 5 and July 30, 2000. From June onwards there will also be an interactive virtual reconstruction of Romanesque Kraków on display.

Wianki 2000 is a two-day event starting on June 23, 2000 and comprising a traditional open-air performance of Stanislaw Wyspianski's plays *The Legend* and *Acropolis*.

The tenth edition of the **Jewish Cultural Festival** will bring together eminent Jewish scholars and artists in the city. The event runs from June–July 2000.

Kraków 2000 Festival Bureau, Ul.Sw.Krzya 1, 31-028 Kraków, Poland
Ⓣ 012/421 86 93 Ⓕ 422 13 81 Ⓔ biuro@krakow2000.pl
Ⓦ http://www.kraków2000.pl

TRAVEL BRIEF

Poland is still largely unknown as a tourist destination, although Kraków is a popular European city-break destination and essential stop on the rail tour of Eastern Europe.

GETTING THERE LOT Polish Airlines operates regular direct flights to Warsaw from New York and Chicago, but there is more choice of timetable and price if you connect via larger European gateways with a range of all major airlines on offer. There are services to Warsaw and Kraków from most European capitals. LOT are the only domestic carriers within Poland. Poland has one of the most extensive and interesting rail networks (PKP) in Europe, with connections to the European system.

ACCOMMODATION Accommodation can be a bit of a lottery in Poland, with prices and star-ratings not always reflecting quality. Several international hotel chains have recently opened up in the major cities, but elsewhere most top-end hotels still belong to Orbis. Also now opening are a variety of heritage hotels in old castles and mansions, many offering activities such as sleigh rides along with the atmosphere. Book sensibly, but there are no unusually large events to cause logjams.

TOURIST OFFICES There are two main sources of tourist information in Poland. The PAPT is the state tourism organisation; Orbis, which grew out of the ranks of the old Communist structure is still the country's largest travel agent, tour operator and hotel chain. National: PAPT, ul. Mazowiecka 9, Warsaw Ⓣ 02/26 62 09; Kraków: ul. Pawia 8, 31-154 Kraków Ⓣ 012/422 6091 Ⓦ http://www.krakow.pl Warsaw: pl. Zamkowy 1/13, 00-262 Warsaw Ⓣ 02/635 1881. UK: PATP: London Ⓣ 0171/580 8811 Ⓕ 580 8866 Ⓔ pnto@dial.pipex.com Ⓦ http://www.poland.net/travelpage US: PATP: New York Ⓣ 212/338-9412 Ⓕ 338-9283; Chicago Ⓣ 312/236-9013; Polorbis: New York Ⓣ 212/867-5011 Ⓦ http://www.polandtour.org/

TOURS UK: Danube Travel Ⓣ 0171/724 7577; Fregata Travel Ⓣ 0171/451 7000; Polorbis Ⓣ 0171/637 4971; Regent Holidays Ⓣ 01983/866129. US: DER Tours Ⓣ 800/782-2424; Eastern European Tours Ⓣ 206/448-8400; Orbis Ⓣ 212/867-5011.

COUNTRY CODE Ⓣ 48

RUSSIA

Moscow will be at the centre of the celebrations in Russia, with up to one million people expected to party the night away in sub-zero temperatures in the capital's **Red Square**. This celebration will be linked to a **World Folk Festival**, bringing together folklore of all different types from the provinces and from overseas. Pop bands and fireworks will also keep the vodka-fuelled crowds entertained. The Moscow authorities hope to complete the restoration of **St Saviour Cathedral** in time for the millennium. The year 2000 will also witness the unveiling of the symbol for **New Russia**.

St Petersburg will be hosting an Imperial Ball (see Travel Brief), whilst the remote Siberian border town of Novosibirisk is planning a **Millennium Rave Party**. The organisers say that 'over 300 rave groups' are expected to attend 'the greatest rave party the Russian bear has ever experienced' and they're hoping to light the night sky with lasers.

Fifteen Russians are spending 1999 on a **Millennium Pilgrimage** from the Siberian port of Vladivostok to Moscow. The walk has received the blessing of the head of the Russian Orthodox Church, Patriarch Aleksiy II, and will be matched by shorter processions from other corners of the Russian Federation. The pilgrims will celebrate Masses, establish new churches and erect crucifixes along the way. They started their 10,000km journey in May 1998 and plan to celebrate Christmas in Moscow on January 7, 2000, in accordance with the Orthodox calendar.

Promoters of the dawn events in New Zealand's Chatham Islands announced in 1999 that they are also creating a 'millennial midnight' initiative in the remote Russian region of **Chukotka** bordering the Bering Strait. "Undoubtedly Chukotka will be the world's first populated area to enter the third millennium and witness the millennium midnight", claims organiser Brad Roberts, who is selling media rights to the event. "This initiative will eclipse all other date-related millennium products", he adds. The project for **Chukotka 00:00:2000** involves using satellite-reflected sunlight to illuminate two people (one from the Russian side and one from the Alaskan/American side) standing on the pack ice in the Strait and shaking hands on the dateline in a gesture of peace.

TRAVEL BRIEF

Russia is a high-risk country for millennium bug problems and some disruption to transport can be expected, particularly on the rail network.

GETTING THERE Moscow is served by direct flights from the UK on Aeroflot and British Airways and from European capitals on national airlines. Aeroflot flies direct from a number of cities in the US.

ACCOMMODATION Hotels are best pre-booked as part of a package.

TOURIST OFFICES Intourist, Mokhovaya ul.13, Moscow ⓣ 095/292 12 78 ⓕ 292 24 75. Embassies: UK: 5 Kensington Palace Gardens, London W8 ⓣ 0171/229 8027. US: 2650 Wisconsin Ave NW, Washington, DC 20007 ⓣ 202/298-5700.

TOURS UK: East-West Travel ⓣ 0171/938 3211; Intourist ⓣ 0171/538 8600; The Millennial Foundation ⓣ 0141/204 2000; Pan Tours ⓣ 0171/233 8458; Progressive Tours ⓣ 0171/262 1676; Steppes East ⓣ 01285/810267; Worldfarers ⓣ 01926/425333. US: East Europe Tours ⓣ 800/641-3456; Maupintour ⓣ 800/255-4266; Pioneer Tours & Travel ⓣ 800/369-1322; Russia House ⓣ 202/986-6010; Russian Travel Bureau ⓣ 800/847-1800.

COUNTRY CODE ⓣ 7

SINGAPORE

Never slow to spot a commercial opportunity, Singapore has jumped on to the millennium bandwagon with the launch of a year-long **'MillenniaMania'** programme. Lasting from June 1999 through to August 2000, the programme includes special millennium editions of regular events such as the Singapore Food Festival, the Dragon Boat Festival, River Fiesta and River Busker's Festival.

The Lion City's ability to capitalise on its varying cultural traditions means that it has few problems harnessing a Christian celebration as well as roping in the annual Hari Raya Light-Up (a Muslim festival) and Lunar New Year Light-Up (a Chinese festival) to their millennium plans. On the other hand, since Christmas now seems to represent little more than an excuse for 'festive shopping', what better place to celebrate than in one of the great shopping capitals of the world.

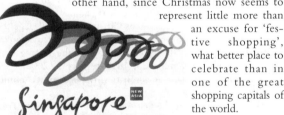

"We are going all out to stage the grandest and most enjoyable events in this country, and this is a celebration list which will be added to as we intensify our preparation and planning", says Mr Yeo Khee Leng of Singapore's Tourism Board. "This is a once-in-a-lifetime marketing opportunity not to be missed."

The MillenniaMania celebrations begin in June 1999, when a specially-commissioned **Countdown Clock** made by Swatch will be unveiled. A national sculpture to capture the spirit of Singapore is also being commissioned.

On September 1, 1999 a huge **Millennium Tree** (or trees) will be erected, and people will be able to hang their wishes and dreams for the millennium on it. The proceeds will go to charity. Traditionally Singapore's main shopping street, Orchard Road, stages a **Christmas Light-Up** with hotels and shopping centres competing for the most dazzling display. The millennium illuminations (November 13, 1999–January 5, 2000) promise to be even more spectacular than usual. The week-long **Christmas Village** is a charity carnival with food, crafts and other merchandise, on the Mall in Orchard Road (December 11–19, 1999).

Billed as the highlight of Singapore's MillenniaMania programme, the **New Year's Eve Street Party** will take place along the length and breadth of Orchard Road, with festivities in hotels, clubs, homes and on the street itself. Half a million people are expected at the Orchard Road bash.

The animal-free Canadian circus **Cirque du Soleil** stage the Asian premiere of their new multicultural extravaganza, **Saltimbanco**, in a 2500-seater Big Top on the Padang over the millennium (November 28, 1999–January 5, 2000). The show combines spectacular acrobatics, trapeze stunts, mime, contortion and juggling.

Trekkies will welcome the first Asian landing of the **Star Trek World Tour** (December 1, 1999–January 31, 2000), which will transform the Singapore Expo in Changi into a ground station for the USS Enterprise (and if the millennium bug hits Asia hard, at least you'll be in the right place to say "beam me up, Scottie").

Ⓦ http://www.millennia-mania.com

TRAVEL BRIEF

GETTING THERE There are direct flights to Singapore from most international airports.

ACCOMMODATION Several of Singapore's hotels are offering special millennium packages, most of which include free champagne and limo transfers from the airport. Hotels participating include the *Conrad International Centennial* Ⓣ 334 8888 Ⓔ conradsg@mbox4.singnet.com.sg; the *Hotel Rendezvous* Ⓣ 336 0220 Ⓔ kellvinong@rendezvous.com.au; *Le Meridien* Ⓣ 733 8855 Ⓔ meriorch@asianconnect.com.sg; the *Regent* Ⓣ 739 3061; and the *Westin Stamford* Ⓣ 339 6633. The only hotel in Singapore that will be witnessing the passing of a century for the second time – *Raffles*, of course – is also offering a special package for the night of Dec 31, 1999 at S$2000 (around US$1250) for two people; the hotel will also be hosting a New Year's Eve Gala Ball with the lobby area transformed into a grand colonial ballroom Ⓣ 337 1886.

TOURIST OFFICES Singapore Tourism Board, 1 Orchard Spring Lane, Singapore 247729 Ⓣ 736 6622 Ⓕ 736 9423 Ⓦ http://www.stb.com.sg UK: London Ⓣ 0171/437 0033 Ⓕ 0171/734 2191. US: New York Ⓣ 212/302-4861 Ⓕ 302-4801Ⓦ http://www.singapore-usa.com

TOURS The Eastern and Oriental Express is operating a seven-day journey from Bangkok to Singapore with an on-board cocktail party on New Year's Eve, concluding with a stay at *Raffles*. UK: Ⓣ 0171/805 5100. US: Ⓣ 630/954-2944

COUNTRY CODE Ⓣ 65

SOUTH PACIFIC

T he South Pacific islands will be one of the principal beneficiaries of the millennium celebrations, with thousands of
people likely to book up 'once in a lifetime' trips to locations
claiming to offer the first glimpses of the new dawn. Countries such as **Kiribati** (pronounced 'Kiribas') and **Tonga**, previously minnows in the South Pacific tourism lagoon, are
gearing up for an unprecedented influx of tourists. The Pacific
islands have, how-
ever, been at the
very centre of the
debate as to exactly
where the sun will
rise first on January
1, 2000.

**MILLENNIUM
OF THE SOUTH SEAS**
crossing the threshold of time

Until recently, the
Kingdom of Tonga
could lay claim to
being the first land-
fall west of the date-
line, and therefore
the first to witness
the dawn of each
new day. It pro-
motes itself as 'the place where time begins' and even has an
International Dateline Hotel in the capital Nuku'alofa. But when
Kiribati 'moved' the International Date Line in January 1995,
the Tongans were deprived of their title. Apparently furious at
being out-manoeuvred by Kiribati, they appealed to the United

Nations and also toyed with the idea of introducing daylight saving time so they could pip everyone else to the post.

The Tongans have had to put a brave face on it and are still going ahead with their millennium plans. "In my opinion, Kiribati moving the dateline does not affect us that much", says Tonga's director of tourism Semisi P. Taumoepeau. "We will be put back in the list of 'the first to see the New Year', of course, but we will maintain the claim that we are one of the first to see the new millennium as well as being the first kingdom to do so", he says.

The Pacific nations have also cast aside their differences in order to promote the region as a whole and have set up the **South Pacific Millennium Consortium**, an offshoot of the Tourism Council of the South Pacific based in Fiji. "Whilst we are doing our best to promote [the first sunrise], we are not stressing the point so that it becomes competitive", says Millennium Co-ordinator Mrs Bernadette Rounds Ganilau. "We are the Pacific and the dawn rises on all of us. It just so happens that one or two of us will receive the rays first. We are doing a solidarity thing so the whole of the South Pacific benefits and not just one or two countries."

The region will also benefit from the fact that you can experience the dawn there twice: first in those countries to the west of the dateline (such as Tonga, Kiribati and Fiji), and then again in those to the east (such as Samoa, the Cook Islands, Tahiti and Niue). The last place on earth to see the sunset on the old millennium is the westernmost tip of Savai'i Island in Samoa, just twenty miles from the dateline.

Apart from countries featured here, some activities are being planned in **American Samoa**, and **Niue** will be holding a National Millennium Events Week (December 26–31, 1999).

South Pacific Millennium Consortium, 3rd floor, FNPF Plaza, 343–359 Victoria Parade, PO Box 13119, Suva, Fiji ⓣ 304177 ⓕ 301995 ⓔ spice@is.com.fj ⓦ http://www.tcsp.com/millennium/mill.htm

The Global Broadcast

It was perhaps one of the easiest things to predict about the coming millennium – that there would be a global broadcast, linking dozens of countries in different time zones for a 24-hour celebration on television. Around fifty broadcasters around the world have now signed up for 2000 Today, which will be the most ambitious live television event ever staged. This complex technical operation will bring together over two hundred camera crews around the world and require at least sixty satellite paths to feed in links.

Co-produced by the British Broadcasting Corporation and WGBH Boston, 2000 Today will start at 10.30 GMT on December 31, 1999 and is expected to reach an audience of around 800 million people. Every hour there will be a top-of-the-hour spectacular (ten minutes either side of midnight) from each time zone as the millennium arrives; the rest of the hour will feature cultural performances and live entertainment from countries in that time zone. The programme will also explore the history of the planet, scientific achievements, the state of the environment, and link up with the *Mir* space station. Breaking news on the millennium bug will undoubtedly add a certain frisson to the global broadcast as everyone waits with bated breath to see whether the twenty-first century will arrive with a bang or a whimper.

Cook Islands

The Cook Islands lie around 500 miles/800km to the east of the International Date Line, and as such cannot compete in the sunrise stakes. Nonetheless, the main island of Rarotonga will be buzzing, particularly since large numbers of expat islanders will return from New Zealand to visit family and friends for the occasion.

Some party-goers are also planning to arrive from Fiji, two hours' flying time away on the other side of the dateline, to celebrate their second millennium New Year's Eve, although there are no scheduled services on that day and there is doubt about whether airlines will be flying anyway.

Visitors will find they can have the best of both worlds here: Christmas services in the picturesque local churches will be particularly enchanting, with Polynesian village choirs singing in heavenly harmony, and New Year's Eve itself will be a full-blown Polynesian ceremony, with *umukai* (feasts baked in underground ovens), drumming, chanting, singing, and the sensual *tamure* dancing at which the Cook Islanders excel.

The programme for the **Millennium Turou Celebrations** (December 1, 1999–January 1, 2000) kicks off with a musical stage show, *Maui Catching the Sun* (December 3, 1999), an epic that is staged annually. Various events will then lead up to the grand *turou* ('welcome') ceremony on New Year's Eve. From dusk onwards, the **Turou Festival** begins on the west coast (where the sun sets), with people lining up along the beach from the west, through the south coast, and around to the east of the island. The **Drums of Polynesia** will echo through the night, reverberating down the line along the beach until sunrise. The rising sun will be welcomed with chants, prayers, dancing, drumming and singing.

On New Year's Day the Turou Celebrations will continue with the **Ceremony of the Stones,** a revival of the sacred custom of Polynesian migrants, who would carry rocks with them from their homeland, placing them on the land they arrived in to symbolise the linking of their past with their future. The Cook Islands are creating a park where people from all over the world can join the tradition by placing rocks from their homeland in this sacred area to mark the millennium. The day will conclude with the regular New Year's Day **Beach Horse Racing** (Muri Beach).

If you don't make it here for New Year's Eve, events during 2000 include Vaka Reti (traditional outrigger races, April); the Coconut Festival (May); the Polynesian Music Festival (October); and Gospel Day (October 26), which commemorates the arrival of Christianity with open-air performances of biblical stories by whole villages, complete with colourful costumes and singing.

TRAVEL BRIEF

GETTING THERE Air New Zealand flies from Australia, New Zealand, Hawaii, Tahiti and Fiji, with links to North America and Europe. Canada 3000 connects Rarotonga with Auckland, Honolulu, Toronto and Vancouver.

ACCOMMODATION At press time hotels were still only half full. Backpacker's hostels and guesthouses are another option (the tourist board produces a brochure with email and fax details for reservations). Note that it is not permitted to land in the Cooks without a reservation, and sleeping on the beach is not permitted.

TOURIST OFFICES Cook Islands Tourism Corporation, PO Box 14, Rarotonga, Cook Islands Ⓣ 29435 Ⓕ 21435 Ⓔ tourism@cookisland.gov.ck Ⓦ www.cookislands.com; Australia: Sydney Ⓣ 02/9955 0446. New Zealand: Auckland Ⓣ 09/366 1100. UK: London: TCSP Ⓣ 01344/717496. US: Los Angeles Ⓣ 888/994-2665.

TOURS UK: Air New Zealand Ⓣ 0181/741 2299; Austravel Ⓣ 0171/734 7755; Bridge the World Ⓣ 0171/209 9427; Flightbookers Worldwide Ⓣ 0171/757 2444; Travel Pack Ltd Ⓣ 01617/887885; Travel 2/Travel 4 Ⓣ 0171/561 5850.

COUNTRY CODE Ⓣ 682

Fiji

Fiji is hoping for a millennium boom. With a well-developed infrastructure and good air links to Australia and elsewhere, it is in a strong position to capitalise on the event; the Fiji Visitors Bureau estimates that the millennium will generate an extra £42 million (US$70m) in tourism revenues.

Millennium
Fiji
Islands

Where the 3rd
Millennium
Begins....

Fiji is one of only two countries in the world where the **180° Meridian** touches land (the other is Siberia), and the Fijians are claiming that the country is 'the first to enter each new day, year and the new Millennium'. Fiji is also witness to the last sunset of each day, year and the present millennium. The islands also boosted their claim to one of the first sunrises by introducing Daylight Saving Time for the first time in late 1998, putting their clocks forward one hour from November through to February annually. Officially, the change was made in order to 'improve productivity' (clearly, a high priority in the languid South Seas). Fiji's capital, Suva, is home to the **South Pacific Millennium Consortium**.

Fiji's official celebrations, which have a strong local emphasis, will last from December 1999 through to early January 2001. Preliminaries include a **Millennium Song Competition** (September 1999), a **National Painting Competition** (the winning design will become the first in a series of First Day covers), and a **National Essay Competition** on the topic of the millennium (four winners will deliver their messages to the UN in New York). There will be a **'Unity Torch'** relay around local communities (December 25–31, 1999). The

National Millennium Committee also plans to award **Millennium Medallions** to citizens who have contributed to the development of the country.

Fiji's second largest island, **Vanua Levu**, is one of the three Fijian islands crossed by the 180° Meridian, and there are ambitious plans for a **Millennium Monument**. The other two islands crossed by the line are neighbouring **Rabi** and **Taveuni**.

New Year's Eve parties are planned for resort islands such as **Beachcomber** and **Naitasi Island Resort** (see Travel Brief) as well as at major resort hotels. **Vatulele Island** is offering the entire resort to thirty-six people for eleven days (December 24, 1999–January 3, 2000).

The most expensive millennium weddings in the world will take place on **Turtle Island**, an American-run resort which is one hour ahead of the rest of the country ever since a Hollywood crew arrived to film *The Blue Lagoon* and reset the clocks to suit their shooting schedule. Several couples have apparently registered for the £120,000 (US$200,000) wedding package.

Fiji is a port of call (March 18–21, 2000) for the **Millennium Round the World Yacht Race** (see p.297). On December 31, 2000 the islands will also host two thousand Japanese who have booked up to witness the first sunrise of the year 2001.

National Millennium Committee, Fiji Visitors Bureau, GPO Box 92, Suva
Ⓣ 302433 Ⓕ 300970.

Rabi

This small island, which reaches a height of 472m at its wooded summit, is home to a community of Kiribatians who were moved here by the British when their own home (Ocean Island) was ravaged by phosphate mining. Eco Dive-Tours, based in Savusavu on Vanua Levu, are planning a historic **Millennium Dive** on the 180° Meridian just offshore from Rabi. Participants will descend from the dive boats just before midnight, emerging after 1am on January 1, 2000 to enjoy an all-night party on the island.

Eco Dive Tours, PO Box 264, Savusavu, vanua Levu Ⓣ 850122 Ⓕ 850344
Ⓔ seafijidive@is.com.fj Ⓦ http://www.BulaFiji.com/ecodiver/ecodiver.htm

Taveuni

Taveuni is Fiji's third largest island and features its second highest mountain, Desveoux Peak. Plans are still under wraps as to what will be happening here, although there will definitely be a millennium party at *Susies Plantation Resort* and the 4000-acre Taveuni Estate will be hosting events, including the last game of golf in one millennium and the first in the next on their Robert Trent Jones-designed course.

Vanua Levu

Udu Point is a remote, wild area situated at the northeastern tip of Vanua Levu, Fiji's second largest island. This is one of the very few places where the 180° Meridian crosses land, and for this reason it has been chosen as the site for Fiji's showcase millennium project, the national **Millennium Monument**.

The main site of the monument will be laid out in a five-point star design, and will feature **Time Walls** (for storing thousands of time capsules) and a **Time Museum** (featuring a 'sun lens' that will cast the sunlight onto the 180° Meridian inside the museum each New Year's Day for the next century). A landscaped **Meridian Park**, planted with indigenous trees and plants, will surround the site. They also hope to create a **Millennium Forest** as an extension of this park.

The park will be near the centre of the 3km-long **Meridian Walkway**, which leads to the coast on either side of the island. The organisers claim that you will be able to watch the first dawn of the new millennium at Sunrise Beach at one end, celebrate millennium day, and then walk to Sunset Beach to watch the last sunset of the old millennium on the eastern side of the line.

As late as January 1999 the site consisted of nothing more than a pole marking the spot in a clearing, but Prime Minister

Rabuka remains confident they will succeed. It is also difficult to get to (involving a three-hour drive from Vanua Levu airport, a canoe ride and a three-hour trek through the forest) but the plans call for improved land and sea access, including new jetties.

Millennium Fiji, Private Mail Bag, Suva Ⓣ 384399 Ⓕ 370399
Ⓔ info@MillenniumFiji.com Ⓦ http://www.MillenniumFiji.com

Vitu Levu

The capital, Suva, will host a special millennium edition of the annual **Festival of Praise** (December 26, 1999–January 2, 2000), with a grand finale on the last day when participants from around the world will give cultural performances from their home country. Suva is also the venue for the **Millennium Hibiscus Festival** (December 21–31, 1999), with the crowning of the Millennium Hibiscus Queen on New Year's Eve. The country's young people will march from Sukuna Park to the central celebrations at Albert Park in a **Marching to the New Millennium** procession.

London nightclub *The Ministry of Sound* has proposed a **New Year's Rave** on Vitu Levu, and California-based FACE (the Foundation for the Arts and the Environment) is hoping to stage **Millennium 2000 – Fiji Islands Festival**, a global festival of international music and the arts under the banner of 'A Celebration of Planet Earth'.

TRAVEL BRIEF

GETTING THERE Fiji is served by Air Pacific, Air New Zealand, Qantas, Korean Airlines and Royal Tongan Airlines, with 85 international flights per week.

ACCOMMODATION Fiji has a wide range of accommodation, from luxury resorts to backpacker's beach hostels. All the top hotels have been block-booked by overseas tour operators but some islands still have vacancies. The popular resort island of Beachcomber will be the venue for a six day/five night

Millennium Bug Party for 150, with some places left at AUS$2050 (£760/US$1275); contact 41 Harris St, Brisbane, QLD 4171
Ⓣ 07/3395 7888 Ⓕ 3395 6688 Ⓔ bula@b150.aone.net.au
Millennium packages at the *Naitasi Island Resort* are bookable through Hideaway Holidays, 994 Victoria Rd, West Ryde, NSW 2114
Ⓣ 612/9807 4222 Ⓕ 9808 2260 Ⓔ sales@hideawayholidays.com.au

Vatulele Island is available for 36 people, fully inclusive for US$500,000 (£230,000); contact the Managing Director, Sydney Ⓣ 02/9326 1055
Ⓕ 9327 2764 Ⓔ vatu@magna.com.au Ⓦ http://www.vatulele.com

TOURIST OFFICES Fiji Visitors Bureau, Thomson Street, Suva, Fiji
Ⓣ 302433 Ⓕ 300970 Ⓔ infodesk@fijifvb.gov.fj Ⓦ http://www.BulaFiji.com
Australia: Sydney Ⓣ 02/9264 3399. New Zealand: Auckland Ⓣ 09/373 2133.
US: Los Angeles: Ⓣ 310/568-1616.

TOURS UK: Airwaves Ⓣ 0181/875 1188; All-Ways Pacific Travel
Ⓣ 01494/875757; Contiki Holidays Ⓣ 0181/290 6777;
Destination Pacific Ⓣ 0171/336 7788; Jetset Ⓣ 01612/366657.
US: Adventure Bound Tours Ⓣ 602/968-3338 Ⓕ 968-8811
Ⓔ tours@adventure-bound.com; Prasad Associates Ⓣ 905/785-0360
Ⓕ 785-0504 Ⓔ prasad@nexusds.com
Ⓦ http://www.nexusds.com/prasadtravel/

COUNTRY CODE Ⓣ 679

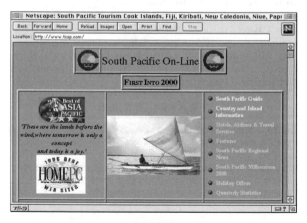

Kiribati

Kiribati is well placed to take advantage of the millennium celebrations on New Year's Eve, 1999 in view of the fact that, since it moved the dateline, three of its islands in the Line and Phoenix group witness the sunrise before anywhere else in the world. These are **Kiritimati** (05:31 local time), **Millennium Island** (05:43) and **Flint Island** (05:47).

Most of the celebrations will be concentrated on **Kiritimati** (Kiritimati is the local translation of Christmas Island, so named by Captain Cook because he arrived here on Christmas Eve in 1777). The island will also be undergoing considerable infrastructure improvements for the millennium. The islanders are holding a **song writing competition** (these competitions are a part of the national culture), with the winning song being performed at the dawn ceremony.

Millennium Island has no infrastructure at all, and very little fresh water. The government is planning a special **Millennium Ceremony**, and is holding talks with tour operators about erecting tents for visitors on the island. Several cruise ships might also be here, along with private yachts.

TRAVEL BRIEF

GETTING THERE Air Marshall connects Kiribati with international routes, and Air Nauru flies to/from Nauru. Aloha Airlines also has services between Hawaii and Christmas Island.

ACCOMMODATION The country has fewer than one hundred hotel rooms and only four hotels of a reasonable standard (two in South Tarawa, one on Abemama, and one on Kiritimati). The official view is that anyone who wants to stay in a hotel is going to have to pay premium prices for the privilege. However, the president has said that independent travellers will not be ripped off and he is happy to extend a traditional welcome to anyone who wants to come provided they are prepared to stay in the *maneabas* (large, palm-thatched meeting houses) or local guesthouses.

TOURIST OFFICES Kiribati Visitors Bureau, PO Box 261, Bikenibeu, South

Tarawa, Republic of Kiribati Ⓣ 26157 Ⓕ 26233. UK: TCSP
Ⓣ 01344/717496. US: TCSP Ⓣ 916/583-0152.

TOURS UK: Airwaves Ⓣ 0181/875 1188; All-Ways Pacific Travel
Ⓣ 01494/875757; Austravel Ⓣ 0171/734 7755; Comet Tailormade
Ⓣ 01702/301666; Destination Pacific Ⓣ 0171/336 7788; Tana Specialist
Travel Ⓣ 01789/414200; Trailfinders Ⓣ 0171/937 8499; Travelmood
Ⓣ 0171/258 0280.

COUNTRY CODE Ⓣ 686

Samoa

Samoa is the last landmass to the east of the International Date
Line and, as such, will be the last to witness the end of the
twentieth century. Samoa (formerly Western Samoa) consists
of two large islands, Upolu and Savaii: the capital, Apia, and
the Faleolo International Airport are located on Upolu.

The **Samoa Millennium 2000** Society has put in place a
Millennium Clock in Apia. All visitors to Samoa during
1999 are eligible for a **Millennium Certificate** which comes
in two parts: an A4 copy to take home, and a smaller version
which will be placed (along with any messages you may wish
to add) in a **Robert Louis Stevenson Treasure Chest**. The
time capsule will be sealed on June 30, 2001 and stored at the
Robert Louis Stevenson Museum (the writer's former home
in Vailima), to be opened in 2100; certificates cost WS$20
(£5/US$9).

Samoa is also planning to celebrate the traditional Polynesian
art of tattooing with the **Tatau Millennium Convention**
(November 7–12, 1999). The island's main **Millennium Celebrations** (December 25, 1999–January 1, 2000) will include
boat parades, village and school cultural performances, floral
parades, choir singing and feasting.

The last sunset of the millennium takes place over the eastern
tip of Savai'i Island, at Cape Mulinu'u Beach near the rainforest reserve at Falealupo, where various ceremonies will also

take place. The sunset is also visible from beaches along the northwest coast such as Fagmalo and Manese.

The *Vaotuua Beach Resort* on Manono Island is planning a two-week Eco-Millennium Festival (see Travel Brief).

TRAVEL BRIEF

GETTING THERE The national airline, Polynesian Airlines, operates services to Samoa from New Zealand, Australia, Fiji, Tonga, American Samoa, Hawaii and Los Angeles. Other airlines flying to Samoa include Air New Zealand, Royal Tongan Airlines, Air Pacific and Samoa Air.

ACCOMMODATION Samoa has around five hundred hotel rooms, and most of these (including the famous *Aggie Greys Hotel* in Apia) have been fully booked since 1995. Some budget accommodation may still be available, bookable through Island Hopper Vacations (Samoa), PO Box 2271, Apia, Samoa Ⓣ 26940 Ⓕ 26941 Ⓔ islandhopper@samoa.net

Another alternative is to stay in a traditional beach *fale* (an open-sided thatched-roof hut), located throughout the islands. Equipped with mattress, linen and mosquito net, they cost from US$20 (£12) per day; a full list is available from the Samoa Visitors Bureau.

The Eco-Millennium Festival at the *Vaotuua Resort* takes place from December 24, 1999–January 4, 2000; the cost is £90 (US$150) per day, fully-

inclusive. Contact: Eco-Tour Samoa, PO Box 4609, Matautu-uta, Samoa
ⓣ 22144 ⓕ 26941 ⓔ ecotour@samoa.net
ⓦ http://www.samoa.net/ecotourism_winners/eco-mill.htm

TOURIST OFFICES Head office: PO Box 2272, Apia, Samoa ⓣ 63500
ⓕ 20886 ⓔ samoa@samoa.net ⓦ www.samoa.net
New Zealand: Auckland ⓣ 09/379 6138. Australia: Sydney ⓣ 02/9824 5050.
UK: TCSP ⓣ 01344/717496. US: TCSP ⓣ 916/583-0152.

TOURS UK: Airwaves ⓣ 0181/875 1188; All-Ways Pacific Travel
ⓣ 01494/875757; Austravel ⓣ 0171/7347755; Comet Tailormade
ⓣ 01702/301666; Destination Pacific ⓣ 0171/336 7788; Tana Specialist
Travel ⓣ 01789/414200; Trailfinders ⓣ 0171/937 8499; Travelmood
ⓣ 0171/258 0280.

COUNTRY CODE ⓣ 685

Tonga

Tonga is not about to be elbowed aside by Kiribati's decision
to move the dateline and has prepared a detailed millennium
programme. The kingdom marked the start of the one thousand day countdown to the millennium on April 6, 1997 with
a dawn ceremony at the historic Ha'amonga 'a Maui, attended
by His Majesty King Taufa'ahau Tupu the Fourth, ministers,
church leaders and hundreds of guests. From Tonga you can
hop over by plane to Samoa for double celebrations.

The wide variety of events planned so far include a New
Millennium Festival Week, Tongatapu (July 1999); Whale
Watch New Millennium Festival, Vava'u (September 1999); as
well as gamefishing, windsurfing and surfing tournaments.
The main event, the one-month-long **New Millennium
Festival** (December), will feature concerts, dancing, sports
events, tree planting, a regatta, arts and craft exhibitions, and
canoe races.

On New Year's Eve there will be a prayer festival, cultural
shows and a gala day parade, followed by feasting and *lakalaka*
(traditional Tongan dancing). At 10pm a massed choir will sing

in the Queen Salote Memorial Hall, followed by a 'meet and greet' session with their Majesties (invitation only). An 'international fiesta of wine, music and song' will then go on through the night on the Nuku'alofa foreshore.

Saudi businessman Hussein Kashoggi is planning a major Millennium Celebration in Tonga and hopes to build a huge circular stage on the Queen Salote Wharf in Tonga's main harbour. The event would feature international artists and performers and be watched by thousands of people on board several cruise ships and private yachts docked in the harbour, with prices from around £36,000 (US$60,000) per person. In a feature on Kashoggi's plans the local magazine *Matangi Tonga* asks 'what's in it for Tonga?', to which the answer seems to be not a lot, apart from 'television exposure which might attract tourism to the Kingdom'.

TRAVEL BRIEF

GETTING THERE Royal Tongan Airlines, Samoa Air, Air New Zealand, Polynesian Airlines and Air Pacific link the kingdom with Sydney, Auckland, Fiji, Samoa, Los Angeles and Hawaii.

ACCOMMODATION Resorts, hotels and even some of the guesthouses have already received bookings for New Year's Eve, 1999, but accommodation is still available. A special Homestay programme has also been set up for independent travellers who would like to stay with Tongan families. Contact the Tonga National Centre Ⓣ 23002 Ⓕ 23520 Ⓔ tncentre@candw.to

TOURIST OFFICES Tonga Visitors Bureau, PO Box 37, Nuku'alofa, Kingdom of Tonga Ⓣ 25334 Ⓣ 23507 Ⓔ tvb@candw.to Ⓦ http://www.vacations.tvb.go.to
Australia: Sydney Ⓣ 02/9519 9700. New Zealand: Auckland Ⓣ 09/634 1519. UK: London Ⓣ 0171/724 5828. US: California Ⓣ 510/223-1381.

TOURS UK: Jetset Ⓣ 01612/366657; Kuoni Ⓣ 01306/740888; TransPacific Holidays Ⓣ 01293/567722; Travel Australia Ⓣ 01603/488664; Travelmood Ⓣ 0171/258 0280. US: Hideaway Holidays Ⓣ 612/9807-4222 Ⓕ 9808-2260.

COUNTRY CODE Ⓣ 676

SPAIN

As a predominantly Catholic country Spain will be celebrating The Great Jubilee in churches and cathedrals nationwide and magnificent processions will also take place during *Semana Santa* (Easter week) and Corpus Christi (early June). The party-loving Spanish are also unlikely to pass up the opportunity for bigger than usual New Year's Eve celebrations in major towns and cities.

A major centre for pilgrimage for over a thousand years, **Santiago de Compostela** is likely to draw the faithful or the simply curious in large numbers, especially since 1999 is a Holy Year, marked by the fact that the birthday of Saint James the Apostle falls on a Sunday.

In **Madrid** New Year's Eve 1999 will be celebrated in bars, nightclubs and restaurants throughout the city, but in particular at the **Puerto del Sol**, officially not only the centre of the capital but also of the nation: a stone slab in the pavement on its southern side marks Kilometre Zero, from where six of Spain's National Routes begin, and from where all distances are measured. It's traditional to swallow a grape at each stroke of midnight as it sounds from the clock tower in the square. The city's Museo del Prado will be staging several exhibitions to mark the 400-year anniversary of the birth of the painter Velazquez in 1999, and in 2000 the city will be celebrating the 500-year anniversary of the birth of Charles V.

Valencia is celebrating the millennium with the completion of a futuristic **City of Arts and Sciences**. It includes a Science Museum built in the shape of a gigantic animal carcass (opens May 1999); a Universal Oceanographic Park (opens

June 1999); and an Arts Palace (opens Spring 2000). The Basque capital of **Bilbão** has completed an ambitious redevelopment programme, **Bilbão 2000**. The centrepiece of the city's renaissance is the stunning new **Guggenheim Museum** on the waterfront, designed by architect Frank Gehry.

On the island of **Fuerteventura** in the Canaries the sculptor Eduardo Chilida is planning to build a gigantic cube, 50m-high, on Mount Tindaya. In May 2000 the historic port of **Cadiz** will welcome over two hundred vessels in the Tall Ships 2000 race.

Santiago

Santiago de Compostela is one of Spain's most beautiful historical cities and has been declared a UNESCO World Heritage site in its entirety. It is the third holiest city in Christendom (after Rome and Jerusalem), thanks to the presence of the supposed tomb of St James the Apostle (Santiago to the Spanish). It became an important centre for **pilgrimage** in medieval times, with over half a million people in the eleventh and twelfth centuries heading south along five well-tramped routes from all corners of Europe. Today these pilgrim routes are still clearly defined by the rows of Romanesque churches, chapels and monasteries that mark the way, each roughly ten miles (one day's walk) from the next. The **Camino de Santiago** (Road to St James) is likely to be especially busy in 1999 and 2000.

Santiago is also one of the **European Cities of Culture 2000**, and will be creating new gardens, parks and museums to commemorate the event. Its theme is 'Europe and the World', and events planned include Faces of the Earth (a hi-tech look at the environment); Faces of the Gods (on different religions and cultures); and a Millennium Music Festival. There will also be a comprehensive programme of theatre, cinema and music events.

SANTIAGO TRAVEL BRIEF

Santiago de Compostela is used to coping with large numbers of pilgrims over the festival of St James each July, but 1999 and 2000 could put a strain even on these facilities.

GETTING THERE There is a small airport with daily flights from the UK, but the nearest major international gateway is Madrid, which is served by frequent flights on many of the world's larger airlines. From Madrid, Santiago is a short flight or long drive or train journey north. There are regular ferries from the UK to Bilbão and Santander.

ACCOMMODATION There are likely to be severe problems finding accommodation in Santiago for much of 1999 and 2000, with very limited options in the picturesque old town. The magnificent sixteenth-century *Hotel de los Reyes Católicos* is already full.

TOURIST OFFICES There is no central tourist office for the country. For nationwide information (within Spain) Ⓣ 0901/300 600
Ⓦ http://www.tourspain.es
Every one of the nineteen autonomous regions has its own tourism office. Galicia: Casado del Alisal 8, 28001 Madrid Ⓣ 91/595 4214 Ⓕ 595 4209; Madrid: Duque de Medinacela 2 Ⓣ 01/429 4951 Ⓕ 429 0909; Santiago de Compostela: Rúa del Villar 43 Ⓣ 81/584081. UK: London Ⓣ 0891/669920 (premium rate; brochure requests) or Ⓣ 0171/486 8077 (information only) Ⓕ 486 8034. US: New York Ⓣ 212/265-8822 Ⓕ 265-8864
Ⓔ oetny@here-i.com
Chicago Ⓣ 312/642-1992 Ⓕ 642-9817 Ⓔ spainil@ix.netcom.com
Los Angeles Ⓣ 213/658-7188 or 658-7192 Ⓕ 213/658-1061
Ⓔ espanalax@aol.com
Miami Ⓣ 305/358-1992 Ⓕ 358-8223 Ⓔ oetmiami@ix.netcom.com
Ⓦ http://www.okspain.org/

TOURS UK: Casas Cantabricas Ⓣ 01223/328721; Individual Travellers Spain Ⓣ 0870/773773; Magic of Spain Ⓣ 0181/748 4220; Mundi Color Ⓣ 0171/828 6021; Tangney Tours Ⓣ 01723/886666. US: Abercrombie & Kent Ⓣ 800/323-7308; Camino Tours Ⓣ 800/938-9311; Catholic Travel Centre Ⓣ 800/553-5233; Latour Ⓣ 800/825-0825.

COUNTRY CODE Ⓣ 34

SWEDEN

T he Swedish government's **Millennium Committee** and the museums of Sweden are jointly staging an extensive programme of exhibitions called **Future Visions** (September 19, 1999–Summer 2000). Stockholm's national cultural history museum, the Nordiska Museet, and numerous regional and local museums are participating in the project, which looks at different visions of the future over time, and their fate. Each museum will choose a time frame and will examine the relevant utopias, visions, ideologies and predictions.

The exhibitions will move from the international to the local and from the past to the present, culminating in a contemporary vision of the future. The project's aim is to generate a nationwide debate on the future of Sweden in the twenty-first century, with participation from schools, businesses, and local communities. Issues to be raised include the dynamics between short-term change and thousand-year-old institutions and the relationships between humanity, technology and the environment.

This is the biggest of the projects being supported by the Millennium Committee, which is also planning to hold a series of public discussions and activities focusing on democracy, human dignity, the distribution of resources, and the environment in the society of the future. It will concentrate particularly on liaising with children and young people, promoting awareness of the role of science in society and stimulating artistic creativity.

Stockholm's Gamla Stan (Old Town) will be the setting for a five-day **Millennium Festival** (December 27–31, 1999) which will feature theatre performances, art exhibitions, and a variety of concerts. The programme will also include readings by one of the country's most respected contemporary authors, Herman Linqvist, who will narrate the history of Stockholm on a daily basis to the backdrop of a laser show projected on to a water screen on the harbour. Throughout the programme historical dramas and ancient games will be enacted.

The festival will culminate in a concert with international performers at **Stockholm Castle**, attended by the Swedish Royal family, with a grand finale 'Big Bang' of lasers and fireworks over the harbour waters.

The city's **Kulturhuset** venue, devoted to contemporary Swedish culture, will be staging the Party of the Century on all seven floors of its rambling premises, with international artists, dance, food and drink.

Future Visions Ⓣ 08/519 560 00 Ⓕ 519 560 01
Ⓦ http://www.framtidstro.org.se
Kulturhuset, Sertels Torg, Stockholm Ⓣ 08/508 31 400.

Millennikommitten, 1033 33 Stockholm Ⓣ 08/405 1000 Ⓕ 405 4967
Ⓦ http://www.millenniekommitten.gov.se/
The official government pages (Swedish only).
Millennium Festival Ⓦ http://www.gamlastan2000.com

TRAVEL BRIEF

GETTING THERE Sweden is served by scheduled and charter services from the UK and Ireland, with five flights per day from London to Stockholm on SAS. American Airlines and SAS fly direct from the US.

ACCOMMODATION Hotel passes can be bought at Swedish Travel and Tourism Offices abroad; there is also an extensive network of youth hostels.

TOURIST OFFICES Stockholm Information Service, PO Box 7542, S-103 93 Stockholm Ⓣ 08/789 24 00 Ⓕ 789 24 50 Ⓔ info@stoinfo.se
Ⓦ http://www.stoinfo.se (bilingual). Swedish Travel and Tourism Council: UK Ⓣ 0171/724 5868. US Ⓣ 212/949-2333.

COUNTRY CODE Ⓣ 46

SWITZERLAND

he only large-scale celebrations planned are in **Geneva**, where an imaginative festival will take place on New Year's Eve, 1999; most other events will be local and very small-scale. Plans to build a giant **Wooden Arch** on the slopes of Mount Rigi have fallen through due to a lack of funding, but the futuristic-looking **Expo 2001** will be up and running from May to October 2001.

Geneva

Geneva's Committee for the Celebration of the Year 2000 is preparing a daily 'surprise' throughout 1999 in the run-up to the millennium celebrations, aimed as much at showing Geneva residents the hidden aspects of their city as at visitors. On December 31, 1999 there will be a free festival themed on the Four Elements and Time. **The Festival**

of Water at the Bâtiment des Forces Motrices will feature 1950s Swing bands performing on floating platforms around the building, with a dance show on the footbridge and an illuminated spectacle on the Rhône itself; the **Festival of Air** at the Halles de l'Ille will feature tightrope walkers, acrobats, mime artists and magicians performing under a huge white canvas covering the square, where a multi-level disco dance-floor is also being built; the **Festival of the Earth** at le Parc des Bastions will have a magic forest for children, a country-style feast, and a salsa stage; the **Festival of Fire** at Caserne des Vernets will feature pyrotechnicians, fire eaters, lasers, a heated dance floor and barbecues; the **Festival of Time** at la Plaine de Plainpalais will feature a choreographed spectacle in the countdown to midnight, a banquet, and the turning over of a giant hourglass at the stroke of midnight.

Signé 2000, Comité Genevois pour les Fêtes de l'an 2000, 35 rue des Pâquis, Genève ⓣ 22/741 2000 ⓕ 741 2010 ⓔ signe2000@worldcom.ch ⓦ http://www.signe2000.ch/

Three Lakes District

Spread over the **Three Lakes District** in western Switzerland, **Expo 2001** (May 3–October 29, 2001) encompasses Lakes Bienne, Morat and Neuchâtel as well as the cities of Biel-Bienne, Murten-Morat, Neuchâtel and Yverdon-les-Bains. Given Expo's aquatic base, the organisers have come up with an ingenious idea for holding the exposition on a series of floating platforms moored in the lakes offshore from each of the four cities; the platforms, known as *Arteplages*, will contain restaurants, events venues and even hotels as well as the exhibits themselves. A fourth mobile platform, the Jura Arteplage, will circulate among the lakes.

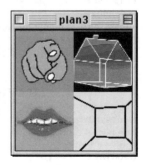

Expo 2001 will reflect the same sort of themes on the future of humanity in the next millennium as those being explored in Expo 2000, the Millennium Dome, and France's Forums for the Year 2000. The

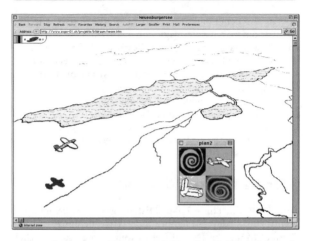

main rubriks are: 'Power and Freedom' (Biel-Bienne); 'Moment and Eternity' (Murten-Morat); 'Nature and Civilisation' (Neuchâtel); 'The Universe and I' (Yverdon-les-Bains); and 'Change and the Meaning of Change' (Jura). Despite these abstract-sounding titles the organisers promise considerable hands-on involvement and the opportunity to try out the latest technologies.

Expo 2001 is aiming for around six million visitors, two million of these from outside Switzerland. Twenty specially built catamarans, each capable of carrying four hundred passengers, will ferry people between the different Arteplages.

TRAVEL BRIEF

Expo 2001, Rue de la Gare 4, 2001 Neuchâtel, Switzerland Ⓣ 0800/88 2001 (in Switzerland) Ⓣ 0800/2002 2001 (from abroad) Ⓔ info@expo-01.ch Ⓦ http://www.expo-01.ch

COUNTRY CODE Ⓣ 41

UNITED STATES

The majority of plans for millennium celebrations in the United States have so far focused on mega-parties for New Year's Eve, 1999 offering a huge range of musical and cultural events, spiced up with massive fireworks and laser shows, with everyone claiming to be the biggest and the best. New Year's Eve in Times Square is, of course, the 'Big Daddy' of them all, and will be supplemented by equally flamboyant celebrations in many states and cities across the country.

Special events are being laid on at hundreds of top hotels and restaurants, and many of the more desirable spots in New York, Miami and Los Angeles are already booked out. The first booking for New Year's Eve, 1999 was made in 1983 by a man from upstate New York who contacted the *Marriott Marquis* (in a prime position on Times Square) when building work began on the hotel. His foresight has been rewarded by a complimentary suite for the night. The Seattle Space Needle has been booked for a private party for nine hundred people, and Disney World is already fully booked, with long waiting lists, even though they have not yet announced their plans for the millennium. But you might still be able to get into top party destinations: Las Vegas, for instance, will be building 17,000 new rooms before the year 2000.

Despite the emphasis on parties, many millennium committees and groups across the country are determined to provide something more lasting. Numerous projects are taking shape whose aim is to celebrate the past, in the form of local heritage and culture, as well as concentrating also on the future and the twenty-first century. The **White House Millennium**

Program, for example, will 'highlight projects that recognize the creativity and inventiveness of the American people', focusing on art, culture, scholarship, scientific exploration and technological discovery.

A major development in the US has been the growth in the number of **millennial cults** across the country, ranging from the right-wing militias that gave rise to the Oklahoma City bombing, to New Age groups, to quasi-religious groups who have adopted the imminent arrival of extraterrestrials as their creed. The most infamous of these was the **Heaven's Gate** cult, who committed mass suicide in March 1997, but they were by no means the first, nor will they be the last to emerge.

In January 1999 a Doomsday cult originally from Denver, Colorado, known as the **Concerned Christians** were expelled from Israel after they were discovered plotting to hasten the arrival of Armageddon and the return of Jesus Christ, by committing violent acts in the city of Jerusalem.

As the potential havoc that may be caused by the Y2K or millennium bug problem becomes apparent – our very own, self-made technological apocalypse – so too has the **Survivalist** movement gathered strength. Communities and households are stocking up on essential supplies and food in preparation for what many believe will be a breakdown of essential services as the clock ticks over into the year 2000 (see FAQs pp.31–33).

Whether this will happen, no one knows. One thing is for sure – apocalypse or not, most Americans are determined to 'Party Like It's 1999'.

California

LA is hosting the **Los Angeles Millennium Show** on New Year's Eve, 1999 at the LA Memorial Coliseum and Sports Arena. It will start with a street festival, followed by a 90-minute 'visual extravaganza hosted by some of the top names in the entertainment business'. The climax will be one of the 'longest and largest fireworks and laser displays the US has ever seen'. After midnight, the arena will become a dance hall for a party until dawn. The Mayor's office is also planning a programme of millennium events kicking off with the opening of the North American segment of the **World Festival of Sacred Music** by the Dalai Lama.

Down the coast **Long Beach** will hold the **Parade of a Thousand Lights** (December 20, 1999) with decorated boats in the harbour, and a huge countdown to midnight party on December 31 including fireworks and lasers on Pine Avenue. On the shoreline up to six thousand people will be partying on board the **Queen Mary**, with seven separate bands providing the entertainment and offering every kind of music, from Latin to Country. At **Huntington Beach** the Turn of the Century Committee is organising fireworks from barges along the shoreline, performances by major entertainers and a city-wide Sunday brunch at the beach. The 31 communities of Orange County are planning a two-year celebration under the title of **Orange County Class of 2000**; events scheduled include a Salute to the Military, a Millennium Festival, and a Technology Conference. In Anaheim, **Disneyland** was fully booked even before they announced plans for celebrating in the Magic Kingdom. In **Pasadena** the celebrated New Year's Day Rose Parade will be even more flamboyant than usual with the theme of 'Celebration 2000: Visions of the Future'.

Inland, **Death Valley**, with its magnificent scenery, is expected to be one of the busiest National Parks over the millennium holiday. Further to the south, the Mojave Desert near Palm Springs will witness the sight of **One Million Pagans** enjoying a three-day event (December 30, 1999–January 1, 2000) which will include rock operas, games, and shamanistic rituals. The event is free, and they hope to create the world's largest drumming and chanting circle. Near the Arizona border **Party 2000** has been in the planning stages for several years, with the aim of attracting two and a half million peole to a five-day bash (December 28, 1999–January 1, 2000) featuring headline rock acts and dozens of other performers. However, like many millennial dreams, Party

2000 fell to earth with a crash when it was announced in March 1999 that negotiations over the 5000-acre site had ground to a halt through lack of funds. Unless a 'white knight' steps in, the event will probably be cancelled.

In **San Diego** they're anticipating 250,000 will attend **Exposition 2000**, during which the city's Balboa Park will be transformed into a 'cultural extravaganza', with stages for entertainment, jazz and rock bands, food stalls, hospitality tents, crafts and fireworks. The organisers of the **Millennium 2000 Wedding** are hoping that up to two thousand couples will choose to either get married or renew their vows in the San Diego Convention Centre on December 31, 1999.

The San Diego **Marathon 2000** will take place on January 1, 2000. **San Francisco** will have numerous galas and parties in the Bay Area's hotels and restaurants and will also host one of six **New American Expos** taking place across the country.

Los Angeles: 633 West 5th St, Suite 6000, Los Angeles, CA 90071 – there are several information points scattered around the city Ⓣ 213/624-7300
Ⓕ 624-9746; California: Ⓣ 800/GO-CALIF (US and Canada) or 916/322-2881
Ⓕ 322-3402 Ⓦ California: http://gocalif.ca.gov
Los Angeles: Ⓦ http://www.lacvb.com
Los Angeles 2000 Ⓦ la2000.com/information.htm

Long Beach Area Convention & Visitors Bureau, One World Trade Center, Suite 300, Long Beach, CA 90831-0300 Ⓣ 800/4LB-STAY Ⓕ 562/436-8606
Ⓦ http://www.golongbeach.org

Hotel Queen Mary, 1126 Queens Highway, Long Beach, CA 90802-6390
Ⓣ 562/435-3511 Ⓔ queenmary@gte.net Ⓦ www.queenmary.com/

One Million Pagans, 10240 NE 12th Street, Suite D-307, Bellevue, WA 98004
Ⓕ 425/455-5703 Ⓔ thorrr@hotmail.com
Ⓦ http://www.AMysticalGrove.com/PTM

Party2000, 8033 Sunset Blvd, Suite 238, Los Angeles, CA 90046
Ⓣ 888/PARTY-2000 (805/723-5501) Ⓔ celebrate@party2000.com
Ⓦ http://www.party2000.com

Florida

New Year on **Miami's South Beach** will be a free event with four sound, light and video towers set out at 300ft intervals along the beach. A stage will be built between the centre towers presenting live entertainment, music, and 'the hottest DJs and fashion shows'. Fireworks set off from barges will light up the sea and the beach at midnight. Gloria Estefan is also reportedly opening the millennium with a gig in the city. In Orlando **Disney World** is sold out, with the celebrations rumoured to include a commissioned millennium symphony and the premiere of Fantasia 2000, an update of the classic cartoon. In **Fort Lauderdale** the Millennium Council is planning a celebration as well as the restoration of the **Old Courthouse** in downtown West Palm Beach. **St Petersburg**'s Millennium Commission is staging a series of events throughout 1999, culminating in a tailored First Night celebration on the downtown waterfront, plus at least one 'lasting monument to the city's present, past and future'.

Miami Convention and Visitors Bureau, 701 Brickell Ave, Ste 2700, Miami, FL 33131 Ⓣ 800/753-8448 (US and Canada) or 305/539-3000 Ⓕ 539-3113
Ⓦ Florida: http://www.florida.com
Ⓦ Miami: http://www.miamiandbeaches.com

Hawaii

With its combination of lively nightlife, top-class hotels, great beaches and hedonistic lifestyle, **Waikīkī** will be a popular choice for millennium travellers. Honolulu has a well-established **First Night** celebration, one of the largest in the US, and over 150,000 are expected to take part on New Year's Eve, 1999. On the Big Island there will be Hawaiian-style festivities, **No'ono'oikala Kalikimaka** (December 17–29, 1999) with choirs, carols, and Santa arriving by canoe.

Georgia

The city of **Atlanta** is thinking big for the millennium and planning a 600ft-tall steel monument, called the **Leap of Faith**, which would be shaped like the letter A with the top missing; the silhouette of a person, jumping from one side of the truncated A to the other, would top the monument. Other

Millennium Miscellania

● Hollywood is producing a rash of disaster movies based on the millennium bug. Warner Brothers are producing *Y2K: The Movie*, which is due for release in Autumn 1999. Set in New York, the film features Chris O'Donnell as a computer programmer who comes across dangerous information as the clock ticks down to December 1, 1999. Other studios, including MGM, are said to be planning millennium bug disaster movies; one script involves a Boeing 747 crashing into the Empire State Building as its critical systems fail. Also on a millennial theme Arnold Schwarzenegger will battle Satan in *End of Days*, and Winona Ryder stars in a still-untitled film about a young woman who discovers a conspiracy to enable Satan to return to earth in human form.

● A nationally televised series called *Millennium Minutes* throws the spotlight on the people, events and achievements of the last 1000 years and is being broadcast throughout 1999. The lavishly-produced series, made by the Great Projects Film Company, is being distributed by PBS PLUS.

● Bookmakers are predicting that the song '1999' by the Artist formerly known as Prince will top the charts as 2000 approaches but the musician is far from happy, since he failed to secure the song's re-release rights when he parted company with Warner Brothers in 1996. He has posted an online petition demanding the rights back, and meanwhile issued seven remixes of the hit on *1999 – the New Master*. The Artist has never licensed a song for commerical use, but advertising agencies have been offering £600,000 (US$1m) to use the hit.

● The US Postal Service is issuing several sets of commemorative stamps in its Celebrate the Century programme, featuring the most memorable and significant people, events and trends of the twentieth century. For the first time ever, the public has been invited to submit designs.

ideas being considered include designating March 4 as 'March Forth' day, a holiday during which Atlantans would celebrate marching towards their dreams, and creating the world's largest photographic mural, with photos of every Atlantan.

Illinois

The city of **Chicago** has come up with a new variation on the millennium theme, a **2000 Minute Party** that will last from 8am on Dec 31, 1999 through to 5.20pm on January 1, 2000. The theme for the New Year's Eve celebrations is 'water and light', with the Navy Pier's 150ft-high ferris wheel acting as a countdown clock for the final seconds before a laser, light and fireworks display at midnight. There will also be alcohol-free family events citywide, and a family day at Navy Pier on New Year's Day. The Chicago suburb of Aurora is building a **Millennium Plaza** which will be the focus of New Year's Eve celebrations.

Chicago 2000: Ⓦ http://www.chigacotime.org/

Kentucky

Newport, on the banks of the Ohio River, is going for a record with the world's largest swinging bell, the **World Peace Bell**, which will form the centrepiece of their **Millennium Monument**. The 33-tonne bell was cast in Nantes, France, in December 1998 and shipped to New Orleans in Spring 1999 before being transported to Newport up the Mississipi and Ohio rivers. On New Year's Eve, 1999 it will ring in each time zone around the world with a message of 'freedom and peace to all nations, religions and people'. It will be sited in a special pavilion in front of a planned 300m-high Millennium Monument Tower.

Louisiana

New Orleans is always a hot spot for partying, and many of the city's top hotels, nightclubs and restaurants are planning millennium specials. Candlelit carols, madrigal dinners, parades and bonfires traditionally feature in the month-long festivities for **Christmas – New Orleans Style** (December 1–31, 1999) whilst on New Year's Eve itself the focus is on the central **Jackson Square** in the French Quarter. Mardi Gras 2000 will be a rollicking, raucous finale to the carnival season.

Maryland

Maryland's **Commission for Celebration 2000** has launched a countdown clock and is planning a year-long, state-wide celebration which will include a travelling arts project, a tree-planting programme, educational events and historic preservation programmes. New Year's Eve parties will take place at several sites across the state.

Massachusetts

Boston 2000 is aiming to establish several major projects, including creating a new park, planting a commemorative tree on the site of the original Liberty Tree and building a 100-acre park along Charles River. The Boston 2000 Millennium festival will take place from July1–16, 2000. Boston is also the home of what is now the nationwide First

Night celebrations, and First Night Boston '99 will include over a thousand artists and performers at over fifty indoor and outdoor venues in the city.

Boston 2000, World Trade Center, 164 Northern Ave, Suite 717, Boston, MA 02210 Ⓣ 617/439-5200 Ⓕ 439-5205 Ⓔ info@boston2000.org Ⓦ http://www.boston2000.org/

Minnesota

The Twin Cities of **Minneapolis** and **St Paul** are planning a six-day long party costing around US$8 million (£5m). The event would give the twin lakeside cities two huge New Year's Eve parties, which would involve family activities as well as top-line bands and other acts (St Paul will also host its usual alcohol-free A Capital New Year). The extensive celebrations will encompass the Metrodome, the Convention Center and the Target Center and will feature an interactive exposition with movie sets and props, sports memorabilia, and displays on science and literature.

Nevada

In **Las Vegas** all the big hotels will be staging millennium spectaculars, and the Las Vegas Boulevard will be the focus of a huge open-air party on December 31, 1999. Barbra Streisand will perform at the **MGM Grand**, having pulled out of playing Madison Square Gardens because of her fears over travelling and the Y2K bug. Earlier in the month you can catch the finish of Desert Race 2000, which will cover 160 miles between Barstow and Vegas in early December.

First Night Celebrations

The traditional, booze-soaked image of New Year's Eve has been facing a major challenge in the US from the concept of First Night Celebrations – alcohol-free events intended to appeal to the whole family. First Night originated in Boston in 1976, when a group of artists had the novel idea of celebrating New Year's Eve with a programme of visual and performing arts that was not only accessible and affordable but also alcohol-free.

It quickly became a great success, with annual attendances in excess of 1.5 million people. Since then this tradition has spread across small towns and big cities alike, with nearly two hundred festivals taking place in recent years in communities right across the US and Canada. In Hawaii, First Night was inaugurated in 1990 under the slogan 'Arts, Not Alcohol' with 40,000 people attending, and by 1998 more than 120,000 had joined in.

Each First Night is unique. In New York, they've had dance parties, jazz performances and stand-up comedy; in Tampa, roving entertainers, art mazes and outdoor music; in Calgary, over one hundred artists have taken part in performances at twenty locations; in Ocean City, they've staged magicians, dancers, bands and more; in Boston, ice sculptures and a grand procession are regular features. First Night '99 nationwide promises to be even bigger and better than previous years.

Ⓦ http://www.firstnight.org/

New York

The Big Apple annually hosts one of the biggest bashes in the country, and in 1999 it will be even more spectacular than usual. Public celebrations in **Times Square** began nearly a century ago when the *New York Times* held its first rooftop party at One Times Square on New Year's Eve, 1903. Three years later they decided to lower a reflective ball down the flagpole to coincide with the arrival of midnight, a tradition that has continued ever since. 1999 will mark the debut of a brand new Times Square Ball, which will be the centrepiece

New Year's Eve

of **Times Square 2000: the Global Celebration at the Crossroads of the World**. The countdown to the New Year will begin with the lighting up of the ball at dusk, and at one minute to midnight lasers will illuminate its descent as 15,000 helium ballons are released and 3500 pounds of confetti floats down from the buildings around the square. More than forty giant searchlights and a 50K 'space cannon' will create a 'cathedral of light' above the square as lasers and spotlights scan across the half-million strong crowds. This year also sees the debut of Father Time, a 16ft tall, 24ft long puppet that will drift through the square prior to midnight.

Giant video screens will broadcast celebrations from around the world, beginning with Fiji at 7am EST. There will also be a wacky, costumed **Midnight Footrace** in Central Park, with champagne at the finish line.

Plans are in hand at the Statue of Liberty for **Liberty Island 2000: Celebration of a Lifetime**, with performances focusing on 'peace and freedom in the next millennium'. There is intense interest in celebrations at two other city landmarks, the World Trade Center and the Empire State Building, but both are keeping their plans under wraps until later in 1999.

Celebration 2000 is hosting the **Party of the Century** at the Jacob Javits Convention Center Celebration 2000, where 40,000 guests will enjoy a twelve-hour celebration to include big band dancing, discos, comedy shows, and fireworks over the Hudson River. It will take place on all four levels of the 22-acre complex, which will also host a week-long **Legends of Sport** event (December 24–31, 1999) honouring the century's greatest athletes.

Big parties will, of course, also take place in major hotels and venues such as the *Rainbow Room*, the *Marriott Marquis*, the *Ritz Carlton*, the *Brown Palace Hotel*, the *Waldorf Astoria*, *New York Hilton & Towers*, and the *Crowne Plaza Manhattan*. Floating parties will also take place on board dozens of boats in the harbour.

Themed exhibitions in the pipeline include 'Millennial Visions: Utopian Dreams and Prophecies in American Folk Art' at the Museum of American Folk Art (September 1999–January 2000); and a major retrospective on 'Twentieth-century Art' at the Museum of Modern Art (October 1999–August 2000).

In 2000, New York Harbour will be the backdrop for **Opsail 2000** (July 3–9, 2000), the largest tall ship parade in history.

Celebration 2000, 155 East 55th St, New York, NY 10022 ⓣ 212/644-8900
ⓕ 688-1883 ⓦ http://www.celebration2000.com

The NYCVB's Millennium Club provides news on events to members. It costs US$20 (£12) to join. Contact NYC Millennium Club, NYCVB, 810 Seventh Ave, New York, NY 10019 ⓣ 212/941-9527.

NYCVB visitor information ⓣ 800/NYC-VISIT (692-8474; US and Canada) or 212/484-1242 ⓕ 247-6193 ⓦ http://www.nycvisit.com

Times Square 2000 ⓦ http://www.times-square.org
Details on New Year's Eve events.

Pennsylvania

The **Millennium Philadelphia** celebration runs from July 5, 1999 through to January 1, 2001, starting off with the **Photo of the Century**, featuring one hundred people born on the Fourth of July, one for each year from 1900 to 1999. The Pennsylvania Convention Center's Great Hall will host a **Bridge to the Millennium** experience (December 24, 1999–January 1, 2000) which focuses on the past, present and future of Philadelphia and the world. The center will also hold **All the World's a Stage** on December 31, 1999, a 24-hour celebration with themed hours linked to each country as they ring in 2000. New Year's Day will be the centenary of the **Mummers Parade**, with thousands of elaborately-costumed mummers. The tall ships of Opsail 2000 will visit in June, 2000.

Philadelphia Convention & Visitors Bureau, 151 Market St, Suite 2020,
Philadelphia, PA 19102 ⓣ 215/636-3327 ⓕ 636-3300.

Texas

Dallas is staging an indoor fair and science and technology exposition, **The Turn: America at the Millennium**, which will run from Thanksgiving weekend 1999 to January 3, 2000. The event will be held at the city's Fair Park, which will be covered with a ten-storey vaulted dome for the occasion. Three more geodesic domes will hold themed attractions and the event will also include a big New Year's Eve party.

Washington

Seattle will be staging a week-long event, **Seattle 2000: Celebrate the Future** (December 26, 1999–January 2, 2000) featuring performances and programmes in the arts, culture, technology, entertainment and education. There will be fireworks displays on Puget Sound and from the famous **Space Needle**, although the tower itself has been booked for a private party for several years. A state-wide **Spirit of 2000** committee has been formed to co-ordinate activities in cities, towns and villages across the region.

Spirit of 2000, 1904 Third Ave, Suite 700, Seattle, WA 98101 ⓣ/ⓕ 206/623-5967 ⓔ gdideas@gte.net ⓦ http://www.spirit2000.com

Washington DC

The year 2000 is the anniversary of a number of symbolic milestones in Washington's history, namely the 200-year anniversary of presidents occupying the White House, the 200-year anniversary of the first meeting of Congress in the Capitol, and 200-year anniversary of the creation of the Library of Congress. Celebrations will focus on these anniversaries as well as a number of other projects in the White House Millennium Program (see box overleaf).

The White House Millennium Program

The program's goals include connecting every classroom and library in the country to the Internet, an expansion of space exploration, preserving the environment and reviving the spirit of citizen service. Amongst the initiatives and projects are:

● **Save America's Treasures**: A US$30 million (£18m) programme to preserve important artefacts such as the Bill of Rights.

● **Millennium Evenings at the White House**: Lecture series with prominent scholars, visionaries and musicians talking or performing (public access is via cybercast or satellite download).

● **Millennium Trails**: Creating a network of trails across the country, including twelve national millennium trails commemorating trails of discovery and migration.

● **The Presidential Millennium Awards for Design Excellence**: Honouring a century of design.

● **National Digital Library**: The Library of Congress intends to put part of its collection online.

● **Festival of American Folklore 2000**: The Smithsonian Institute will expand its annual festival to include two hundred children from around the world.

● **The Millennium Stage**: At Washington's Kennedy Center, with free performances at 6pm daily.

● **Millennium Minutes**: The National Endowment for Humanities will sponsor a TV series covering humanity's last thousand years.

● **Leadership Project for the Millennium**: The National Endowment for the Arts is to tell America's story through the arts. Teams of photographers will be sent across the country to capture their images of America at the turn of the century.

The White House Millennium Council, 708 Jackson Place, Washington DC ℡ 202/395-7200 Ⓔ millennium@whitehouse.gov Ⓦ http://www.whitehouse.gov/Initiatives/Millennium/

TRAVEL BRIEF

With multiple time zones to choose from between Hawaii and New England, the US has plenty of time to party and intends to take full advantage of it.

GETTING THERE The US has probably the busiest air network in the world, with flights to everywhere, both domestic and international, led by the giant US airlines – American, Continental, Delta and United. All are prepared to add some additional flights should it prove necessary. Some disruption to the transport infrastructure is to be expected due to the Y2K bug.

ACCOMMODATION Most top hotels and romantic restaurants in New York, Miami and Los Angeles are full. If you want to spend the millennium in luxury in the US, look for the remote, out of town resorts and even then, book now. Ski resorts are also filling up fast.

On the bright side, Florida, southern California and New York are all awash with more ordinary hotel beds, are used to handling mass events and don't see the Millennium as anything out of the ordinary. Sensible advance booking is advised.

TOURIST OFFICES UK: New York: New York Convention and Visitors' Bureau, 33–34 Carnaby St, London W1V 1PA ⓣ 0171/437 8300 ⓕ 437 8100; California: ABC California, PO Box 35, Abingdon, Oxon OX14 4SP (send £2/US$3 for a brochure pack) ⓣ 0891/200278 (premium rate); Miami: ABC Florida, PO Box 35, Abingdon, Oxon OX14 4SP (send £2/US$3 for a brochure pack) ⓣ 0891/600555 (premium rate) or London ⓣ 0171/792 0087 ⓕ 792 8633.

TOURS UK: American Connections ⓣ 01494/473173; Destination USA ⓣ 0171/253 2000; Jetsave ⓣ 01342/327711; North America Travel Service ⓣ 0171/938 3737; Travelbag ⓣ 01420/88380. US: Collette Tours ⓣ 800/340-5158; McBride Tours ⓣ 802/372-4719; Moore Fun Tours ⓣ 414/432-3226; Outbound Tours ⓣ 612/777-7366.

COUNTRY CODE ⓣ 1

THE MILLENNIUM

CONTEXTS

Some Millennial History

Preoccupations with the end of the world (the apocalypse) and universal transformation are clear manifestations of the millennial myth, a defining archetype in Western consciousness which has run like a thread through the beliefs of cults, prophets, New Age visionaries and Doomsday sects over the last two thousand years. But where did it all start – and what lies in store for the year 2000? Read on . . .

The Roots of Apocalypse

Belief in the apocalypse has its roots in the ancient teachings of **Zoroaster**, an Iranian prophet who lived around 1500 BC. Zoroaster's vision was of a wise and powerful God, **Ahura Mazda**, who was plagued by an evil twin, **Angra Mainyu**. The prophet held the theory that the long and arduous battle between these two would eventually result in victory for Ahura Mazda. The complete transformation of the world would then occur, leading to a universal resurrection and the elevation to perfect immortality of believers. In other words, Zoroaster more or less invented the notion of heaven and hell.

Zoroastrianism is thought to be the world's first eschatological faith – that is, there can be no return to a former paradise, but a total transformation into another state. The historical cycle of time effectively ends.

The Book of Daniel

Zoroaster's prophecies had an important influence on early Judaism, which is most apparent in the **Book of Daniel** (written around 168 BC). This particular text marked a decisive shift away from previous Jewish prophecies by suggesting that there would indeed be a final cataclysm, a battle between good and evil, and a resurrection of the dead followed by a golden age.

A crucial concept in the Book of Daniel is that salvation is imminent, and it is this shared belief in the imminent arrival of the apocalypse that has become the hallmark of millenarian movements throughout history. Although Daniel was cryptic about the actual date ('a time, two times, and half a time'), he left enough numerical clues to generate speculation for over two thousand years, and his words are still being scrutinised today by those who believe that the year 2000 heralds the apocalypse and/or a new dawn.

The Revelation of St John the Divine

Just over fifty years after the death of Jesus, Nero launched the first great persecution of Christians, which continued throughout the reign of the Emperor Titus Flavius Domitianus. It was around this time (between 65 and 100 AD) that a believer called John (his exact identity is uncertain) was exiled to the Greek island of Patmos, where he wrote the hugely influential and enigmatic **Book of Revelation**. "I was in the Spirit on the Lord's Day," he recorded, "and heard behind me a great voice, as of a trumpet, saying 'I am Alpha and Omega, the first and the last: and, what thou seest, write it in a book, and send it unto the seven churches which are in Asia'" (Rev 1: 10–11).

The dramatic vision that enveloped him unfolded as a series of bizarre images – beasts with multiple eyes and wings, locusts 'with the hair of women and the teeth of lions', great dragons, lakes burning with brimstone, glass seas, and 'foul spirits like frogs' – which take on a hallucinatory quality as the whole of creation is sucked into a vortex of destruction and renewal.

The imagery of the Book of Revelation owes more to religious cults of the Middle East, Greece and Egypt than it does to the conventions of early Christian writings, but its crucial significance lies in its depiction of the pattern of events leading up to the **Second Coming of Christ** and the **Last Judgement**.

Although many of Jesus's followers lived in daily expectation of the apocalypse, after his death the focus shifted to the Second Coming, which Jesus had implied would occur in their own lifetimes. When this failed to happen some explanation was needed, and the Book of Revelation adequately served this purpose. For persecuted Christians it not only reiterated the scale of the reward that awaited them in the eternal kingdom, but also partially explained the delay in Christ's Second Coming by revealing the full horror of the battle between good and evil which was still taking place.

Although John was not the first to suggest that the 'end-time' sequence had begun, it is largely due to his writings that the notion of an imminent apocalypse gained widespread currency. His cosmology represents the quintessential millennial myth, a vision that explains the death and rebirth of the world.

The Seven Seals

Part of John's vision describes a door opening into heaven to reveal a throne surrounded by 24 elders, clothed in white with crowns of gold. 'There was a rainbow round about the throne' and 'out of the throne proceeded lightnings and thunderings and voices' (Rev 4: 3, 5). The Holy One holds in his hand a book with seven seals, which 'no man in heaven, nor in earth, neither under the earth, can open' (Rev 5: 4), but a lamb with seven horns and seven eyes (signifying Christ) appears and takes the book. As the first four seals are broken the Four Horsemen of the Apocalypse appear, the last of whom is Death. 'Hell followed with him. And power was given unto them over the fourth part of the earth, to kill with sword, and with hunger, and with death, and with the beasts of the earth' (Rev 6: 8).

With the opening of the fifth seal all those martyred for Christianity arise. With the sixth, 'lo, there was a great earthquake; and the sun became black as sackcloth of hair, and the moon became as blood; and the stars of heaven fell unto earth. And the heavens departed as a scroll when it is rolled together; and every mountain and island were moved out of their places' (Rev 6: 12–14).

Thus the Wrath of God gives a foretaste of things to come, whilst the chosen 144,000 who are to be saved are marked by four angels of the wind.

With the seventh seal there is a temporary peace until seven angels blow their trumpets to unleash the real apocalypse. The world is subjected to hail and fire mingled with blood. Mountains are cast into the sea, the star Wormwood falls from the sky, the sun and the moon are dimmed, and unbelievers are tormented by scorpions and beasts arising from a fiery pit.

In the midst of the deluge, a pregnant woman appears, accompanied by a seven-headed red dragon. As the woman gives birth the dragon tries to devour the baby, but it is defeated by St Michael. The dragon (who is Satan) appears in a new form, a beast rising out of the sea, 'having seven heads and ten horns, and upon his horns ten crowns' (Rev 13: 1). This creature is the Antichrist, the Beast of the Apocalypse, 'and his number is six hundred threescore and six' (Rev 13: 18).

The chosen ones ascend to Mt Sion with the lamb and, as Babylon falls, they witness the torment of the infidels. A white horse appears, mounted by a figure 'clothed with a vesture dipped in blood, and his name is the Word of God' (Rev 19: 13). He wages war on the beast and his followers, and Satan is cast into a bottomless pit and bound for a thousand years.

The Importance of Revelation

John's account of the Seven Seals heralds the beginning of Christ's **millennial reign**. 'And I saw a new heaven and a new earth: for the first heaven and first earth were passed away' (Rev 21: 1). A new Jerusalem descends from heaven, and all suffering is eradicated: 'And God shall wipe away the tears from their eyes, and there shall be no more death, neither sorrow, nor crying, neither shall there be any more pain, for the former things are passed away' (Rev 21: 4). The delights of the new Jerusalem, with its walls of jasper, streets of gold and twelve pearly gates, are described in some detail.

John ends with a warning to anyone who might consider meddling with his manuscript: 'If any man shall add unto these things, God shall add unto him the plagues that are written in this book' (Rev 21: 18).

The Book of Revelation has had, and continues to have, "a greater effect on human behaviour in the Western world than any other single piece of writing", claims one millennial commentator. "It is perhaps the most powerful source of utopian hope in Western civilisation", says another. Certainly, the Book's concepts and images – the Battle of Armageddon, the Four Horsemen of the Apocalypse, and the Great Beast whose number is 666 – have occupied a firm position in the iconography of Western consciousness through the centuries.

The Montanist Heresy

By the second century the Christian church was well established and, although there was still speculation on the Second Coming, the church hierarchy was able to gloss over this issue in the interests of maintaining the status quo. But the situation of relative calm was soon disturbed with the arrival of the first heretical apocalyptic cult, the **Montanists**.

Founded in Phrygia, Asia Minor, in the second century AD, the sect was led by a Christian convert called **Montanus**, together with two priestesses, Priscilla and Maximilla. Speaking in strange tongues, the group prophesied that the new Jerusalem was about to descend to earth in the region of Phrygia, and they encouraged Christians to abandon their villages and follow them to the appointed place. When the 'new heaven and new earth' failed to materialise, Montanus and his priestesses are thought to have committed suicide. The sect survived without them for another seven hundred years, however, spreading throughout Asia Minor, despite condemnation by the church.

The Montanists are significant not only because they represented the first heretical challenge to the orthodox church but also because they were one of the first clearly defined examples of what anthropologists call **millenarian movements**. Often arising in times of social and cultural upheaval, millenarian movements thrive on the promise of a better life, a utopia lurking around the corner. The fact that they flourish as a result of discontent with the established order often places these movements in conflict with the dominant culture. Frenzied behaviour, coupled with mass migration to the spot where they will await the new millennium, is also a characteristic of apocalyptic cults that has manifested itself throughout the centuries.

Medieval Millennialism

Was the year 1000 marked by a sense of impending apocalypse? Historians differ, but the popular view is that the masses did succumb to some form of millennial fever. In his book *Millennium Prophecies,* Stephen Skinner writes, "For a few short months in 999 AD people could talk of nothing else but the Second Coming. In Europe generally a sort of mass hysteria took hold as the year end approached. This atmosphere led to some astonishing happenings. Some men forgave each other their debts; husbands and wives rashly confessed infidelities; convicts were released from prison; poachers made a truce with their liege lords....December saw fanaticism reach new heights as communities attempted to rid their area of the ungodly."

Damian Thompson disagrees with this account, however, in *The End of Time.* "The 'Terrors of the Year 1000' appear to be a romantic invention of sixteenth-century historians", he asserts. "The main reason for disbelieving accounts of apocalyptic expectations in the year 1000 is that at the time the majority of the population had no notion of what year it was anyway."

The Middle Ages were, nonetheless, ripe for outbreaks of millennialism. It was a time of social turmoil which saw whole populations suffer wars, famines, plagues and invasions, as well as economic and social dislocation as international trade routes opened up and people began to travel more widely. At the same time, the notion of an imminent end to the world was central to popular religious beliefs. The stage was set for the emergence of numerous apocalyptic prophets and messianic cults.

The Crusades

In the first millennium after Christianity the established church tended to make light of 'end-time' beliefs, and apart from a few isolated examples such as the Montanists, there is little evidence of any powerful millenarian movement. But from the eleventh century onwards the church hierarchy began to turn millenarian beliefs to their own advantage. This new strategy began with the holy wars that became known as the **Crusades**.

The two hundred year period of the Crusades began in 1095. The aim of the western European kingdoms was to wrest control of Jerusalem and other sacred sites in the Holy Land from the Muslim powers, and the Christian church mounted at least eight major expeditions to this end before it was finally expelled from Syria in 1291. The millennial myth was used by some clerics to justify the campaign of aggression. The seizure of Jerusalem was judged a prelude to the arrival of the Antichrist; its overthrow would hasten the final Battle of Armageddon.

But whilst the church had envisaged well-disciplined and well-equipped armies of chivalric knights in its ranks, the call to liberate the Holy Land also took root amongst the peasantry. At the end of the eleventh century northern Europe had been through a succession of floods, droughts, famines and plagues, and since these were precisely the sort of prophetic 'signs' that were taken to herald the beginning of the end, the masses formed their own ragged army of crusaders and began travelling across Europe.

This was the **People's Crusade**, a chance for many to escape their intolerable lives and seek salvation in Jerusalem. "Gradually, the image of real Jerusalem became confused with the perfect New Jerusalem of scripture; rumours circulated of a miraculous realm where common people lived like princes", writes Damian Thompson, who describes it as "classic millenarianism".

The Third Age

During the thirteenth century, millenarian movements, nourished by the mass anxieties of the time, experienced vigorous growth throughout Europe. This period also saw the emergence of a new kind of millenarianism which was to prove highly influential in later centuries. The latest prophetic voice was that of **Joachim of Fiore**, a Calabrian abbot who had a vision (sometime between 1190 and 1195) of a complex pattern underlying history which revealed humanity's progress through three successive stages: the **Age of the Father**, the **Age of the Son** and the **Age of the Spirit**.

Anchoring the three different ages within the numerology of the Bible, Joachim reckoned that the **Third Age** was due to arrive around 1260 and that it would be a golden age of love, freedom and joy which would last for a thousand years until the Last Judgement. The prevailing orthodoxy at the time was that the Kingdom of God was already present, and by declaring that utopia had yet to occur within history, Joachim was inadvertently subverting the church.

The abbot's vision had an important influence on European mythology and, centuries later, its central tenets surfaced in secular revolutionary movements such as **Marxism** and the idea of the **Third Reich** – the Nazi concept of the glorious thousand-year reign.

Roving Flagellants

Penitential **self-flagellation** was common in monasteries from the eleventh century onwards, but in the thirteenth century it came to be embraced by the masses – amid millennial overtones. Earliest demonstrations occurred in Italy, where priests bearing sacred candles and banners led processions from town to town. Arriving at a church, the flagellants would whip themselves for hours on end using leather scourges armed with iron spikes. Eventually, many thousands joined in this practice as the processions moved further across the countryside.

Mass **flagellant movements** also sprang up in southern Germany and France and continued to reappear for the next 200 years. In Germany this concept of contrition evolved into a more militant messianic movement, with leaders urging the populace to disobey (and in some cases stone to death) the clergy and appropriate the church's wealth. The flagellants also massacred numerous Jewish communities, fuelled by rumours that the Jews had caused the outbreak of the Black Death by poisoning the drinking water.

Doomsday Cults

The flagellants were one of the first millenarian groups to preach armed resistance to the church. Founded in 1260, the **Apostolic Brethren** believed that they alone were the beneficiaries of God's word and that the pope and all his cardinals would soon be destroyed in a final conflagration. Led by **Fra Dolcino**, the Brethren retreated to the Alps to arm themselves for the decisive battle, but they were eventually defeated at Monte Rebello in 1307.

The movement's destruction was one of the first examples of a **Doomsday cult** locked into a self-fulfilling prophecy that eventually led to their own demise, a pattern of self-destructive millenarian behaviour that has continued until the present day (the bloodbath at Waco in 1993 is a classic example). "Of all the apocalyptic mutations, none has appeared with such tragic regularity as the small group which hides behind fortifications in expectation of glorious deliverance from a cataclysmic onslaught by the forces of evil", writes Damian Thompson. "The believers jump the gun by taking up arms themselves, and the onslaught materialises."

The Doctrine of Free Love

Self-flagellation was not the only trend in medieval millenarianism veering towards the socially dysfunctional. For nearly five centuries a belief known as the **Heresy of the Free Spirit** appeared in various guises (it was also known as 'Spiritual Liberty' and the 'Spirit of Freedom') throughout Europe. Adherents believed that they had obtained absolute perfection and were not only therefore incapable of sin, but expected to do things that were forbidden. In Antwerp, one adept of the Free Spirit, **Willem Cornelis**, preached that since poverty abolished all sins the poor could indulge in sex as much as they liked. Cornelis himself was said to have been 'wholly given up to lust', and it took the church authorities more than twenty years to try and stamp out his promiscuous beliefs in the city. Elsewhere, the Brethren of the Free Spirit preyed on lonely widows or unmarried women in the towns and cities.

Predictably enough, the doctrine of spiritual emancipation through eroticism proved highly popular. Similar beliefs were found amongst the **Adamites**, a millenarian cult in fifteenth-century Bohemia who preached free love and 'danced naked around camp fires'. These states of mystical ecstacy were an essential part of a belief in the return to a state of innocence, of perfection on earth.

Nostradamus

Born in Provence in 1503, **Michel de Nostradame** is the most famous prophet of the last thousand years, and his predictions have been studied avidly for the last four and a half centuries. He was known simply as Nostradamus (the Latinised version of his name), and his predictive talents were encouraged by his grandfather, who was physician to King René of Provence. Having shown an early aptitude for astrology and maths, Nostradamus was sent to study the arts in Avignon, but upset his teachers by defending astrology and the theories of Copernicus. He then studied medicine at Montpellier and became well known as a plague doctor before losing his own wife and children to the Black Death when he was just 34.

Nostradamus wandered in self-imposed exile in Italy and southern Europe, the tragedy turning his energies inwards to the occult for the next ten years, a time during which he is said to have developed his prophetic vision. In 1544 he returned to Provence, married a rich widow and devoted himself wholeheartedly to the predictive arts. He began writing an annual almanac and was sufficiently encouraged by its success to embark on what was to become his most famous work, the seven-volume *Centuries*, intended as a future history of the world.

In 1556 Nostradamus predicted the death of Henry II of France in a jousting accident, which drew him to the attention of the queen, **Catherine de Medici**. In 1559 Henry II was duly killed as foreseen, making Nostradamus the talk of the courts of Europe. Crowds burned effigies of him before the Inquisitors, and he was only rescued from death by Catherine, who later encouraged Charles IX to elevate him to the status of Counselor and Physician in Ordinary.

Just eighteen months later, Nostradamus died as he himself had prophesied: 'On his return from the embassy, the King's gift put in place. He will do nothing more. He will be gone to God. Close relatives, friends, brothers by blood will find him completely dead near the bed and the bench.'

Nostradamus's *Centuries* comprises a series of 942 four-line quatrains. Written in a combination of French, Latin, Greek and Provençal, the poetic and obscure nature of the prophecies has proved a fruitful source of material for interpreters, who have been able to read into them whatever they want. Nostradamus consciously made them enigmatic, jumbling time sequences and historical allusions to protect himself against potential repercussions.

Century 3, Quatrain 95

This particular quatrain is said by commentators, among them Stefan Paulus, to have predicted the fall of communism:

The Law of More people
will be seen to fall:
After a different one a
good deal more seductive:
Dnieper first will fall:
Through gifts and language to
another more attractive.

'More' as used here is said to refer to **Sir Thomas More**, who published his *Utopia* when Nostradamus was a student, the inference being that utopia was an allegory for communism.

Democracy is seen as a 'different one' (political system) which replaced communism because it was 'a good deal more seductive'. The **Dnieper** runs through Kiev, the capital of the Ukraine, which was one of the first breakaway states from the USSR. And the transition came about peacefully, 'through gifts' (pledges of aid) and 'language' (diplomacy).

Century 10, Quatrain 72

Dozens of volumes have been written on Nostradamus's enigmatic quatrains, all of them offering different interpretations, but most scholars seem to agree that the prophet's most compelling prediction concerning the millennium is Century 10, Quatrain 72:

The year 1999,
*   the seventh month,*
From the sky will come
*   a great King of Terror;*
Resuscitating the great
*   King of the Mongols,*
Before and after Mars
*   to reign happily.*

It is one of the very few quatrains to mention a specific date but, despite this, some argue that the original French word, 'sept' might be short for September. The 'great King of Terror' is thought to imply the imminent arrival of a comet, which would collide with the planet, or indeed a nuclear war. The reference to the **King of the Mongols**, Genghis Khan, is interpreted as pointing the finger at northwest China, but there again, others maintain that the reference alludes to an advanced alien civilisation which will be able to clone Genghis Khan's cells to resurrect the Antichrist. Some commentators have also made much of the proximity of this date to a major planetary alignment which will take place in August 1999, when the last solar eclipse of the century will be followed by a Grand Cross of the planets in the fixed signs of the zodiac (Taurus, Leo, Scorpio and Aquarius) which correspond to the Four Horsemen of the Apocalypse in John's Revelation.

The only prediction that is 100 percent certain is that books on Nostradamus will continue to be churned out well into the next millennium.

Nineteenth-century Prophets

Millenarian movements have always had to deal with the consequences of their own blunders as the date set for the apocalypse passes by uneventfully. In medieval Europe theological obfuscation was often deployed to gloss over the disappointment, but in later centuries this trick became more difficult, especially once the arrival of newspapers ensured that predictions of a Second Coming achieved much wider publicity, and that these 'false profits' were mercilessly exposed to public ridicule.

Joanna Southcott

The daughter of a Devonshire peasant, **Joanna Southcott** began prophesying in 1792 and drew a large following owing to her increasingly accurate predictions concerning events such as the French Revolution. In 1802 she began annointing the 144,000 people who were to enjoy Christ's millennial reign, among them many clergymen. In 1814 the 64-year old virgin became convinced that she had been impregnated with the Holy Ghost and would give birth to the child 'Shiloh', a new Christ-figure who would redeem the world. Seventeen of the twenty-one doctors who examined her pronounced that she was probably or definitely pregnant, and dozens of people camped outside her London home awaiting the event. She died in 1815, ten days after the baby was due, and an autopsy revealed no evidence of pregnancy, nor could it establish the cause of death.

A later Southcottian follower, **Helen Exeter**, founded the **Panacea Society** and sealed Southcott's writings in a box that had once belonged to her. The Society, which still exists today, believes that opening the box will usher in a new era, but that it must be opened in the presence of all the bishops of the Church of England – a gathering that is highly improbable, despite newspaper advertisements placed by the Society demanding that the event takes place.

Charles Hindley and the Mother Shipton Prophecies

Although they first appeared in the mid-fifteenth century, the prophecies of **Mother Shipton** achieved widespread popularity in the nineteenth century when an editor named **Charles Hindley** decided to publish the predictions, adding a few of his own along the way. Numerous legends surround the birth of Mother Shipton (Ursula Southiel 1488–1561), including one that she was born in a cave after her mother had been impregnated by a superhuman being. She became famous as a seer whilst in her twenties, correctly predicting **Henry VIII's invasion of France** in 1513, the destruction of the **Spanish Armada** and the **Great Fire of London** in 1666.

The Millerites

The **Millerites**, a millennial cult that took hold in Boston and New York in the mid-nineteenth century, was founded by **William Miller**, a farmer who began scrutinising the books of Daniel and Revelation and who became convinced that the Second Coming would occur during the year 1843. His preaching attracted a large following, particularly after the appearance of a meteor in 1833 which was interpreted as a signal that the time was nigh. A Boston pastor founded several newspapers (including one called *Signs of the Times*) to promote Miller's ideas, which fell on fertile ground in New York

State as floods and crop failures exacerbated the effects of the depression, encouraging 50,000–100,000 people to join the movement.

Miller announced the date for the Second Coming as sometime between March 21, 1843 and March 21, 1844. When the first date came and went without incident, it was described as 'The Great Disappointment', and many followers abandoned the movement. But others decided a recalculation was necessary, and hit upon October 22, 1844 as the second plausible date. Members moved to the hilltops to await the great event, and when nothing occurred, the disappointment was overwhelming: 'we wept and wept until the day dawned', said one disciple.

Thus was born the comic stereotype of the Doomsday prophet, surrounded by his followers 'staring up in disbelief at an empty sky'. It was the first time in history that an apocalyptic movement had become the laughing stock of the public.

The Ghost Dancers

Millennial prophecies found a receptive audience amongst Native Americans, eager for a redemptive vision as they witnessed the erosion of their culture, loss of their lands, and social upheaval caused by the introduction of alcohol. One of the most celebrated movements was the **Sioux Ghost Dance**, inspired by the visions of the shaman **Wovoka** in 1886. Wovoka foresaw a cataclysm that would overwhelm white civilisation, bring back the Plains buffalo, restore Indian culture, and resurrect those they had lost.

The Sioux were urged to dance nonstop for five whole days in an attempt to bring about the impending apocalypse, scheduled for the spring of 1891. "When the earth shakes at the coming of the new world, do not be afraid; it will not hurt you", claimed Wovoka. The Sioux dressed themselves in 'ghost shirts' which they believed had the magical ability to protect them against the bullets of white troops, but in 1890 nearly 300 men, women and children were massacred during the battle at Wounded Knee Creek.

Another Native American messianic movement was the **Earth Lodge**, who predicted that floods and earthquakes would swallow up white culture. Adherents built large, circular underground chambers where they could shelter when the apocalypse arrived.

Jehovah's Witnesses

Founded by **Charles Taze Russell** (1852–1916) in Pittsburgh in 1872, the **Jehovah's Witnesses** are one of the best known of Christian millennial cults, largely due to their door-to-door evangelism. Witnesses believe that the Battle of Armageddon is imminent and that it will cleanse the earth for the arrival of the Kingdom of God, which will last for a thousand years.

The date Russell first predicted for the establishment of the Kingdom of God was 1874, and when this failed he settled on October 1914. This date was then reinterpreted as the year in which Christ was enthroned in Heaven, and the timetable for Armageddon was reset to 1975. It was then revised many more times until, in 1995, the church's journal, *The Watchtower*, pronounced that no more dates would be set.

Jehovah's Witnesses must refuse to serve in the armed forces or vote. Estimates vary as to their numbers, which are thought to be anything between four and eleven million people worldwide.

Edgar Cayce

Known as 'the sleeping prophet', **Edgar Cayce** (1877–1945) has been called America's Nostradamus. He predicted a number of events with a high degree of accuracy – and many more that were completely wrong. During consultations he would lie down to sleep, allowing his 'inner light' to channel communications, claiming to remember nothing when he woke. Just before the Wall Street crash in early 1929 he advised clients not to invest in stocks and shares, predicting a 'downward movement of long duration'.

His followers claim that he also foresaw the downfall of communism, both world wars, the assassination of President Kennedy, and independence for India and Israel. Other less successful predictions included California falling into the sea in 1969, the emergence of new islands in the Caribbean, and China becoming a 'new cradle for Christianity'.

In 1934 Cayce gave a trance reading in which he predicted that there would be a shift in the earth's axis in 1999, leading to widespread natural disasters, as well as World War III. The year 2000, his followers believe, will see the Second Coming of Christ and the advent of the New Age. His well-documented predictions are maintained by the **Association for Research and Enlightenment**, based at his former home in Virginia.

Mormons

Mormons are members of the **Church of Jesus Christ of Latter-Day Saints**, a millennial group often confused with the Jehovah's Witnesses, since both proselytise on doorsteps. Mormons hold firm beliefs in the imminent end of the world – members are required to stockpile a year's supply of food, clothes and emergency supplies in preparation for the approaching Armageddon.

The church was founded by **Joseph Smith** (1805–44), who is said to have had his first divine revelation at the age of 14 when he went into the woods and met two figures, God and Jesus, who told him to have nothing to do with established religions. Later, an angel called Moroni appeared and instructed him to translate a secret history of North America, written on golden tablets, conveniently located on a hillside near his home. This became the **Book of Mormon**.

The Book of Mormon claims that America was discovered by various Hebrew tribes around 600 BC, some of whom perished, but others of whom survived internecine wars to become the nucleus of the people who were later known as Red Indians. The Book also rejects the conventional Christian doctrine of the one true God.

After it was published, Smith established the Church of Jesus Christ of the Latter-Day Saints and attracted a considerable following. But he also met with fierce local opposition from the established churches, and the 'saints' (as Mormons refer to themselves) were chased out of Vermont. They went first to Ohio, then to Missouri, then Illinois, and finally to Utah, where they founded **Salt Lake City** – still the worldwide headquarters of the movement.

In 1844 Smith announced that he was running for the US presidency and opposition reached fever pitch. After smashing up a newspaper office hostile to the Mormons, Smith and his brother were thrown into jail, but before they could be charged, a mob broke into their cell and killed them both.

The newspaper Smith attacked had been exposing the Mormon practice of polygamy, which is a central tenet of their faith and one of the reasons they have attracted such widespread hostility. **Brigham Young**, Smith's successor, fathered 56 children with sixteen wives. In 1890 polygamy was outlawed in the US, a condition that was imposed on the Mormons by the federal authorities to allow them to form their own state, but fundamentalists continued to practise it despite threats of excommunication.

In recent years, polygamy has made a comeback amongst Mormons, with breakaway groups setting up their own churches to recognise plural marriages. The church currently has around £18 billion (US$30b) in assets, and invests £3 billion (US$5b) annually in property acquisitions. It has ten million members worldwide (around 180,000 in the UK).

Modern Cults

'In the event of the rapture, this car will be unmanned' reads a bumper sticker in the US midwest. As the year 2000 approaches, belief in the forthcoming apocalypse has moved beyond the realms of religious fundamentalism and into everyday life, tapping into basic concerns about the fate of the world. Issues such as nuclear war, population growth and the global ecological crisis have become the present-day equivalents of the plagues, famines and wars that fanned apocalyptic flames in the Middle Ages.

The millennial myth still retains a powerful hold on the imagination, adapting to the idioms of the age: fundamentalists believe that angels descending from heaven will save the faithful, but for other eschatological cults the apocalypse will be followed by the descent of gods in spacecraft, to save believers who have reached a higher plane of consciousness.

Detailed below are some of the better known postwar millennialist movements and cults. They are unlikely to be the last. In the US, the **Cult Awareness Network** warns of a new wave of Doomsday cults committing mass suicide as the millennium approaches. Millennial fever is also being stoked up by evangelists like the Rev. Jerry Falwell, who announced in 1999 that the Antichrist is probably alive today and that the Second Coming of Christ would occur within the next decade.

Aetherius Society

The **Aetherius Society** was formed by London taxi-driver **George King** in 1955 after he heard a mysterious voice telling him he had been selected by the 'Cosmic Masters' to become a spokesman for the 'Interplanetary Parliament' who would soon usher in a utopian age on earth. King channelled messages claiming that the Star of Bethlehem was a flying saucer which brought Jesus to earth, and that Jesus and other religious leaders such as Rama-Krishna and Buddha are now living on Venus.

Aetherians believe that the world is in great danger but catastrophe has been averted many times thanks to their efforts in storing thousands of hours of prayer in special 'radionic batteries', based on gold and crystals, which are used to release spiritual energy at times of crisis. His Eminence Sir George King, the great Aquarian Master, left the physical world on July 12, 1997 'to return to his true spiritual home amongst the great ones'.

Raëlians

The **Raëlians**' central belief is that life on earth was created by aliens known as the **Elohim**. The cult was launched by a former sports journalist, **Claude Vorilhon**, who claims that the Elohim abducted his mother, inseminated her and then erased her memory of the experience. Vorilhon changed his name to Raël, claiming to be the last in a long line of prophets, when his mission (and his origins) were revealed to him in the 1970s.

Raël claims that we have entered the 'age of apocalypse', and after the cataclysm the Elohim will descend to save those who have entered a higher plane of consciousness.

Combining New Age and Doomsday beliefs, the movement claims to have around 35,000 members (mostly in Europe and the US) who are required to tithe 10 percent of their income to Raël. In the past the Raëlians have attracted controversy due to the overtly sexual nature of some of their practices, notably 'sensual med-

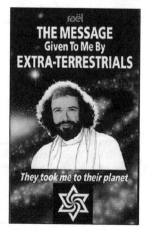

THE MESSAGE
Given To Me By
EXTRA-TERRESTRIALS

They took me to their planet

itations' intended to banish adherents' sense of Judaeo-Christian guilt, which take place at 'courses of awakening' in discreet rural locations.

More recently, the cult announced that they were offering a service giving infertile or gay couples the chance to have a child cloned from one of them in laboratories which the Raëlians are building for this purpose. Launching **'Clonaid'** in late 1997, Raël said that "cloning will enable mankind to reach eternal life".

Branch Davidians

The siege at Waco, Texas, in 1993 in which at least 85 members of the **Branch Davidian** sect died is one of the most recent examples of a Doomsday cult whose apocalyptic beliefs turned into a self-fulfilling prophecy. The Branch Davidians, a breakaway group from the mainstream Seventh-Day Adventists, established a centre at Waco in 1935, naming it Mount Carmel. In 1959 they predicted the end of the world and the resurrection of the faithful; hundreds gathered on the appointed day, but the hour merely passed them by.

The sect languished until the late 1980s, when a 'semi-literate rock guitarist' called **Vernon Howell** took over as leader. Howell, who later changed his name to **David Koresh**, had a hugely detailed knowledge of the Bible and reinvigorated the sect with his beliefs, in particular that the prophecy of the 'Seven Seals' was now being fulfilled and that the apocalypse was imminent. He fortified Mount Carmel and started stockpiling automatic weapons. This attracted the attention of the Bureau of Alcohol, Tobacco and Firearms (ATF), who mounted an ill-conceived raid on February 28, 1993 in which four ATF agents were killed. A full-scale siege began, ending 51 days later when the authorities rammed the compound with tanks, causing a conflagration in which Koresh and most of his followers perished.

Aum Shinrikyo

Aum Shinrikyo ('Aum Supreme Truth') is a Japanese Doomsday cult that hit the world headlines in March 1995 when its members released clouds of deadly Sarin gas in sixteen stations of the Tokyo subway, killing twelve people and putting 5500 in hospital. A series of raids on 25 Aum centres around Japan unveiled stockpiles of chemicals and AK-47 automatic rifles; the cult had already bought a Russian helicopter and was planning to buy tanks.

With around 10,000 followers at the time of the 1995 attack, the cult was led by a half-blind guru, **Shoko Asahara**, whose doctrines combined yoga, Buddhism and Western apocalyptic tendencies. Asahara had used LSD and truth serum on his followers (who were required to wear strange headsets) and had murdered more than a hundred of them, using a cement grinder to dispose of their bones.

One former member of the cult has already been sentenced to hang by a Tokyo court for his part in murdering an entire family by injecting them with potassium cyanide. Shoko Asahara is still on trial even though proceedings began in 1996, and they are likely to drag on for years as his lawyers prolong the case. But there is little doubt about the outcome, and he will eventually hang.

In December 1998 it was reported that a Doomsday cult known as Sukyo Mahikari, with links to Aum Shinrikyo, had set up a base in London. It had recruited more than three hundred members and was preparing to hasten Armageddon with a 'baptism of fire' some time in 1999.

Order of the Solar Temple

Alongside the events precipitated by Aum Shinrikyo, the activities of the **Order of the Solar Temple** rank amongst the most shocking of the cult dramas during the 1990s. Founded in the 1980s, the cult claimed to trace its lineage back to the

solar/temple/paraphernalia

Back Forward Stop Refresh Home Favorites History Search AutoFill Larger Smaller Print Mail Preferences

Address: http://www.total.net/~dldz/soltem.html   Go

A policeman of the Sureté du Quebec shows a cross being part The Solar Temple paraphernalia, found in the house of St-Casimir, Quebec, were members of the Order committed a collective suicide.

Internet zone

medieval legend of the Knights Templar, and its ceremonies involved elaborate rituals with robes and swords. Its leader, **Luc Jouret**, believed that the world was about to undergo a massive environmental disaster, and that this was the apocalypse foretold in Revelation. Those who joined the Order would be saved and lifted off across space to the star Sirius, where they would be reincarnated as 'Christ-like solar beings'.

The cult, originally based in Switzerland and Canada, first hit the headlines in September 1994. In Canada, a young couple and their baby were ritually murdered, after which other cult members set up a petrol bomb which burned them all alive. A few hours later fire broke out at the cult's farmhouse in Switzerland, and police discovered an underground chapel with 22 bodies arranged in a circle around an altar; nineteen had been shot, and three suffocated. Shortly afterwards, two more petrol bombs exploded in Swiss ski chalets, and 25 more bodies were discovered.

One of the documents left behind by the cult stated that 'the initiates who are evolved enough...will now voluntarily leave this world and reach the Absolute Dimension of Truth. They are in fact helped to escape a fate of destruction now awaiting the whole wicked world in a matter of months, if not weeks'.

Sixteen more cult members died in 1995 in the French Alps, and a further five in Canada in March 1997. On January 8, 1998, the Spanish police arrested 31 cult members in Tenerife just hours before they planned to follow their leader to the 3718m summit of the Tiede mountain on the island in order to commit mass suicide, in the belief that the world was to end at 8pm that day. The group, believed to have been an offshoot of the Order of the Solar Temple, told police that a spaceship would land to collect their souls and transport them to another planet.

Heaven's Gate

On March 22, 1997, 39 members of a cult known as **Heaven's Gate** committed mass suicide in a San Diego mansion. Cult members 'exited' their bodies ('vehicles') with the help of phenobarbitol, vodka and suffocation with plastic bags, believing they were on their way to join a spaceship travelling in the wake of the comet **Hale-Bopp**.

The cult was led by self-styled guru **Marshall Herff Applewhite** (known as 'Do'), and its doctrine was a bizarre cocktail of apocalyptic Christianity, New Age mysticism and alien-abduction lore. It was the Christian heritage updated for the science fiction age: Mary was impregnated on a spacecraft, and the aliens were returning to beam up believers to the 'level above human'.

Despite the cultic UFO trappings, the cornerstone of the Heaven's Gate worldview was the mainstream apocalyptic belief that has dominated American evangelism for over a century.

Books

Many of the books listed below are in print and in paperback – those that are out of print (o/p) should be easy to track down in secondhand bookshops. Publishers follow each title; first the UK publisher, then the US. Only one publisher is listed if the UK and US publishers are the same. Where books are published in only one of these countries, UK or US comes after the publisher's name.

Children's Books

Bob Fowke, *The Millennium: The Unofficial Guide* (Hodder Children's Books, UK; 1999). An entertaining guide for older children, illustrated with the author's witty cartoons and packed full of intriguing information despite the jokey approach.

Anne Love and Jane Drake, *The Kid's Guide to the Millennium* (Kids Can Press, US & Canada; 1998). Full of great ideas for kids to celebrate the millennium, from how to make countdown calendars to creating your own time capsule. A timeline of key events and discoveries throughout history runs throughout the book.

Futuristic

Adrian Berry, *The Next 500 Years: Life in the Coming Millennium* (Headline; W H Freeman & Co; 1995). Looking ahead to cities on Mars, terraforming planets, the storage of human personalities on disk, three-million tonne bombs which can blow up planets, and other fantasies.

Marshall T Savage, *The Millennial Project: Colonising the Galaxy in Eight Easy Steps* (Little, Brown; Empyrean; 1992). The whole process begins with the growth of oceanic cities, followed by building a bridge into space, establishing habitable eco-spheres on other planets, colonising the moon, transmuting solar matter and finally going to live on the stars. What could be simpler?

History & Millenarian Movements

Marina Benjamin, *Living at the End of the World* (Picador, UK; 1998). A perceptive survey of millenarian cults, institutions and religious movements.

Asa Briggs and Daniel Snowman (eds), *Fins de Siècle: How Centuries End 1400–2000* (Yale University Press, US; 1996). Six eminent historians each examine a century's end (starting in 1390) and reflect on the prevailing consciousness of time. They conclude that a 'sense of ending' seems to have pervaded each period studied – and with good reason – since epoch-making events have tended to be clustered around the turn of centuries, but otherwise the essays (originally part of a radio series) fail to hang together in any meaningful way.

Norman Cohn, *The Pursuit of the Millennium* (Pimlico; Oxford University Press; 1978). A classic of scholarship, Cohn's often-cited work examines the revolutionary millenarians and mystical anarchists of the Middle Ages.

Felipe Ferna'ndez-Armesto, *Millennium: A History of Our Last Thousand Years* (Bantam; Touchstone; 1995). A monumental (830-page) and idiosyncratic work that charts the shifting influence of cultures over the centuries. The author argues that the historical initiative in human affairs originated in the Far East, from where it passed to 'Atlantic civilisation' with the rise of capitalism, and is now shifting back to the Pacific Rim.

Michael Grosso, *The Millennium Myth: Love and Death at the End of Time* (Quest; Theosophical Publishing House; 1995). Michael Grosso's book follows a well-trodden route in tracing the history of apocalyptic and millennial visions from biblical and medieval times through to contemporary cults and the New Age movement, but he parts company with more objective accounts in his belief that 'forces are awakening everywhere, propelling humanity to powerful transformation'. He has in fact fallen for the millennium myth.

Robert Lacey and Danny Danziger, *The Year 1000* (Little, Brown, UK; 1999). An absorbing and eye-opening account of what life was like in England around the year 1000. Although based on interviews with leading archeologists and historians for accuracy's sake, the text is evocative and highly readable. This book was waiting to be written, and the authors have made a commendable job of it.

Philip Lamy, *Millennium Rage: Survivalists, White Supremacists and the Doomsday Prophecy* (Plenum Press, US; 1996). A perceptive and illuminating book that links the rise of the far-right militias, white supremacists and other 'survivalist' cults to the apocalyptic and millennial traditions in mainstream American culture and religion. Lamy's disturbing analysis sheds light on phenomena such as the Unabomber, the Branch Davidians, and the Oklahoma bombers to show how they have distorted apocalyptic symbolism to their own ends, gearing up for Armageddon in this world rather than the next.

Damian Thompson, *The End of Time: Faith and Fear in the Shadow of the Millennium* (Vintage, UK; 1999). Timely update and paperback publication of this thoughtful analysis of millenarian cults which traces the millenarian time-line from the Bible through medieval movements to Aum Shinrikyo, Waco and Heaven's Gate. A new chapter brings Thompson's razor-sharp perception to bear on the Millennium Dome and the millennium bug.

Party Guides

Harden's Mumm Millennium Party Guide for London (Harden Guides, UK; 1998). An impressive compilation of over 1000 venues, from dance halls to museums. Includes a full directory of services from professional party planners to toastmasters.

Susan Jones and Catherine Jones Juvan, *New Year's Eve 1999!* (Open Road Publishing, US; 1998). If you can wade through the slushy descriptions of romantic venues this is a useful guide to New Year's Eve in (predominantly) the top US hotels and resorts. A 1999 update would be appropriate, but none is planned.

Prophecy

John Hogue, *The Millennium Book of Prophecy* (HarperCollins; 1994). Features 777 visions and predictions from Nostradamus, Edgar Cayce, Gurdjieff, Madame Blavatsky and many others.

A T Mann, *Millennium Prophecies: Predictions for the Year 2000* (Element Books, UK; 1992). Encompasses everything from pyramidology to Aquarian predictions.

James Manning, *Prophecies for the New Millennium* (Thames and Hudson, UK; 1997). Beautifully produced and illustrated with a striking series of original collages, this compact compendium romps through all the main strands of millennial prophecy and predicts an era of galactic harmony brought about by the arrival of the Age of Aquarius, the turning of the Buddhist Wheel of Dharma, and the advent of the Hindu 'Krita Yuga', the Age of Gold.

Stefan Paulus, *Nostradamus 2000: Who Will Survive?* (Michael O'Mara Books, UK; 1997). One of the best of the current crop of Nostradamus books.

Stephen Skinner, *Millennium Prophecies* (Virgin Books; 1994). A large-format, highly illustrated guide that leads down some fairly idiosyncratic paths concerning prophecies over the centuries.

Religion

Harold Bloom, *Omens of Millennium* (Fourth Estate; Riverhead Books; 1997). A fascinating study of gnosticism, angelology, and dreams through several centuries of religious thought, and their relationship to the approaching millennium. According to Bloom,

65 percent of Americans believe in angels, and he predicts that 'angels will be at least partially restored to their equivocal glory as the millennium nears'.

Robert G Clouse (ed.), *The Meaning of the Millennium: Four Views* (InterVarsity Press; 1977). Four theologians debate the significance of Christian millennial texts.

Michael Drosnin, *The Bible Code* (Weidenfeld & Nicolson; Simon & Schuster; 1997). Controversial best seller that claims to have cracked a code 'buried' in the Bible which foretells events thousands of years after it was written, including the assassination of Yitzhak Rabin in 1995. The book's apocalyptic predictions will no doubt fuel millennium fever amongst those gullible enough to believe it.

Revelation, with an introduction by Will Self (Canongate Books, 1998). One of a series of mini-paperbacks covering standard texts from the Bible, reissued with prefaces by contemporary writers. The pocket *Revelation* caused controversy on publication, largely due to the intriguing introduction by novelist Will Self.

Science and Time

Nicholas Campion, *The Great Year: Astrology, Millenarianism and History in Western Tradition* (Penguin Books; 1994). An important and often-quoted study on the links between concepts of linear and cyclical time and societies' views of their place in the cosmos, this scholarly work (700 pages, with almost 100 pages of notes and references) is not for the faint-hearted.

David Ewing Duncan, *The Calendar* (Fourth Estate; 1998). A fascinating account of humanity's efforts to compute time, embracing science, religion, superstition and politics across continents and centuries. Charting the wobbly development of the Gregorian system since its introduction in the sixteenth century the author notes that it was not until October 1, 1949, when Mao Zedong announced that China would follow the Gregorian calendar, that the whole world agreed what the date was.

Stephen Jay Gould, *Questioning the Millennium: A Rationalist's Guide to a Precisely Arbitrary Countdown* (Jonathan Cape; Thomas T Beeler; 1997). Bearing all the usual erudite hallmarks of Gould's questioning mind, this elegantly written little volume explores the religious and rational roots of our fascination with the millennium and our compulsion to impose time-schemes on the universe. The last chapter is particularly compelling: it relates the story of an idiot savant who, like Dustin Hoffman in *Rain Man*, has the power to instantaneously calculate dates deep into the past and the future. The identity of this young man, whose gift is but an offshoot of the curse of autism, is revealed in a moving peroration.

Michael S Hyatt, *The Millennium Bug: How to Survive the Coming Chaos* (Regnery Publishing, Inc, US; 1998). After overviewing the worst possibilities, the author concludes that the US Army will be in such a state of disarray that the country will be vulnerable to invasion by the low-tech Chinese army. One of numerous alarmist texts on the millennium time bomb, it fails to recognise that a 'big bang' on January 1 is unlikely, and that serial failures throughout 1999 and 2000 are predicted instead.

Simon Reeve and Colin McGhee, *The Millennium Bomb* (Vision Paperbacks; 1996). The first in-depth analysis of the millennium time bomb problem to appear in book form.

Margo Westrheim, *Calendars of the World: A Look at Calendars & the Way We Celebrate* (Oneworld Publications; 1993). A good introduction to the numerous solutions to the problem of measuring time from different cultures around the world, and the associated rituals and festivities.

THE MILLENNIUM

DIRECTORIES

The Millennium on the Net

The millennium could have been tailor-made for cyberspace, or vice versa. The global scale of the celebrations about to take place has been echoed on the Internet's **World Wide Web and Newsgroups**, which are littered with millennial visions and plans, reflecting the collective fascination with the arrival of the year 2000.

The Internet is a natural home for conspiracy theorists, doomsday merchants, UFO enthusiasts, eco-prophets and believers in the 'end-times', all of whom are having a field day in the uncensored realms of cyberspace. The flip side of the coin, the dawning of a New Age, and how best to transform the world into a twenty-first century utopia, also occupies gigabytes of the network. Other preoccupations that emerge include the millennium time bomb (Y2K) problem, and far too many fruitless debates about when the millennium actually starts.

Plenty of opportunists are attempting to float money-making millennium schemes, many of them doomed to failure, but a lot of fun ideas have also emerged for parties, celebrations and general mayhem as the big date approaches. You'll also find some first-rate sites on topics such as time and calendars, and studies of millennial cults.

The listings that follow are just a selection of millennial Web sites we found interesting. Depending on which search engine you use, a search on 'millennium' can yield anything between 200,000 and 370,000 hits ('apocalypse' brings up 80,000 matches, and 'doomsday' a respectable 24,000).

There is plenty more to discover by following the links on the pages listed here. As with any Web guide, however, usual caveats apply: the Web is nothing if not a fast-changing environment, and Web addresses can change, move or disappear with alarming regularity.

General Sites and Events

Club2000

http://www.club2000.com/

News, events, groups, kids 2000, contests, webstore, museum, etc., – there's something for everyone on this US site. It includes a Y2K section which has some information on and from US firms who are already experiencing Y2K computer crashes. On the partying front, 'Mr Millennium' will keep you informed of 2000-related events and you may register your own events with him. Well-presented site, definitely worth a look.

Earth Day

http://www.earthsite.org/

Explains the genesis of Earth Day and how you can get involved locally, with links to different countries and world regions. Envirolink news headlines can be found here along with 'Green Dream Jobs' and an organic marketplace. Awarded a 'Times Pick' by *Los Angeles Times*.

Everything 2000

http://www.everything2000.com

Millennium information – events, Y2K problems, travel/party destinations, up-to-date news, shopping, life, etc. It has excellent links to other sites focusing on peace, religion, the environment and the apocalypse, amongst others.

General Sites & Events

http://www.simmer2000.nl/2000links.html

Quite simply, a page of links to some useful and interesting millennial sites.

Millennium Alliance

http://www.igc.apc.org/millennium/alliance/index.html

The Millennium Alliance for 'Peace, Justice and Sustainability' was founded in 1996 as a project of the Millennium Institute. Their pages contain data on what they call 'threshold observances' taking place around the world, but a lot of it is out of date.

Millennium Concentrate

http://home.earthlink.net/~hipbone/MilCon.html

Contains links to current apocalyptic, millennial and futuristic ideas.

Millennium's Eve Parties: The International Register

http://www.jepa.co.uk/shopping/party.html

This site contains everything from a knees-up in someone's front room to a champagne gala in a castle. It lists parties for New Year 2000 and 2001 and has a message board for those wishing to meet and party with others.

Millennium Hell

http://www.millenniumhell.com

Entertaining spoof site which pokes fun at all the millennium hype.
Includes the FU2K Store, Mindless Millennium Rumours, and a
Millenium Hype-O-Meter. One of the hottest new sites in 1999,
well worth a visit.

Millennium Portal

http://www.skywebs.com/earthportals/milenport.html

Nice graphics, but the content is outdated.

Millennium Society

http://www.millenniumsociety.org/

'Do something great for civilisation and have a ball doing it.'
Founded in 1979, it claims to be the oldest and largest millennium
society in existence.

Millennium Trance Party

http://www.southafrica2000.com

Musicians in South Africa are hoping to attract top trance DJs and
bands from around the world for this scheduled event to take place
on top of Table Mountain.

Talk2000

http://hcol.humberc.on.ca/talk2000.htm

Jay Gary's site covers a wealth of material relating to millennium
movements, from folklore and festivities to the darker side of
cults.

The Billennium

http://www.billennium.com

They're planning a big event for New Year's Eve, 1999 – details will
be unveiled here. Their recent survey (http://www.2000survey.com)
contains some surprising results about what people are planning to
do for New Year's Eve 1999.

The Electronic Millennium Project

http://emp2000.ukonline.co.uk/

The E.M.P. is a co-operative, non-profit making, Internet-based enterprise working towards celebrating the year 2000 and the Millennium by constructing a Global Virtual Web site. A truly excellent site offering a wealth of resources, source codes, etc. It's been awarded several accolades including the Lighthouse award for 'Excellence', Ladybird's 'Lamp of Enlightenment', Ark's award for 'Elegance' and it's also 'Site Inspector' approved.

Apocalypse and Prophecy

Atlantis Rising

http://www.atlantisrising.com/

If you want to know about Atlantis and its prophesied return to the surface, then this site may well be the authority on the Web. Published by the magazine of the same name, it includes Edgar Cayce's famous prophecies on the subject. You can subscribe to the magazine online.

Branch Davidian Revelations According to Prophecy

http://www.branchdavidian.com

This site details the revelations found in the book *Seven Seals*. The book itself can be downloaded from the site and the site's authors offer to send you a free hard copy. They claim to be amongst some of the survivors of the David Koresh/Waco siege in Texas. Interesting stuff all the same.

Conspire.Com

http://www.conspire.com

They're all here – enough to make you totally paranoid, should you believe all these conspiracies. Very entertaining site with well-presented information.

Counter-Culture – End of the World News

http://www.disinfo.com/

Excellent site offering all manner of doom and gloom prophecies from the biblical kind to killer viruses. Well worth a visit, but be warned, there's a lot to read.

Cybotron: The Cyber Lord Apocalypse Project

http://pages.prodigy.com/cybotron

Cybotron – a pop band who claim to be influenced by Kraftwerk, Giorgio Moroder and Parliament, offer us a potent brew of weird music in their music boulevard, some apocalyptic texts and some sexual imagery. Strange and suitable for adults only.

Futurecast

http://www.futurefate.com/

Learn about the world's future fate – a collection of predictions, scientific data, truths of the past etc., reside on this site. They have an online chat feature coming soon, and a new section called preparedness.

Millennium I : Our Times

http://www.aquarianage.org/

Contains over 500 pages of New Age-related information ranging from Stargate to Astrology to a Healing Arts magazine. The site also has Web casts and a forum, and will prove rewarding if you're looking for New Age contacts.

Nostradamus Society of America

http://www.nostradamus.com/

The one they're all talking about, unedited. An interesting Nostradamus site, exploring the infamous quatrains, offering astrology, links, membership and more.

Prophecy, Earth Changes and the Millennium

http://www.are-cayce.com/millen.htm

Some of Edgar Cayce's prophecies are paraded here on the Web site of the Association for Research and Enlightenment, based at the Atlantic University, Virginia Beach (US), which Cayce founded. Also listed are sections on the paranormal, dreams, holistic therapies, psychic abilities and more.

Christian

Jubilee 2000

http://www.xibalba.com/solt/jubilee

'A World Celebrating His Birth and Message'. This is not a Vatican-affiliated Jubilee site, but it has some useful links to other Christian sites, and is very well presented.

The Rapture Truth Home Page

http://users.cyberzone.net/siscokid

Christian Scientists' page declaring that even Christians will not be saved from the Great Tribulation.

The Timeline from 750AD to 250 years into the Millennium

http://www.cynet.com/Jesus/timelin4.htm

Verily, the Empire of the Antichrist is about to be established, the US and Russia will be destroyed in the Battle of Armageddon, and in the year 2000 (give or take a few years) Jesus will set up an Earthly Kingdom for his Millennial Reign. The Fundamentalist take on events.

Third Millennium & Jubilee Year 2000

http://www.nccbusco.org/jubilee/vatican/prayer.htm

Official Web site from the National Conference of Catholic Bishops detailing the preparation for and celebration of the Jubilee Year 2000 in the United States.

Cults & Conspiracies

End of the Millennium

http://www.ufomind.com/para/spirit/prophesy/millennium

Theories, controversies and commentaries concerning the end of the millennium. Some interesting links available here.

Planetary Activation Organisation

http://www.paoweb.com/

The Planetary Activation Organisation is preparing for Close Encounters of the Third Kind with the Galactic Federation.

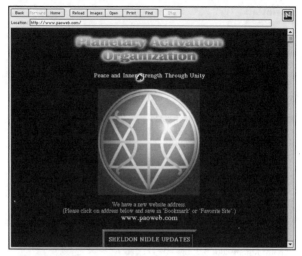

The UNARIUS Academy of Science

http://www.serve.com/unarius/

Another bunch of UFO-nutters, this lot are expecting a giant spaceship to land in the Caribbean.

UFOs, Aliens, Mars and Antichrist

http:/www.geocities.com/Area51/Vault/3040

The Watcher Ministry's pages claim that Satan was exiled to Mars and that UFOs are controlled by the fallen Sons of God. Other pages lead into detailed studies of biblical texts.

Virtual Suicide Cult

http://www.ArsNova.org/vmall/vcult.html

It had to happen …'with our popular new programme, there's no need to suffer the inconvenience and expense of belonging to a full-time, live-in suicide cult'. For only US$99 (£69) you too can be reincarnated in an Eastern metaphysical cult, South American Indian cult, and so on.

Music, Media & the Arts

Big Opera Mundi
http://www.quadrant.net/

Big Opera Mundi (BOM) plans to stage a live 'great world opera' with artists from all over the globe connected via the Internet to create a 24-hour symphony.

Casual Nexxus
http://www.quadrant.net/bom2000

Casual Nexxus – the necessary connection between cause and effect. Sandhya Padmanabh has developed Interfocus 99 – a collaborative, synthetic, new media event. It will involve live acts both in Paris and in Canada. They're also interested to know of your media projects and millennial artwork.

Millennium Art
http://www.art1.com/

Well-designed site offering an art gallery, an art forum, a gift shop and a good links page to similar New Age-type sites.

Millennium Renaissance
http://www.well.com/user/tcircus/Cyberlab7/index.html

Visual realities, millennium events and planet change projects are on view here, thanks to San Francisco's CyberLab 7.

Millennium Time Machine
http://www.mda.org.uk

The Millennium Time Machine team have been busy committing Britain's museum collections to the digital world and onto this site for everyone to see. Ironically, the site itself is poorly designed.

The New Millennium
http://www.garfnet.org.uk/new_mill

Nice graphics, but the content is parochial.

World Action for the Millennium
http://www.wam2000.org/

Explains the thinking and operational plans behind WAM's scheme to link the inhabitants of the earth to share a musical message on January 1, 2000. Available in a host of languages, but note, the site map is not in English.

New Age

Being Millennial

http://www.geocities.com/Paris/2313/meta.html

Fairly extensive links through the 'philosophies of the third millennium [and] resources to help guide your path into the next age of humankind', including mysticism, prophecies, UFOs and spiritual pages.

Calendarsign

http://web.vip.at/calendarsign/

An Austrian site aimed at raising awareness of the dawning of the Age of Aquarius (from an 'archeo-astronomical' standpoint). Their pages include several zodiac graphs, essays, a bibliography (German only), and an online shop where you can order their symbolic 1000-day Countdown Calendar.

First Millennial Foundation

http://www.millennial.org

Web site of Marshall T Savage's book of the same name, with links to FMF Chapters in the US and UK, discussion groups, newsletters, projects and articles relating to his theory that we should create space colonies in the oceans before venturing off the planet. The first colony – Aquarius Rising – is now 'in the planning stage'.

Global Visions

http://www.globalvisions.org/

'Your guide to People, Projects, Organisations and Events for a Better World'. A clearinghouse of information concerning 'spiritual and humanitarian activity on the planet'. Also offers a Global Visions store with art, books, games etc., on offer.

Lightshift 2000

http://www.lightshift.com

A fairly typical New Age millennial site, Lightshift 2000 proposes that we 'turn on the light of the world' with a series of global meditations.

Lookout for 2000, the millennium

http://caroling.holyoak.com/Lookout/lookout.html

Would you like to spend New Year's Eve, 1999 looking out from a watchtower over an ancient forest near the sea, in New Zealand? You can, virtually.

Millennium Matters

http://www.m-m.org/jz/intro.html

This site offers matters of spirit, earth prophecy, a sphinx group – to name but a few. It has its own Bazaar shop plus a host of Internet accolades and awards to its credit including a *Los Angeles Times* 'Times Pick' and a *USA Today* 'Hot Site'.

Omega

http://deoxy.org/omega.htm

Entertaining and eclectic site covering Gaia, Hopi prophecies and futuristic thinking. Good graphics.

2001: A Journey to the next Millennium
http://www.sun2001.com

Billed as a 'full service metaphysical site', the Web Prophet's pages include features on reincarnation, astrology, runes, the tarot and 'transformation', as well as offering psychic counselling by email and rune jewellery.

Peace Movements

World Peace 2000
http://www.worldpeace2000.com/

A global network of eight hundred organisations promoting the 'count-up' to 2000. Includes links to the Earth Rainbow Network, Peace 2000 Proclamation, the UN International Year for Culture and Peace, and more.

Year 2000 Campaign to Redirect World Military Spending to Human Development
http://www.fas.org/pub/gen/mswg/year2000/

Initiated in 1995, the campaign hopes to involve all countries in talks to reduce armaments by the year 2000.

Publications & Studies

Armageddon Books
http://www.armageddonbooks.com/

The world's largest biblical prophecy bookstore with a huge range of stock covering everything from premillennialism to the Rapture and the Antichrist. Also features a prophecy chat room and links to prophecy sites on the Web.

Center for Millennial Studies
http://www.mille.org

The Center for Millennial Studies carries some thoughtful analyses of millennial and apocalyptic movements. Good links pages, with sites differentiated according to various shades of apocalyptic beliefs. Also has a comprehensive online bookstore for millennium-related titles, plus details of conferences.

Millennia Monitor

http://www.fas.org/2000/index.html

The Federation of American Scientists (FAS) set out a framework for monitoring apocalyptic groups. Includes links to other pages studying millennial movements. Predictions of space weather to come, including Cycle 23, abound on this site.

Millennium Whole Earth Catalog

http://www.well.net/mwec/home.html

'Integrating the best tools from the past 25 years with the best tools for the next 25 years', the Catalog takes its original inspiration (communities, self-help, and whole systems) into cyberspace, providing access to resources and ideas on everything from the environment to telecommunications in the next millennium.

The Millennium Institute

http://www.igc.org/millennium

Formerly the Institute for Twenty-First Century Studies, the Millennium Institute aims to promote 'long-term, integrated global thinking' to create sustainable lifestyles for the next millennium. The site includes links to events and papers by millennial scholars.

The Millennium Watch Institute
http://www.channel1.com/mpr/mpr.html

The Millennium Watch Institute's pages contain a series of objective, in-depth features on various millennial cults from back issues of their Millennium Prophecy Report. Founder Ted Daniels is one of the foremost authorities on millennial cults in the US, and this site is well worth browsing. You do need to be a member to read the back issues.

The Skeptical Inquirer
http://www.altculture.com/aentries/s/skepticalx.html

Extracts from the *Skeptical Inquirer*, published by the Committee for the Scientific Investigation of Claims of the Paranormal. Insightful analyses on topics such as Heaven's Gate, UFO mythology and so on.

Round-the-World Journeys

Millennium Round The World Yacht Race
http://www.millennium-rtw.co.uk

This commercial race departs from Portsmouth in October 1999, heading westwards to circumnavigate the globe. Participants pay to join particular segments; places available.

Odyssey 2000
http://www.kneeland.com/02KFull1.html

Leaving California on January 1, 2000, the ride aims to cover 32,000km in 366 days, travelling through 46 countries and across every continent except Antarctica. Fully booked.

River 2000
http://www.river2000.co.uk/

Planned as the first expedition ever to 'transnavigate' the world by the rivers, lakes, canals and inland seas of Eurasia, North America, South America and Africa, River 2000 will also conduct a series of scientific and environmental surveys that will link into a schools' education programme.

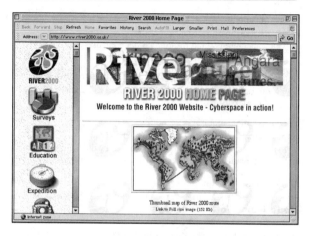

The Millennium Peaceride
http://www.peaceride.org

Endorsed by UNESCO, the bicycle ride is already underway across the continents of the world. Their Web pages include a detailed route map of the ride's progress and a daily chronicle with pictures.

Times Clipper 2000
http://www.clipper-ventures.com

Fifteen yachts will take part in this ten-month race, which covers 34,000 miles (the longest of all round-the-world yacht races) and departs from the UK in October 2000. Another commercial race, places available.

Tour du Monde 2000
http://www.tdm-wcc.com

Starting from London in late 1999, the Tour du Monde 2000 will allow two hundred cyclists to complete a 23,000km journey around the world by June 1, 2000. No prices have been set, places available.

Time & Calendars

A Base for Calendar Exploration in Time
http://ghs1.greenheart.com/billh/

Bill Hollon's new site with comprehensive information on calendars and time from all corners of the world and all dimensions.

A Walk Through Time
http://physics.nist.gov/GenInt/Time/time.html

Appealing pages from the US National Institute of Standards and Technology (NIST) that go back to basic explanations of calendars, clocks, atomic time and world time scales.

Calendarzone
http://www.calendarzone.com/

An excellent resource with links to almost everything conceivably connected to calendars – celestial, cultural, religious, interactive, perpetual and Web calendars, to name but a few.

Earth Calendar
http://www.geocities.com/TheTropics/Cabana/6218/index.html

A good-looking site offering comprehensive international information on events, public holidays, famous birthdays, etc. The site has won numerous awards including 'Best of the Web '98 Bronze', 'Hot Site', 'Critical Mass' and the 'Global Award for Home Page Excellence'.

Exactly when does the new millennium arrive anyway?
http://www.mohawk.net/~barbaria/millennium.html

Heavy-going, verbose trawl through the date problem. Suggests we move the date forward so that the year 2000 coincides with the birth date of Christ. Could be a spoof if it showed any traces of irony – but sadly it doesn't.

US Naval Observatory (USNO)
http://tycho.usno.navy.mil/

An excellent reference source for questions concerning time and the millennium. Awarded 'Coolest Science Site' by the National Academy Press.

Yahoo!™ Calendars

http://www.yahoo.com/text/Reference/Calendars/

Good compilations of links to calendar sites, including Mayan, Hebrew and Aztec calendar sites, to name but a few.

Year Zero Campaign

http://www.gozero.com

Home page of the people who want to wind the calendar back to zero at the beginning of the next millennium. This site won 'Best Bizzare Site' by the Sacramento Internet Excellence Awards Committee 1998.

Time Capsules

Keo

http://www.keo.org

Groovy graphics but it takes a while to get to the meat of this site, which is a non-profit-making French enterprise to put a satellite in space for 50,000 years with messages stored on CD-ROMs. So far Keo has backing from the ESA (European Space Agency), Aerospatiale, and several other corporations. Send them a message – it might just happen.

The Millennium Project

http://www.USTimecapsule.com

Nicely presented site for the proposed US Time Capsule Monument which is being planned for the Boston Mountain Range in Winslow, Arkansas. The final design will depend on the results of a fund-raising drive in 1999, but the organisers claim to have six hundred reservations so far.

Timecapsule 2000

http://www.arctic.ca/LUS/Timecapsule2000.html

An electronic time capsule is being created in Canada, co-ordinated by Industry Canada and sponsored by the SchoolNet scheme (which aims to put the country's schools and libraries online). The capsule will be sealed on December 31, 1999, and reopened on July 1, 2020. Individuals, families and communities are invited to participate.

Year 2000 'Time Bomb' Web sites

Microsoft TechNet – the Year 2000 problem

http://www.microsoft.com/technet/topics/year2k/

If you use Microsoft software and/or MS Windows™ environments, give this site a visit. Fixes are available by download along with some useful tips and a welcoming message from Bill. Also has articles on Y2K and links to other sites.

Millennium Bug

http://www.bug2000.co.uk

Action 2000 bring you a business and home Y2K bug check. The site has very nice graphics, is easy to follow and has a wealth of really useful information. For the home, it has a list of appliances that may be affected along with the insurance implications, etc., and other useful consumer advice.

RighTime

http://www.RighTime.com/

This site offers a free fix for PC users (DOS v3 or later, IBM OS/2 and Windows except NT). Contains links to diagnostic software that will help you determine if your computer is at risk.

The Good, the Bad and the Ugly

http:/www.demon.co.uk/dita/year2000/ye02001.html

Lists PCs that fail the date rollover test and explains how to test yours.

The Mac and the Year 2000

http://devworld.apple.com/dev/technotes/tn/tn1049.html

Macs should be safe until 2019 ... but, what the heck, here's a reference if you experience any glitches. It's regularly updated for this and all kinds of other Mac problems.

The Year 2000 Information Centre

http://www.compinfo.co.uk/y2k.htm

Contains links to dozens of commercial consultants in the millennium debugging business and numerous background features.

US Government Y2K Council

http://www.y2k.gov

If you want to know what the US government is doing for the Y2K problem, then visit this site. It contains a copy of the 'Year 2000 Information and Readiness Disclosure Act' which outlines the US government's commitment to solving the millennium bug, and regular updates on issues such as Y2K and social security payments.

Year 2000 Support Centre
http://www.support2000.com
> Very useful resource for organisations no matter how small or large.
> There are plenty of articles on Y2K, tips for assessing your
> vulnerabilities, and advice on how to overcome the problems that
> arise as a consequence.

Y2K Cinderella Project
http://www.cinderella.co.za/cinder.html
> Excellent pages detailing a number of zero-cost, minimal-impact
> solutions; includes one of the best links listings for Y2K issues.

INDEX

Picture Credits

p.1, 20 National Maritime Museum
p.34 David Austin
p.41, 90 Eden Project
p.46 Tourism New South Wales, Australia
p.58 Rio Convention and Visitors Bureau
p.60, 70, 75, 89 Hayes/Davidson/NMEC
p.76, 78 Jeremy Young/Foster and
  Partners
p.85 Mark Edwards/Still Pictures
p.95 LPL Public Relations

p.98 Earth Centre, Doncaster
p.104 Marius Alexander/Unique Events
p.108 National Botanic Garden of Wales
p.143, 281 Expo 2000, Hannover
p.155 Dublin Corporation
p.167 Bethlehem 2000 Project
p.174 John Pottle/Esto Photographics
p.180 Jeroen van Putten
p.217 Island Hopper, Samoa
p.247 @Bristol Project

KNOW WHERE YOU'RE GOING?

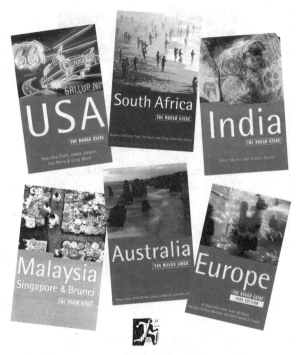

ROUGH GUIDES

Travel Guides to more than
100 destinations worldwide

AT GOOD BOOKSTORES • DISTRIBUTED BY PENGUIN